Long 'on' the Tooth

Long 'on' the Tooth

Dental Evidence of Diet

Christopher W. Schmidt
University of Indianapolis, Indianapolis, IN, United States

ELSEVIER

ACADEMIC PRESS
An imprint of Elsevier

Academic Press is an imprint of Elsevier
125 London Wall, London EC2Y 5AS, United Kingdom
525 B Street, Suite 1650, San Diego, CA 92101, United States
50 Hampshire Street, 5th Floor, Cambridge, MA 02139, United States
The Boulevard, Langford Lane, Kidlington, Oxford OX5 1GB, United Kingdom

British Library Cataloguing-in-Publication Data
A catalogue record for this book is available from the British Library

Library of Congress Cataloging-in-Publication Data
A catalog record for this book is available from the Library of Congress

ISBN: 978-0-12-824306-0

For Information on all Academic Press publications
visit our website at https://www.elsevier.com/books-and-journals

Publisher: Stacy Masucci
Acquisitions Editor: Elizabeth Brown
Editorial Project Manager: Mariana L Kuhl
Production Project Manager: Swapna Srinivasan
Cover Designer: Christian J. Bilbow

Typeset by MPS Limited, Chennai, India

CONTENTS

PREFACE

Human teeth are made of mineralized tissues that regularly make contact with objects foreign to our bodies. Their sizes and shapes are products of changes wrought over millions of years of human history—a history we can view by simply smiling at ourselves in a mirror. What we see is a reflection of the forces that shaped them throughout our evolutionary journey. If we look closer at their biting and chewing surfaces, we see evidence of the forces our teeth experienced during our lives, a permanent record of their use.

Our teeth can crush small animal bones as well as hold our pen; they can soften a frozen seal hide or tear a piece of thread. Whatever uses we have for our teeth, most of the time they can handle it. There are limits, of course. Moving hockey pucks and flying fists (often found at the same event) can fracture teeth, in part because they are better at handling end-on forces rather than those coming from the side, like a slap shot or haymaker. Human activities of the more typical sort put teeth through a multitude of daily demands, usually without issue. Their primary purpose is to reduce mechanically the foods we consume. To do this, teeth are part of a masticatory complex that includes the muscles of mastication, the upper and lower jaws, the lips, and the tongue. All of these work together to provide an efficient means of preparing food for additional digestion in the gut. Furthermore, teeth have material and structural components that offset the mechanical forces brought forth by chewing. These components are important because teeth must function for many years with no mechanism to heal or replace broken or worn-out parts.

Our tooth crowns, that part which is visible when we smile, has an outer layer made of an acellular material called enamel. Having no cells, enamel is a lifeless tissue. This means that if our hockey player referred to above takes a puck to the face, the only way to repair the broken enamel would be with the aid of a dental professional because, otherwise, a broken tooth is broken forever; your body will shed a tooth before it fixes it. By contrast, bones have many living cells within and surrounding them and broken bones can repair themselves in as little as 6 weeks. Thus, your enamel, in particular, and your teeth, in general, are unique bodily structures.

Only enamel, however, is acellular and there are living dental tissues. Deep in your teeth, lining the pulp cavity, are cells, blood vessels, and nerves. If a dental injury only affects the enamel, like when a tooth is chipped, there will be no blood or pain at the site of the chip itself. On the other hand, if you have ever had a dentist check the depth of a cavity with a metal probe, you know that parts of your teeth are very much alive and capable of detecting pain! Despite the presence of these living cells, dentin is not much better than enamel at healing; it can do little to hinder an insult and nothing to correct a fracture. I discuss it more in the following chapter, but for the most part, dentin's only response to any problem is to plug up the pulp cavity.

Most bodily tissues will not last a lifetime without the ability to repair or grow. Replacing or adding cells to tissues is something that happens throughout the body, from replacing red blood cells to growing hair. When you look at the skin of your arm, you are not seeing the same skin cells you had as a young child. Your body has replaced those cells over-and-over since your birth. In fact, much of the dust in your home is dead skin cells sloughed from the people, and pets, who inhabit it. There is, however, no tooth dust. Likewise, living tissues can add to existing cells as needed. We see increases in muscle mass in athletes and people who are active. Throughout our lives, much of our bodies change dramatically in size, shape, and composition. Yet, dental structures remain the same. If you look at the labial (lip) side of your front teeth, you are seeing the same surface you had on those teeth when they emerged in your mouth as a child.

Your first molar likely erupted when you were around 6 or 7 years old, since that is about the average age of eruption for first molars in human beings. If a person experiences average first molar eruption timing and goes on to live for an average life expectancy, that person would have had a first molar facing daily usage for seven decades without repair. In archeology, we frequently see old people who died still having their first molars intact. Some of these people lived to quite advanced ages, which indicates their molar tissues lasted for perhaps eight or nine decades! Usually their enamel is worn thin, and in places worn through, but the fact that teeth can persist in our mouths for so long with no means to forge a living response makes them truly remarkable.

Enamel's durability relates to its initial anatomical conditions. Once fully formed, enamel is primarily mineral, like a rock; and, like a rock, it bears etchings made by objects that abraded it. Perhaps you have seen large granitic stones having long, deep scratches and gouges on them, carved out as glaciers slid over or past them. Similarly, our enamel has scratches and gouges on it caused by hard and abrasive elements of the foods we eat. Since dental enamel can neither add nor subtract material once it forms, changes to the enamel that occurred during life persist even after death, usually long after death. In fact, as long as the teeth stay undamaged by their post-depositional environment, and the information they carry, they will preserve for millions of years.

The permanent record of tooth use enamel maintains is cumulative, but recent losses of enamel replace older ones. Tiny fragments of enamel are scraped from our crowns each time we chew hard or abrasive foods, and every day we lose small amounts of our enamel crown (Is that tooth dust? No, these microscopic particles are far too small to see and remain in our saliva or swallowed). Over time, our crowns reduce in height. This is normal; our thick enamel is set up for lots of wear. If a diet is particularly abrasive, however, the wear can become severe enough to remove entire tooth crowns. People experiencing this degree of wear often have little more than polished tooth roots by the time they die. In agricultural populations, usually disease rather than extreme wear destroys teeth. As sugary foods became dietary staples, cavities became emerged as the primary purveyor of dental damage.

So, what is in the record that teeth retain? First, teeth preserve the overall pattern and degree of tooth wear you can see visually; we call this macrowear. It also preserves the microscopic wear caused by daily use; we call this microwear. Finally, diseases like dental caries (i.e., cavities) leave a permanent mark. Together, these three consequences of tooth use, particularly as they relate to food consumption, are the focus of this book. Collectively, they provide insight into the foods that people ate over their lifetime (e.g., macrowear and oral pathology) as well as within the last few weeks or months before they died (e.g., microwear).

Thus far, I have avoided most of the jargon associated with dental studies. From here on, the terminology gets gradually more technical due to the need to explain things precisely. Hopefully in this book I have limited jargon to where it is necessary and jettisoned it elsewhere in order to open this research up to as many potential readers as possible. Archeologists, bioarcheologists, and students are the target audience, which means the writing must bridge a wide range of backgrounds and training. To do so means, at times the professionals may feel some explanations are too basic, while at other times the nonprofessionals may feel I made points without appropriate simplification. It is my hope that instances like these are minimal.

A critical archeological matter that needs addressing early on concerns the people studied herein, who are Native Americans from precontact Indiana who lived from about 5000 to 500 years ago. It is important at the onset of this book to recognize that their descendants are still in Indiana and surrounding states and that ancient Native Americans and living Native Americans are the same people. It is a privilege for me to learn from them, but the ancient people I studied did not ask for analysis of their remains. Frankly, neither did their descendants. Their study raises important ethical issues addressed toward the end of this book; but from the beginning, it is vital that we recognize that Native American remains come from people; human beings like you and me in every way—just as intelligent, inquisitive, thoughtful, loving, caring, and giving. Aliens did not help them. There is no connection between them and any tribes of Israel. Native Americans built every mound in the United States that existed before Europeans arrived. In fact, none of the all-too-sad tales told to undermine Native American achievements have even a modicum of truth. The Native peoples of the Americas were scientists, engineers, midwives, political leaders, teachers, mentors, friends, caregivers, and, when necessary, warriors. In all, Native Americans, then and now, are people of a continent who have a brilliant history to share. I strongly recommend reaching out to living Native peoples to directly learn from them. I think there is tremendous value in studying past peoples, but in the end, information gained through archeology is just part of the story.

I also want to make a point that this study focuses on ancient Native American populations that typically do not get a lot of attention, public or otherwise. How many popular documentary programs discuss people from Indiana? Despite its name, even professionals tend to overlook Indiana's ancient cultures. To be fair, large earthworks in Ohio, Kentucky, and Illinois surround the state. Sites, such as Adena, Hopewell, Newark, Indian Knoll, and Cahokia are truly extraordinary and important; but as incredible as they are, they still only represent certain groups at certain times. The people of Indiana also built earthworks and other remarkable structures, had wonderful customs and traditions, and they too deserve our attention.

The lack of attention received by Indiana sites is something scholars have noted for some time. In 1924, a noted archeologist of the day, E. Y. Guernsey wrote, "Compared with our neighboring states, Indiana has been rather more negligent of the study and preservation of archeological material than the rest (Guernsey, 1924: 1)." Having given this admonition, it would be misleading to make it sound as if Indiana gets no archeological attention. Noted scholars include Glenn Black, Robert Pace, James Kellar, Don Janzen, Cheryl and Pat Munson, Jocelyn Turner, Curtis Tomak, Don Cochran, Beth McCord, Della Collins Cook, B. K. Swartz, Ron Hicks, Evelyn Bowers, Elizabeth Glenn, Russell Stafford, Mark Cantin, Mike Anslinger, Jeff Plunkett, Susan Spencer Helfrich, Ken Tankersley, Andy White, Steve Mocas, Bret Ruby, Brian Redmond, Bob McCullough, Anne Bader, Leslie Bush, Mark Schurr, Sarah Surface Evans, Ed Smith, and Chris Moore. I have known most of these folks for many years, and, sadly, some are no longer with us. Together they form a small but distinguished cadre of dedicated researchers, whose work is important and rigorous, and I hope you feel inspired to look it up.

There are many people to thank when one pulls together a study like this one, which draws from decades of work, including my 1998 doctoral dissertation. I am particularly thankful for the aid of Jerry Rose of the University of Arkansas. Even though I completed my dissertation at Purdue University, Jerry served as my *de facto* doctoral advisor and I am forever thankful for his help and guidance. I also thank Peter Ungar who introduced me to the scanning electron microscope-based software, Microwear, and later on to dental microwear texture analysis. I am indebted to Clark S. Larsen for his mentorship and training, and to Anne Grauer and Steve Ousely for their guidance. Others who have given me support regarding pathology and dental anthropology include, Maria O. Smith, Della Collins Cook, G. Richard Scott, Joel Irish, Debbie Guatelli-Steinberg, Greg Nelson, Loren Lease, Cheryl Johnston, B. Holly Smith, Jim Watson, and Peer Moore-Jansen. Colleagues and former students who were integral to the research herein include Richard Blanton, Matthew Williamson,

Chris Moore, Steve Nawrocki, Lindsy Frazer, Laura Wonderly Chiu, Ashley Remy, Beckie Van Sessen, Curtis Tomak, and Melissa Zolneirz.

Kind permissions for access to remains came from Kit Wesler and Hugh Matternes, then of the Wickliffe Mounds Research Center; Della Collins Cook of Indiana University; Don Cochran and Beth McCord, formerly of Ball State University; Russ Stafford of Indiana State University; George Crothers of the Webb Museum at the University of Kentucky; and Steve Nawrocki of the University of Indianapolis.

Special thanks go to Greg Reinhardt, who has been a mentor, colleague, and friend; Curtis Tomak who generously shares his archeological knowledge; Chris Moore who provided vital edits to the archeology section of this book; and Mackenzie Vermillion who helped assemble the bibliography.

My family has helped me tremendously with this project. My wife, Molly Hill Schmidt, has been an unwavering friend, field companion, colleague, and she made critical edits to several chapters. Likewise, my children Emma, Will, Joey, and Lucy have helped as loving offspring, but also as compatriots in the field and lab. My mother, Saundra, edited very early versions of this manuscript. This book benefits from insights and editorial assistance provided by skilled and knowledgeable friends and colleagues. Nonetheless, any errors in it are strictly mine.

Finally, I am grateful to Liz Brown, Mariana Kuhl and Swapna Srinivasan of Elsevier who made this book possible, and to those who funded various aspects of this research including the National Science Foundation; the University of Indianapolis; the Indiana Academy of Science; and the Indiana Department of Natural Resources, Division of Historic Preservation and Archeology.

CHAPTER 1

Taking a bite out of teeth

Introduction

This book's focus is reconstructing diets for precontact people from Indiana by examining their dental remains. Teeth from archeological settings can be difficult to study because they are small and bear the effects of heavy wear and disease. I will not deny the toils of dental study or the challenges brought forth by their worn and decayed conditions. The tediousness of studying ancient teeth is surmountable, however, because the wear and disease provide answers to the questions bioarcheologists like me have, concerning tooth use in the past. Pristine teeth might be easier to identify, but they hold no information regarding what people ate.

Since this study uses teeth as its source for dietary information, the following provides a brief overview of their anatomy and function. Its intention is to clarify the circumstances that lead to teeth expressing and preserving evidence of their use. For detailed descriptions of teeth and the means by which dental anthropologists study them, there are a number of excellent volumes (e.g., Kelley and Larsen, 1991; Hillson, 1996, 2012; Scott and Turner, 1997; Irish and Nelson, 2008; Irish and Scott, 2016; Guatelli-Steinberg, 2016; Ungar, 2010, 2014, 2017; Edgar, 2017; Scott et al., 2016).

Anatomy

Humans have 32 adult and 20 deciduous teeth. Like most mammals, we have two generations of teeth; one set that is small and temporary to accommodate the mouths of young children, and one that is larger that we keep for the rest of our lives. There are three primary dental tissues: enamel, dentin, and cement (also called cementum). Embryologically, enamel derives from a layer of epithelium formed by the ectoderm, which among other things, produces the skin. Initially, a primary epithelial band surrounds what will become the mouth and a

Long 'on' the Tooth. DOI: https://doi.org/10.1016/B978-0-12-824306-0.00004-5

layer of that band, the dental lamina, intermittently dips into underlying connective tissue, the mesenchyme. These dips, or invaginations, become the enamel organs, which eventually initiate the mesenchyme to differentiate into cells that produce dentin and cement, as well as produce enamel. Teeth will not form if disruptions take place in the developmental processes leading up to the formation of the enamel organ (i.e., ectodermal dysplasia [Mikkola, 2009]). Bones, in contrast, develop from mesenchymal-derived cartilaginous precursors that do not require ectodermal incursions. Thus, teeth are distinct from bones due to their developmental history (e.g., Ten Cate, 1998; Harris, 2016).

Each tooth has three primary anatomical components, the crown, root, and pulp cavity. The crown is that part of the tooth that is visible in the mouth and used for chewing, biting, and holding. Its enamel cap has rounded eminences called cusps. Some teeth have single cusps while others have multiple. Beneath the enamel is the dentin. If the enamel cap were removed in its entirety, the underlying surface of the dentin would share a similar contour, which is an artifact of the manner by which the enamel organ establishes the shape of the crown before it initiates dentin and enamel production (odontogenesis and amelogenesis, respectively). In addition to forming part of the crown, the dentin makes up the root. Within the root is the pulp cavity that houses the blood vessels as well as the sensory receptors necessary for proper mastication. The roots fit into bony sockets called alveoli; the upper teeth attach to the maxilla, the lower teeth are in the mandible (Hillson, 1997; Ten Cate, 1998; Legge and Hardin, 2016; Tang et al., 2016). In humans, the alveolar regions of the maxilla and mandible are the only places where teeth typically form, although ectopic teeth occur, particularly in the face and palate (Pindborg, 1970).

Enamel is the hardest tissue in the body. The mineral component of enamel is hydroxyapatite ($Ca_{10}(PO_4)_6(OH)_2$). Where bone is about 65% mineral, however, enamel is 97%–99% mineral (Ten Cate, 1998). The rest is primarily a protein called enamelin and a very minute quantity of water. Enamelin is scarce in mature teeth, but very important; it helps to anchor the mineral crystallites. Enamel's structure is fascinating; it is not a homogenous blob of rock on top of a root. Rather, it has offset rows of microscopic rods running from the deepest layer of enamel to its outer surface. The rods look like rebar rods in concrete; but instead of being rods of a different material coursing through a matrix, like true rebar, enamel rods are the enamel. Moreover, these rods are wavy for about two-thirds of their lengths, which helps the crown resist fracture (Hillson, 2014). The complex structure of enamel is one reason why it can last for years, even several decades, without repair.

For all its strength, enamel has one serious limitation. It is quite brittle. Recall that enamel has the same mineral as bone, but bone is about one-third collagen, which means it has a soft tissue component that buffers the brittleness of its mineral content. Enamel has few non-mineral components, so it relies on the underlying dentin to provide some plasticity. Dentin is about 75% mineral and quite rigid, but less so than enamel. Together enamel and dentin create a durable, composite anatomical structure that in most cases has just enough give to avoid shattering. Dentin is ivory. Even though we may associate ivory with large mammals like elephants and walruses, we have it too, and it makes up most of each tooth. In addition to supporting the enamel, it makes up the entire root. Deep in the tooth is secondary dentin, a thin layer of living dentin cells that surround the pulp chamber; it produces new dentin if special cellular fibers detect an insult like encroaching wear or disease. The dentin can only place new dentin (called tertiary dentin) in the pulp cavity, making it a meager mechanism for protection. It does not repair or replace broken dental elements (Ten Cate, 1998).

Between the tooth root and the walls of the alveolus is a bone-like substance, cement. Its job is to hold the tooth in the socket by providing attachment points for the periodontal ligament, which consists of multiple collagenous strands coursing from the alveolus to the root. Cement in some ways is like a less structured bone material. It has a similar mineral content, but it is less organized. Mature bone has a microscopic organization that looks like bundles of straws, the hollows of which house blood vessels. Cement lacks these straw bundles, called osteons, but it has layers like bone and houses cells like bone. Cement accumulates throughout life like rings in a tree (Huffman and Antoine, 2010). In cases where disease leads the maxilla or mandible to resorb, cement deposits can become very thick, a condition known as hypercementosis (Pindborg, 1970). This condition is useful for identifying teeth from compromised alveoli, even when found in isolation.

There are four classes of teeth in the human mouth: incisors, canines, premolars, and molars. Incisors are the anterior-most teeth. They are spatulate in shape and their primary function is to bring food into the mouth with help from the lips and tongue. There are four upper and four lower incisors. Distal, or behind, the incisors are the canines. In our primate kin, canines can be very large and dimorphic; in most cases, that means male canines are much larger than the females' are. In humans, canine dimorphism remains, but it is modest (Keiser, 1990; Viciano et al., 2011; Guatelli-Steinberg, 2016; Schmidt, 2015). For the most part, our canines are incisiform, meaning they look and act more like incisors than large, piercing canine teeth. There are two upper and two lower canines.

Distal to the canines are the premolars; they have two cusps and at times are referred as 'bicuspids,' usually in clinical settings. They are multifunctional teeth in humans that help with ingestion and mastication. Rigid foods that need more force to snip off (think of a carrot) are side-loaded into the mouth at the location of the premolars rather than front loaded near the incisors. Premolars can chew too. Having more than one cusp means they can assist the crushing and grinding of food. There are four upper and four lower premolars.

Behind the premolars are the molars. From an evolutionary standpoint, there is only one generation of molars. When molars erupt they do not replace a deciduous tooth (the deciduous molars are molarized premolars that are replaced by adult premolars [e.g., Luo et al., 2004]). The upper molars have four cusps and three roots, the lowers have five cusps and two roots. The multiple roots help to stabilize these teeth, which are the primary chewers in the mouth. The multiple cusps make up the occlusal surface and provide precisely matched upper and lower "hills and valleys" that sheer, crush, and grind food (Kay and Hiiemae, 1974). Humans have low and rounded molar cusps and they have been low and rounded throughout the millions of years of our natural history (Guatelli-Steinberg, 2016). In fact, our molars are similar to our ape kin as well. In nature, low and rounded cusps tend to be in omnivorous creatures, those that eat both meat and plants. Bears have low and rounded cusps on their distal molars and pigs have low and rounded cusps on all of their molars. Not surprisingly, both of these animals are omnivorous (Ungar, 2010).

We do not chew with our incisors and canines, but we do bite with them. The biting edge of incisors and canines is termed the incisal margin. On all teeth, the crown of the tooth and root meet at the neck or cervix. If you look at your smile in the mirror, your gums, or gingiva, attach to the teeth at or around the cervix. Teeth are usually closely packed on each tooth row and they touch each other on their mesial (forward) and distal surfaces. For example, the canine touches the incisor in front of it and the premolar behind it. This is true for all the teeth, except the third molar, because it is the last tooth in the back of the mouth. The point where adjacent teeth touch is the interproximal contact facet (IPCF). Teeth move very slightly in their alveoli and this motion creates small wear facets at the point where teeth make contact. The IPCFs are usually small, less than a millimeter, but they can become large and lead to increased dental macrowear; cavities sometime form at IPCFs, because they like to live in the protected spaces between teeth.

Function

True teeth first appeared on earth over 430 million years ago in the earliest jawed fishes (Fraser et al., 2010; Zhu et al., 2013; Ungar, 2016). Teeth may have evolved independently a few times in vertebrate history, but the ancestral forms of our teeth derived from scales, the same kind of scales girding sharks today (Fraser et al., 2010). As fish evolved into their myriad forms, so too did their teeth. Nearly every variety of extant, jawed fish has teeth; the exceptions being sea horses and pipefish (e.g., Lin et al., 2016). Four-limbed (tetrapodal) creatures arose from fish around 360 million years ago; the living tetrapods, amphibians, reptiles, birds, and mammals, either have or had teeth (birds lost their teeth millions of years ago, but the earliest varieties had them [Chiappe and Witmer, 2002]). Mammals have an amazing assortment of teeth, ranging from large flat elephant teeth, to tiny, rounded vole teeth (e.g., Ungar, 2010); it is not, however, their variation that makes mammal teeth special. Frankly, fish, too, have a remarkable assortment of teeth from the stilettos of sand tiger sharks to the pavement-like teeth of bat rays (e.g., Peyer, 1968). What is truly unique about mammal teeth is that they include molars (Davis, 2011). Molars, like those we see in our own mouths, appeared in mammals around 100–140 million years ago (Davis, 2011). There were many reasons for the evolution of molars, but the most salient is endothermy, being "warm-blooded." Mammals needed to initiate digestion as soon as foods entered their bodies in order to maintain their high energetic requirements. Today, we see the outcome of this aspect of mammalian evolutionary history in the oral component of human digestion, which includes chemical and mechanical processes. Chemical digestion is the use of enzymes in the saliva to breakdown foods; humans have amylase that digests sugars in the mouth. We also have lingual lipase that turns triglycerides into glycerides and fatty acids, something that is particularly helpful during our milk-consuming time as infants (Kulkarni and Mattes, 2014). Mechanical digestion is chewing, which tears, crushes, and grinds food. Chewed food has a larger surface area relative to mass than un-chewed food; that gives digestive juices more opportunities to penetrate it in the stomach.

The chewing cycle tracks the movement of the mandible during chewing. It starts with the mouth fully open, or at full gape. The first step is the closing stroke; the mandible elevates and moves laterally. In humans, the lateral movement is subtle, but you can see it. Watch your chin in a mirror as you chew gum; you will see it move laterally as you elevate your mandible. In herbivores that eat very fibrous foods, like cows and horses, the mandible moves laterally quite a bit. Carnivorous animals, on the other hand, have almost no lateral movement. They are so dependent on high bite forces that their chewing motion becomes limited. Imagine a pair of scissors that wobble compared to a tight pair with no wobble. Which is likely to cut better? The restricted jaw movement of carnivorous animals is due to the placement of the mandibular condyle, a rounded knob that attaches the mandible to the cranium. In herbivorous animals, the condyle sits well above the tooth row. For carnivorous animals, the condyle sits at about the same height as the tooth row. Humans have the herbivorous condition and we can easily move our jaw from side-to-side. Your pet dog or cat cannot.

The closing stroke continues as the mandible moves from its slightly lateral position to a point where the cusps just start to come into contact. At that point, called intercuspation, the closing stroke ends and the power stroke begins. During the first part of the power stroke, the tongue-side (lingual) cusps of the mandibular molars glide past the cheek side (buccal) cusps of the maxillary teeth. This first part of the power stroke, called Phase I, introduces some shearing of the food and sets up the molars for tight occlusion. Phase II begins as the mandibular buccal cusps hit the maxillary lingual cusps almost head-on. At this point, the bite force is greatest, and crushing and grinding take place. The mandible reaches centric occlusion when the maxillary and mandibular midlines line up and the upper and lower teeth fit tightly together. As the chewing muscles relax, the jaw opens, starting the opening stroke. A single chewing cycle is completed when the jaw returns to full gape (Kay and Hiiemae, 1974).

The chewing cycle is of value because it explains the patterning of wear we see on teeth. First, it explains why upper lingual molar cusps and lower buccal molar cusps wear more than the other cusps. It also helps us to understand what is happening to the molar cusps as they go into and through the power stroke. The shearing nature of phase I of the power stroke means that those cusps are likely to bear numerous microscopic linear scratches. The phase II wear generates microscopic pits and scratches because of the crushing nature of the cusps occluding so forcefully. The microscopic wear is the focus of dental microwear and dental texture analyses, which I used in the current study.

Briefly, macrowear is gross occlusal wear (see Schmidt and Watson, 2019). The crown wears over time; first the cusps round over, then they flatten. Eventually, the enamel wears through and patches of dentin become visible. What happens next depends on the overall abrasiveness of the diet (e.g., Schmidt, 2010). If the diet is mildly abrasive, then people will have some dentin exposure on their molars at the end of their lives but much of their crown will remain intact. This is what we see, for example, in historic populations from the 1800s. On the other hand, as I mentioned in the preface, if a diet is very abrasive it is possible for people to wear down their crowns completely.

The most extensive macrowear I have seen comes from a population discussed in this book who lived about 5000 years ago. A few people had molars worn to such an extent that all that remained were a few isolated maxillary molar roots polished on their sides. Recall that upper molars have three roots. To have only a single root remaining, the tooth must have lost its crown through wear and exposed its pulp cavity. The exposed pulp would have allowed bacteria into the tooth, which led to an infection of the bone. As the body responded to the infection, it resorbed most of the alveolus. Without a socket, the remaining part of the molar fell on its side, held in the mouth by just a few remaining strands of the periodontal ligament. As the person continued to eat, the side of the tooth facing down would have continued to wear. By the time this person died, all that remained were a few single roots polished to the point that they looked like tiny surfboards. Others in the population had heavily worn teeth, too, but the example given here was by, far, the most severe. If you are wondering about pain, the teeth probably only hurt during the early stages of infection and up until the alveolus resorbed. Once they lost a bony attachment, the teeth no longer had nerves and blood supply.

Dental microwear is the microscopic breakdown or removal of dental hard tissues (Teaford, 1991). Typically, it reflects the foods consumed within the last 2–4 weeks since newer microwear features eventually replace older ones (e.g., Winkler et al., 2020a). To study microwear features, it is possible to magnify, count, and measure them. It is also possible to borrow analytical techniques from industry that characterize surfaces rather than quantify features. When manufacturers produce motors, tables, surgical equipment, etc., they make sure their products have appropriately rough or smooth surfaces. The inside of a piston cylinder, for example, has very small grooves to allow oil between the piston and cylinder (see Vorberger and Raja, 1990). Engineers who specialize in measuring surface characteristics analyze three-dimensional variations in surface elevation under low and high magnification (e.g., Vorberger and Raja, 1990). The higher the magnification, the finer the scale; fine-scale fluctuations in surface contours are termed "surface roughness" and it is the roughness of ancient occlusal surfaces that I study. The technique I employ is dental microwear texture analysis (DMTA), which detects fine-scale (submicron) changes in surface elevation. It takes about a 1000 μm to make the width of a dime, thus, those of us engaged in this type of study explore the tiniest details of tooth wear.

Dental macrowear and microwear are normal outcomes of chewing. There are, however, some pathological outcomes, such as degenerative conditions at the temporomandibular joint, and infections caused by oral bacteria. The current study incorporates the infectious condition known as dental caries, that is, cavities. Dental caries results from oral bacteria metabolizing sugars in the mouth, whose acidic waste erodes dental hard tissues (Pindborg, 1970). Foods vary in their sugar content.

Agricultural goods, like maize, are far more cariogenic than foods like walnuts or acorns. People who consume a great deal of cariogenic foods have more dental caries than people who do not. Thus, dental caries is a good marker for when sugary food intake goes up in ancient populations (Larsen, 2015). Dental caries prevalence can increase without a concomitant shift to or intensification of agriculture, but examples of that happening are less common (e.g., Walker and Erlandson, 1986).

Teeth are excellent repositories of dietary information and the avenues of dental analysis I employ with this project (i.e., macrowear, microwear/DMTA, and dental caries) are known from previous studies to be efficacious (e.g., Scott, 1979; Smith, 1984; Teaford, 1991; Scott et al., 2005, 2006, 2012; Larsen, 2015; Schmidt et al., 2019). They are not, however, the only indicators of diet found on the teeth. There are other oral diseases and ways for enamel to be lost. Periodontal disease can lead to bone resorption and tooth loss, and eating hard or frozen foods can chip enamel. Dental calculus (a.k.a. tartar) can accumulate and lead to gingivitis, all the while trapping small food items. Thus, this study does not address every dental phenomenon related to food consumption. Rather, it focuses on particular mechanical and chemical processes associated with mastication for which researchers have developed data collection protocols and analytical techniques known for their reliability and validity (e.g., Molnar, 1971; Smith, 1984; Teaford, 1991; Buikstra and Ubelaker, 1994; Larsen, 2015; Armen et al., 2016; Ungar et al., 2019).

CHAPTER 2

Ambassadors of the past: the archeological record

Introduction

If we, as anthropologists, only studied living people, we would have a limited perspective of human cultural and biological diversity. By looking at all people, from all places, and from all time, we gain a much richer appreciation of human endeavors. Thus, the deceased are ambassadors of our heritage; they are here as formerly living people and they bear knowledge often unattainable from other sources. As we delve into the bioarcheological record, it is important to keep in mind that it is up to us, the living, to make sure that we appropriately treat the formerly living. What they share are important aspects of the human story, and they are unequivocally irreplaceable.

My interest in the people of ancient Indiana stems from interactions with bioarcheologists studying Native populations in the southeastern United States. My M.S. Thesis advisor, Clark S. Larsen, spent decades using biological data to decipher the impact of colonization on the Native Americans in a region called *La Florida*, which stretched from what is today southern South Carolina to Florida. Thanks to his work as well as that of his colleagues, the southeastern part of the United States is one of the most well-documented parts of the New World (e.g., Saunders, 1988; Larsen, 1984, 1990, 1992; Ruff et al., 1984; Larsen et al., 1990, 2001; Schmidt, 1993; Williamson, 1998; Teaford et al., 2001; Stojanowski, 2005; Organ et al., 2005; among many others). Starting nearly 30 years ago, I to applied this bioarcheological approach to populations from Indiana, many of which had never been analyzed fully. There were archaeologists from the early 20th century that described human remains, but for the most part they did not analyze them (e.g., Black, 1933, 1934, 1936, 1967; Dorwin, 1971; Dragoo, 1955; Faulkner, 1960, 1961; Guernsey, 1924; Householder, 1945; Lucas, 1973; Martin, 1954; MacLean, 1931; McAllister, 1932; Neumann and Tomak, 1965; Purdue, 1896; Setzler, 1930, 1932; Weer, 1935; Vickery, 1970;

Long 'on' the Tooth. DOI: https://doi.org/10.1016/B978-0-12-824306-0.00008-2

Winters, 1967). Even into the early 1970s it was rare to see detailed osteological analyses.

Dragoo (1949) made general assessments of skeletal remains from the late precontact Angel site (described in more detail later), but it was not until Georg Neumann became the first physical anthropologist in Indiana that detailed bioanthropological studies commenced. His early interests focused on the "racial" affinities of precontact residents of Indiana (Neumann, 1952, 1960, 1961, 1966). He compared cranial morphological traits to determine ancestral links between populations. This was an antiquated area of study that was replaced with more appropriate means for documenting human variation in human skeletons. In 1961, Herrala studied the prevalence of dental pathological conditions in preagricultural and agricultural populations from Indiana. This somewhat detailed analysis was one of the first cross-cultural bioarcheological studies based in Indiana. Her study also analyzed remains from the Angel site. Black (1967) provided age and sex data on more than 300 individuals from Angel, but provided no analysis of demography, paleopathology, or paleodietary reconstruction.

By the middle to late 1970s, bioarcheological studies of precontact populations were more common (e.g., Glenn, 1973, 1976, 1982). While Glenn was interested in population affinity, she also constructed detailed inventories, determined age and sex for the adults, and described pathological conditions. By the 1980s and 1990s, interest in bioarcheology was increasing, but publications remained scarce. Hilgeman (1988) and Schurr (1992) focused on bioarcheological study of Angel site skeletons; Schurr's work remains one of the most important dietary reconstructions at Angel. Havill and colleagues (1998, 2003), and White (1998) studied pathology and mortuary patterns at three Albee cemeteries, all of which are part of the current study. Also in the 1990s, bioarcheology of the extraordinary earthen Mount Vernon mound commenced (e.g., Beard, 1997). This entailed a tremendous effort that engaged archeologists, bioarcheologists, and numerous other technicians in order to complete the study. I have provided more site details later in this chapter, but it is difficult to capture the extraordinary nature of Mount Vernon via a brief overview. Munson and Cook (2001) documented skeletal materials from the Late Mississippian Hovey Lake site in the far southwest corner of the state. Their work is very insightful and stands as one of the only studies of these Late Precontact people. Another important study that include people of the Late Precontact is Katie Passalacqua's

2015 dissertation regarding biodistance in Late Woodland and Mississippian populations. She found that the Late Precontact was not a time of population movement into the Indiana and that local groups adopted Mississippian ways.

During the 1990s and early 2000s, a number of technical reports came about due to several accidental discoveries of ancient human remains. In Indiana, the Department of Natural Resources, Division of Historic Preservation and Archeology has purview over skeletal materials predating 1940. I was part of a group of bioarcheologists the state would contact to help recover and study these remains (e.g., Schmidt and Helmkamp, 1994; Nawrocki and Schmidt, 1995; Peterson et al., 1996; Schmidt, 2003, 2008; Schmidt and Hill, 2000, 2003; Schmidt et al., 1998, 1999, 2006).

In 1998, I completed my doctoral thesis, which focused on populations from Indiana and Kentucky. Since completing my doctoral work, I have been involved in numerous bioarcheological studies of Indiana populations (e.g., Schmidt, 2001, 2010; Schmidt and Greene, 2003; Schmidt et al., 1999a,b, 2008, 2010, 2016, 2019; Miller and Schmidt, 2018; Schmidt and Osterholt, 2014; Bergman et al., 2014; Casserly et al., 2014; Schmidt and Sharkey, 2012; Schmidt and Williamson, 1998), but I am just one of the bioarcheologists working in the state. Others who are directly or indirectly involved with Indiana bioarcheology include Della Collins Cook, Susan Spencer Helfrich, Holmes Hogue, Shawn Phillips, Mark Schurr, Mike Strezewski, Rachel Sharkey, and Rick Sutter.

Time

Archeologists primarily frame time in two ways. First, we look for layers of cultural materials in the ground to see if artifacts change from layer to layer. Knowing that, for the most part, deeper strata are older than younger strata, we can determine relative ages of artifacts. Once archeologists determine a cultural sequence, they can use that sequence at other sites to determine the relative age artifacts they find there. This means of relative dating does not provide chronometric dates, it simply documents older versus younger. Yet it is how archeologists constructed all chronologies prior to the 1940s, when radiometric dating came about.

To get chronometric or absolute dates, archeologists draw on radiocarbon and other means of radiometric dating to determine an object's age. Dating takes place by directly analyzing the artifact of interest, or another artifact from the same level as the artifact of interest. Radiocarbon dating works on artifacts made of once-living materials, like wood, bone, and shell. If an archeologist wishes to date the age of a stone projectile point from a particular archeological layer, she will have to date organic material from that layer, rather than the projectile point itself. Human bone can be dated using ^{14}C, but in my experience, archeologists usually gather their dates from nonhuman bone, shell, and charred wood.

There are many ways to designate time. A common practice is to use AD and BC, which set a starting or reference point at the year zero in the Gregorian calendar. Another is to use "CE" and "BCE," which mean "Common Era" and "Before the Common Era." To me, this is no better than AD/BC and still requires people to know the Common Era starts around the Gregorian year zero. Thus, in this book I use the abbreviation BP, which simply means "Before Present." If we adhere to archeological tradition, the present is 1950.

A New World

Human beings entered the New World around 20,000 years ago by crossing from eastern Russia into Alaska via the Bering land bridge, either on foot or by hugging the coast in boats (Potter et al., 2018). To me, the word 'bridge' does a disservice for visualizing the land that once connected Asia and the Americas. The Bering land bridge, also known as Berengia, was 600 miles wide and encompassed an area over 600,000 square miles. This massive area still exists today, but it is under nearly 100 m of ocean. During the last glacial advance, global sea levels dropped and exposed the land bridge as well as many other masses of land around the world.

Homo sapiens entered eastern Asia over 100,000 years ago, and by 20,000 years ago, human occupations were widespread at both lower and higher latitudes (e.g., Rybin, 2014). Confounding the matter is that there were Neandertals in western Asia and Neandertal-like people known as the Denisovans in eastern Asia prior to the arrival of *H. sapiens*. This circumstance affected when and where *H. sapiens* (*sensu stricto*) migrated;

it also complicates determinations of site origins because early Paleolithic sites could have had either *H. sapiens* or Neandertal/Denisovans as their founders (e.g., Svendsen and Pavlov, 2003). Further discussion of Neandertals and Denisovans is beyond the scope of this book, but I suspect they played a role in the timing and placement of some of the sites I mention here.

By 36,000 years ago, Paleolithic people moved into the Siberian arctic (Svendsen and Pavlov, 2003) and around 30,000 years ago spread from central into eastern Russia (Medvedev, 1998). The 28,000 Yana RHS site on the Arctic coast of eastern Russia has the oldest examples of late Paleolithic personal ornamentation (Pitulko et al., 2012). A little more than 10,000 years later people inhabited Djuktai (Mochanov, 1970), which is known for its microblade technology that resembles artifacts in Alaska (e.g., Slobodin, 1999). From there people migrated into Kamchatka and Beringia.

By the time humans first set foot on Beringia, they had within their ranks genes from throughout Asia as groups interbred from one end of the continent to the other (e.g., Kemp et al., 2007). People likely followed the Beringian coastline, in part because glaciers covered much of the land. Coastal areas would have had both marine and terrestrial food sources, although the latter may have been more seasonally available. The genetic evidence indicates a Beringia bottleneck, meaning people remained in Berengia for some time before going on to Alaska (Hoffecker et al., 2016). From there, they continued down the west coast of North America and perhaps straight on to South America (e.g., Jenkins et al., 2012). The extraordinary site of Monte Verde near Tierra del Fuego in southern Chile dates to over 13,000 BP and may be older (Dillehay, 1989, 1997). At least some groups turned east and crossed the continent, likely following major and minor waterways, and by 16,000 BP, a few populations were in the eastern United States (e.g., Adovasio et al., 1975; Goodyear, 2005). Today, archeologists call these earliest people the "Pre-Clovis," because they predate the Clovis culture, who archeologists thought until recently were the first to enter the Americas. From the original Pre-Clovis settlers, indigenous cultures emerged and spread throughout the New World (e.g., Dillehay, 1997; Boldurian and Cotter, 1999; Araujo et al., 2012).

The actual names of America's earliest people are lost to time; the names given by archeologists are all we have. Since this book ultimately focuses on people of Indiana, it uses archeologically ascribed designations for groups from the eastern woodlands of the United States. There are four primary precontact cultural groups in Indiana: Paleoindian, Archaic, Woodland, and Late Precontact. Within these primary cultural designations, there are sub-periods based on time—the Early and Late Paleoindian, Early and Middle/Late Archaic, and the Early/Middle and Late Woodland. Historically, these cultural periods represent a temporal sequence from oldest (Paleoindian) to youngest (Late Precontact). The following is a brief summary of these cultures; it is not exhaustive. Its intention is to provide\ a reasonable outline of the Indiana's precontact history. It gives general descriptions as well as touches on social organization, subsistence, and mortuary practices in order to provide context for the subsequent dietary analyses.

Paleoindian

As of this writing, there are no demonstrably Pre-Clovis sites in Indiana, although their presence is likely. Paleoindians of the Clovis variety, dating between approximately 13,000 and 10,000 years ago, lived throughout Indiana (Tomak, 1980, 1994a; Tankersley, 1992). Although living during the late Pleistocene, Clovis Paleoindians in Indiana did not see a glacier in the state; when they lived, the nearest glacier had almost entirely retreated to Canada. The climate was cool and wet, but not arctic. Forests in the northern part of the state had pine and fir trees; deciduous trees dominated the southern part (Tankersley, 1992). The Clovis people saw extinct megafauna, animals like mammoths and mastodons. Some archeologists argue that Clovis people drove the megafauna to extinction via over-hunting. Others feel the period of glacial retreat brought warm temperatures to which the megafauna could not adapt (Meltzer, 2015). Either way, by 10,000 BP, the megafauna were gone.

The Clovis people get their name from a site in Clovis, New Mexico where archeologists recovered fluted points near extinct mammoth bones (Boldurian, 2008; Boldurian and Cotter, 1999). A fluted point has a small channel on either side at the base that runs a few centimeters toward the tip. These channels helped to hold the point on a spear shaft (or foreshaft). A survey by Tankersley (1992) reported collectors found over 400 fluted points from 55 counties in Indiana, nearly half of which came from the valleys of the Ohio and Wabash rivers. Most of the sites that produced Paleoindian points are located on terraces overlooking rivers and in river floodplains. The Paleoindian tool kit was modest and included a variety of bone, stone, ivory, antler, and probably wooden implements. It was indicative of a band-level means of sociopolitical organization and a hunter-gatherer pattern of subsistence (Tankersley, 1992). The best-documented Paleoindian site in Indiana is Alton located on the Ohio River (Tomak, 1980, 1994b). This site produced over 50 projectile points and a number of unifacial tools made primarily of local chert. Archeologists have yet to find Paleoindian domiciles or cemeteries in Indiana, although some exist in nearby states. The Paleoindian diet surely included some now-extinct animals like mammoths and mastodons but primarily they fed on small mammals, birds, fish, and a variety of plants (Meltzer and Smith, 1986; Hollenbach, 2009; Anderson and Sassaman, 2012).

There is a small late Paleoindian site in northwestern Indiana. From 2003 to 2005, colleagues including my wife Molly, Chris Moore, Rachel Sharkey and I excavated the Flora Mastodon site. It was at the edge of what was once a kettle lake; it produced several mastodon (*Mammut americanum*) bones, two giant beaver (*Castoroides ohioensis*) tooth fragments, and a plethora of small mammal, reptile, and fish bones. It also produced a bone awl made from a whitetail deer ulna dated to 10,400 BP (Moore and Schmidt, 2009). The awl came from a rich organic layer immediately above a dense marl that contained the mastodon bones, which dated to just over 11,000 BP (both of these are calibrated dates). Near the location of the mastodon was a small scatter of lithic artifacts that included the base of a late Paleoindian Agate Basin point (Schmidt and Moore, 2003; Moore and Schmidt, 2009). The Paleoindian presence postdated the megafauna, but it indicates Paleoindians exploiting upland wetlands.

Across the United States, mortuary practices for Paleoindians are exceedingly rare and varied in terms of treatment of the body and inclusion of artifacts. The oldest known burials in Alaska were two infants and a cremated child at the Upper Sun River site that dated to around 11,500 years ago (Potter et al., 2011, 2015). The infants, a newborn and a late term fetus, were about 40 cm beneath a residential hearth that had within it the cremated remains of a 3-year-old child (Potter et al., 2015). The cremations and burial likely took place very close in time. The bones of the 3-year-old had evidence of burning, but the bones remained in their anatomical positions. There were hundreds of lithic pieces including bifaces and animal bones from fish, birds, and mammals found near the cremains, but because of the residential nature of hearth, it is unclear if any of these were grave goods. The only exception may be two pieces of ocher found near the skeleton (Potter et al., 2011). The two infants had with them four ocher-covered bibeveled antler foreshafts and two projectile points placed parallel to each other adjacent to the fetal child; there was a third point near the foreshafts. The two points were at the end of the two of the foreshafts and were likely hafted when buried (Potter et al., 2015: 17062–17063).

The 10,000–11,000 year old Spirit Cave site in Nevada produced four Paleoindian individuals, an adult female, an adult male (who naturally mummified), and two cremated people. Unlike Upper Sun River, they were not within a residence. Instead, their remains were within a cave. An adult female was wrapped in woven matting and an adult male found below the female had on moccasins, a breechcloth, and was wrapped in four layers of finely woven textiles. The cremations, located approximately 3 m from the male, were in woven baskets (Edgar et al., 2007). The burial of the nearly 13,000 year-old Anzick child of Montana was below a now-collapsed rockshelter. With just these three examples, we see people buried in open air, cave, and near rockshelter sites. If we included other Paleoindian burials, such as Buhl in Idaho and Horn Shelter No. 2 in Texas, we would see they too had distinct mortuary practices (e.g., Young et al., 1987; Green et al., 1998).

There are no known Paleoindian burials in Indiana. A possible Paleoindian cremation site near Indiana is the Renier site from Wisconsin (Mason and Irwin, 1960). It produced fire-cracked rock and late Paleoindian bifaces. Walthall (1999), however, reassessed the artifacts and argued it could belong to the Early Archaic.

Early Archaic

The Early Archaic period began around 10,000 years ago. The climate of Indiana was no longer as wet and cool as it had been during the periods of glaciation (Newman, 1966) and the flora and fauna took on their current manifestations. Several important Early Archaic sites exist throughout Indiana (e.g., Tomak, 1979, 1994b). The Early

Archaic people continued as mobile hunter-gatherers, although a decline in the distribution of high quality cherts indicates regionalization and the formation of territories (e.g., Cantin, 2000; Moore, 2008). People of the Early Archaic likely remained in a territory for weeks or months before moving on and their movements had them re-visiting known or preferred areas repeatedly. During the Early Archaic, people constructed cemeteries. Cemetery locations varied widely, but that they existed at all meant Early Archaic people considered certain areas to be a place for the dead. In other words, their cemeteries indicate a familial or corporate identity that transcended death; their ancestors linked the group with the area or territory in which they placed the cemeteries (e.g., Charles and Buikstra, 1983; Moore, 2008).

Lithic technology changed somewhat from the Paleoindian to the Early Archaic, leading to new point sizes and shapes related to group identity and hunting functionality (Cantin, 2000; Moore, 2008; White, 2013). For the most part, the Early Archaic tools shared a high level of craftsmanship with the Paleondians, although they did make more expediently manufactured stone points than did their predecessors (Moore, 2008).

A number of Early Archaic sites are in Indiana and one of the better known is Swan's Landing (Tomak, 1994b). This large habitation area sits immediately on the Ohio River; it produced an abundance of pits and hearths and lithic artifacts including scrapers, drills, hammerstones, and small notched points. The preferred raw material for the stone tools was the locally available Wyandotte chert (Smith, 1986). The Swan's Landing artifacts are similar to those from the St. Albans site in West Virginia and Icehouse Bottoms in Tennessee. Its lack of nonlocal cherts indicates it had a locally-based economy (Smith, 1995).

Another well-known Early Archaic site is Jerger (Tomak, 1979). It sits on a sand ridge overlooking what was probably a marshy area adjacent to the White River in the southwest corner of the state. The Jerger people made well-crafted small points with bifurcated bases. The point sizes indicate they were for atlatl darts. The bifurcate-base points at Jerger are similar to points from West Virginia, which date to 8000–9000 BP. Other artifacts included marine shell beads from the Gulf of Mexico or the Atlantic coast, turtle shell, animal bones, and flakes of locally available cherts. The people of Jerger must have had, in addition to their local means of acquiring resources, a way of getting exotic resources through trade or long distance travel (Tomak, 1979).

Jerger is a mortuary site containing the cremated remains of at least 14 people, nine subadults and five adults (Schmidt et al., 2008). The cremains were in a series of pits, each bearing remains from multiple people. There was no attempt to separate the adults and subadults (Schmidt et al., 2008). Jerger shares cultural traits with other Early Archaic people in Indiana who also employed cremation as a primary mortuary custom (Muller, 1986). Not far from Jerger is the Steele site, which had a cemetery of at least five people, two adults and three subadults (Quataert, 2018). To the northeast of Jerger and Steele in east-central Indiana is McCullough's Run, which had cremains for eight adults, eight subadults, and two people of unknown age (Cochran et al., 1997; also see Schmidt et al., 2008).

Middle/Late Archaic

Although often described as distinct cultural episodes, it is becoming clear that the Middle and Late Archaic share many commonalities and there is no archeological reason to divide the two. With the advent of the M/L Archaic (approximately 8000–3000 BP) came a brief environmental change termed the hypsithermal or altithermal (Muller, 1986). For the first 1000 years or so, the climate was drier and warmer than it was previously. The warmer conditions changed the local flora permitting the western prairies to encroach into Indiana.

By 5000 years ago, the climate took on its current conditions. In Indiana, the northern half of the state was generally cooler and had climatic conditions more like that of other Great Lake states. The southern half of the state was warmer and more humid, reflecting climatic conditions commonly found in Kentucky and the northerly aspects of the southeast. To this day, cypress swamps, which are more common to the south, outcrop along Indiana's most southwestern tip. The stable, agreeable climate may have aided the growth in population and technology experienced at this time. In places, this led to the domestication of local weedy plants (see Chapter 3).

A nuance of the cultural practices of the M/L Archaic people of the Ohio River Valley was the creation of shell "mounds." These were not earthworks, that is, intentional earthen mounds built to support a building or a ceremony. Some M/L Archaic people did construct earthen structures; at the Poverty Point site in Louisiana, people built five earthen mounds as well as six concentric low earthen ridges (Sassaman, 2005). In and around Indiana, however, M/L Archaic people did not; rather, they piled mussel shells into enormous mounds. It is unclear if people built the shell mounds to serve the kinds of purposes mentioned above for earthen mounds, but given their sizes, locations, and common occurrences, the shell mounds were likely meaningful to the M/L Archaic people in a way that related to their perception of place and identity (Basso, 1996; Moore and Thompson, 2012).

Winters (1969) found that Late Archaic sites indicated seasonal sedentism driven by maximal exploitation of wild resources, such as deer or mussels. Janzen (1977) too found evidence for increased seasonal sedentism among in the Falls of the Ohio region of southeastern Indiana and northern Kentucky. There, people settled between different environmental zones, which they exploited at different times of the year. This allowed for seasonal food collection from a primary habitation center, without a need for frequent travel (Jefferies, 2008).

There are several M/L Archaic sites with mortuary components in Indiana. The 12Fl73 site in far southern Indiana produced nine individuals, all of whom were eroding from the Ohio River bank. Most burial positions were flexed and on the side. One individual, an adult male had in his grave a cache of 10 human forelimbs from five people, and a bone pin (Schmidt et al., 2010). The cache is unique, but having human remains accompany another in a grave was not. In fact, throughout the eastern woodlands, but primarily in an area between the Ohio and Tennessee Rivers, "trophy taking" was a rare but persistent practice (Schmidt and Osterholt, 2014). At least five Indiana M/L Archaic mortuaries had burials with trophies or had trophy victims; but usually only one person per cemetery had evidence of trophy taking (Schmidt et al., 2010). An exception was the Bluegrass site from southwestern Indiana. This is the largest professionally excavated M/L Archaic mortuary in Indiana, producing around 80 individuals. There, two people had signs of being trophy taking victims. One was an adult female missing her head and left forearm. The other was an isolated rib cage and pelvis bearing several cut marks. It appears this person had all of their limbs and head removed. What is unclear is the context of this person's burial. Often partial body elements end up placed with another person; the partial remains from Bluegrass did not.

More typically, M/L Archaic burials were flexed and on their side. Grave inclusions tended to be bone pins, needles, atlatls, and projectile points (e.g., Jefferies, 2008). Variations in bone pin decoration may have indicated corporate membership (Jeffries, 1997). Beads occur in some frequency in child burials, even when grave goods were otherwise uncommon for others in the cemetery (e.g., Webb, 1946; Schmidt and Hill, 2003). Typically, M/L Archaic graves were single interments, but there were exceptions. In addition to people buried with trophies or caches, some graves had multiple complete inhumations in them. At Millersburg in southwestern Indiana, a group of three adults and three subadults were in a common grave (Zalzala et al., 2015). In Indiana, many of the mortuaries were too affected by erosion or looting to get a good sense for group grave frequency. In Kentucky, group graves made up about 3%–5% of the Green River M/L Archaic burials (Zalzala et al., 2015).

Early/Middle Woodland

The people of the E/M Woodland were hunter/gatherers who also exploited domesticated weedy plants (see Chapter 3). For the most part, the E/M Woodland cultures emerged around 3000 BP and lasted until approximately 1500 BP. Because Early Woodland traditions are so similar to both the M/L Archaic and the E/M Woodland, starting and ending dates vary widely depending on the researcher (e.g., Hicks, 1992: 24; Rick et al., 2015). In the Midwest, the Adena is the most extensively studied cultural entity of the early aspect of the E/M Woodland (Dragoo, 1963; Cassidy, 1984; McCord and Cochran, 2014; Henry and Barrier, 2016). It was a burial cult that linked populations via a shared set of mortuary practices. Adena material culture included circular paired post structures, large "ceremonial circle" earthworks, ditched villages, tubular pipes, various gorgets, Adena ovate-based points, hematite celts, copper bracelets, and Adena Plain and Montgomery incised ceramics (Webb and Snow, 1945; Webb and Baby, 1957; Seeman, 1986: 566; Cochran, 1992).

One of the confounding issues of Adena is the extensive inter-site variation. For example, Webb established 90 separate traits to describe Adena burial practices (Clay, 1990). Clay (1990) proposes that these differences were the result of autonomous peoples having social idiosyncrasies that included nuanced means of burial (Clay, 1990). In no way was Adena a kind of regional polity despite its widespread occurance. Rather, it was a cult that linked tribal-level populations; people made social alliances that eventually spread Adena over wide areas of the eastern woodlands (e.g., Webb and Baby, 1957).

Pottery use became common during the E/M Woodland (Griffin, 1983). In Indiana, the oldest pottery is Marion Thick. As its name implies, it had robust walls ranging from 8 to 12 mm thick. As pottery improved, grit temper replaced sand and grog, giving the newer vessels thinner and less brittle walls. However, they were not sturdy enough for sustained boiling (Braun, 1987). In addition to pottery, Adena people had grinding stones, hammer and nutting stones to process their foods (Griffin, 1983).

In Indiana, Adena mortuary practice included burials in log tombs containing single, extended burials although multiple burials and cremations were present, too (Kellar, 1983). Grave inclusions were elaborate and included artifacts made from copper, bone, and chert. Some of the best-documented early E/M Woodland mortuary sites are from the southern part of the state (e.g., Kellar, 1960; Tomak and O'Connor, 1978). The Nowlin Mound site in Dearborn County is located on an upland formation near the Whitewater River. The elliptical burial mound measured 50.2 m long and 5 m high making it one of the largest burial mounds in the state. Seven extended primary and four secondary burials were recovered from log-lined tombs within the mound. Material culture included corner and side-notched points, bone awls, bone handles, a sandstone "tablet," and a C-shaped copper bracelet (Black, 1936; Kellar, 1983: 39).

The C.L. Lewis Stone Mound in Shelby County is another well-described early E/M Woodland mortuary from Indiana. It overlooks the Flat Rock River and had a mound measuring approximately $15.2 \times 16.8 \times 1.2$ m (Kellar, 1960). It had three building stages; the first created a low embankment. Over this layer was a layer of limestone slabs brought in from a nearby cliff. Finally, a layer of slabs enlarged the mound (Kellar, 1983). The mound had at least 36 individuals placed within it. An ossuary containing a minimum of 14 individuals, both adults and children, was in the central area, covered with burned grass and twigs. Among the limestone slabs, above the ossuary, was a crematory pit and the remains of two partially burned individuals. The site had human remains interred in several ways including extended, flexed and disarticulated; it also had isolated human crania (Kellar, 1983).

Frequently E/M Woodland graves were in mounds and ceremonial centers, but at times, they were in isolated settings. In southwestern Indiana, an E/M Woodland cremation was in an upland region overlooking a former marshland. There is no evidence of a mound or structure at the site, which covered about 0.41 hectares. The material culture from the site includes 15 "leaf-shaped" blades, a grooved sandstone "tablet," a stemmed point, and a drill. Most of the artifacts were immediately associated with a feature that yielded the cremains. The artifacts did not show evidence of heat and were deposited after the body was burned. The burial feature lacked burned soil, indicating the burning of the remains took place elsewhere. The highly fragmented and calcined skeletal remains had red ocher on them, and appeared to represent a single adult individual (Tomak and O'Connor, 1978).

The Hopewell aspect of the E/M Woodland is a continuation of the Adena burial cult (e.g., Applegate, 2008; Carskadden, 2008; McCord and Cochran, 2014). It was once thought to be a distinct cultural entity (e.g., Brose and Greber, 1979), but archeologists continue to find evidence that Adena and Hopewell are the same (e.g., McCord and Cochran, 2014; Henry and Barrier, 2016). The traditions set forth during the early aspect of the E/M Woodland, that is, the construction of large mounds for social and funerary affairs, the use of pottery, and the harvesting of domesticated starchy and oily seed plants, were also important aspects of Middle Woodland life. Likewise, the complex religious and trade networks founded during the Adena continued to link Hopewell people. Thus, the Hopewell aspect of Adena/Hopewell was a fluorescence of religions and economic practices that emerged centuries before (e.g., Carr and Case, 2005; Charles and Buikstra, 2006; Ruby et al., 2006).

Hopewell was a regional phenomenon that bridged people across the midcontinent and beyond. Formerly described as an "interaction sphere" (e.g., Brose and Greber, 1979) today archeologists see it as much more. Archeological evidence points to Hopewell including economic exchange, religion and burial cults, pilgrimages, vision quests, long distance exchanges of medical knowledge, and trade among elites (e.g., Carr, 2006). Some of the trade goods that moved long distances included mica from the Appalachians; marine shells, shark, alligator, and barracuda teeth from the Atlantic coast; quartzite from Arkansas; silver from near Lake Superior; copper from Michigan; and obsidian from the area of Yellowstone National Park (Griffin, 1983; Stoltman, 1978; Seeman,

1979). The Hopewell phenomenon was particularly robust in Illinois, Indiana, Ohio, and Kentucky. The first sites to be designated Hopewell were from southern Ohio where several sites including Mound City, Seip, and Hopewell still exist. At the Hopewell site near Chillicothe, Ohio, 38 conical mounds are present. A road connected the Newark Earthworks, near Columbus, Ohio to Chillicothe in the southern part of the state.

Hopewell was present throughout northern and southern Indiana. The complexity of Indiana Hopewell varied and some sites took on elaborate ceremonial levels comparable to Ohio Hopewell (e.g., Ruby, 2006). Hicks (1992) describes a number of sites containing circular or sub-rectangular earthworks around the modern cities of Anderson, New Castle, Cambridge City in east-central Indiana. In addition, at least two large enclosures were near Winchester and Fountain City. The sites were primarily located near bluff edges overlooking river valleys and distributed relatively evenly throughout the area. By studying the artifactual inclusions and site sizes, Hicks determined the Hopewell sites in east-central Indiana lacked the same level of ceremonialism found at Hopewell sites near Chillicothe, Ohio. People visited the earthwork sites periodically, but for most of the year, people lived in small, short-term hamlets (Clay, 2009; McCord and Cochran, 2014).

Cochran (1992) also looked at Adena/Hopewell in east-central Indiana; he focused on site positions relative to each other and to celestial objects. He and colleagues plotted the locations and orientations of burial mounds, circular enclosures, and earthwork complexes and found that the site landmarks often pointed toward important astronomical features. For example, he found that vectors through the corners of Fudge Mound aligned with the sunrise and sunset at the summer and winter solstices. Interestingly, the Adena and Hopewell sites had the same alignments, indicating a shared cosmology. This cosmological similarity, as well as the co-occurrence of Adena and Hopewell artifacts at these sites, led Cochran and McCord to conclude that Adena and Hopewell were simply early and late versions of the same phenomenon (McCord and Cochran, 2014).

In northern Indiana, Hopewell sites include the Goodall Site, which had 22 mounds, some of which were arranged in a semi-circle (Brown, 1977). Another northern Indiana Hopewell site is the Franz-Green Mound (McAllister, 1932). This mound was 3 m high and just under 70 m in circumference. At least 17 burials of adults and subadults were within the mound. It also had two human hemi-mandibles, which look very much like worked human mandibles from the GE Mound in southern Indiana (Tomak, 1994c). E/M Woodland sites commonly produce ground human and nonhuman mandibles. Some call the mandibles "cut," but they were ground with sandstone primarily on their inferior and distal surfaces (Schmidt and Helmkamp, 1997).

To the south, the Mann and the GE Mound sites belong to Hopewell. The Mann site represents one of the largest known Middle Woodland sites. It extends for over a mile along a high terrace bordering the floodplain of the Ohio River. Mann had 16 earthen structures, including five geometric earthworks, a linear embankment, and 10 mounds; it is the largest Middle Woodland earthwork site outside of Ohio (Cole, 2017: 8). The largest mound, Mound 3, is one of the largest earthen structures known in the Hopewellian realm; it is about 150 m in length, 75 m in width, and 4 m high (Ruby, 1997). The ceramic styles at Mann were unusual for the area and resembled motifs from the southeast (Ruby, 1993). A tremendous number of Mann ceramics indicated domestic activities, which runs counter to ideas that large ceremonial centers lacked residents (Ruby, 1993). Thus, the use of Hopewell ceremonial sites in southern Indiana differs from those in east-central aspects of the state. Evidence for domestic activity at Mann goes beyond ceramics. Perhaps as many as 80 hectares of the site had a thick midden indicative of habitation (Ruby and Shriner, 2005), implying Mann functioned ceremonially and domestically for a long time. The ceremonies likely included mortuary practices, but the realm of the dead may not have been limited to people. Cole (2017) argues that some of the broken artifacts at Mann were "killed" by the inhabitants perhaps as a part of a purification ritual.

Overall, the Mann artifact assemblage is extraordinary. In addition to prodigious amounts of pottery sherds, it produced over 3000 lamellar blades (similar to others found in Ohio), copper earspools, copious amounts of galena, copper headplates, meteoric iron, obsidian bifaces, mica, plummets made from limonite, steatite, hematite, marine shell, copper, crystal quartz, Knife River chalcedony, and sharks teeth (Ruby, 1993, 1997; Ruby and Shriner, 2005; Cole, 2017).

Hopewell burial practices were similar to those of Adena. Byers (2005) sees Hopewell burials as part of a burial process, a series of ceremonies where the dead received visits from the living in order to help move them from this world to the next via stages of processing that eventually ended in cremation. This view is not held by all archeologists, but Hopewell mortuary practices, no matter how explained, are complex and varied. Moreover, it is common for ceremonial centers, particularly those in Ohio, to have huge deposits of cremains. One characteristic of Hopewell is the elaboration of burial for elite individuals, who may have had leadership or religious roles. An example of one of these highly elaborate burials comes from the GE Mound (also known as the Mount Vernon Mound) in far southwestern Indiana, very close to the Ohio River.

The original loaf-shaped mound was 122 m long, 52 m wide, and 6 m high (Tomak, 1994c). Inside was an adult male buried with thousands of local and exotic artifacts, including thousands of partially worked chert blades, so-called cache blades; ceremonial projectile points made of quartzite from Arkansas, and local cannel coal; hundreds of grizzly bear teeth likely from Wyoming, and black bear teeth; copper earspools, panpipes, and some unidentified copper fragments; and over 20 human mandible fragments representing at least 13 people (Tomak, 1994c). The human mandible fragments had holes drilled in them and may have been strung on a necklace or similar piece of ornamentation. The mandible fragments came primarily from young adult males and females, and were made by grinding the inferior and posterior edges against sandstone (Schmidt and Helmkamp, 1997).

More typically, Hopewell graves had people buried within or near domiciles (Griffin, 1983), or placed in log tombs within mounds, as cremations, inhumations, or bundles (e.g., Swartz, 1973; Konigsberg, 1985). It is not clear if all of the people in a single mound or a single log tomb came from a single social or kin group. At times, it appears they did (e.g., Konigsberg, 1985). At other times, Hopewell people may have put their dead in particular mounds or structures based on their societal roles or social status. Thus, members of a single community could have had ancestors in multiple burial locations at a given mortuary site (e.g., Carr, 2006).

Late Woodland

The Late Woodland period began around 1000 BP and lasted for approximately 200 years. The elaborate log tombs, worked copper, and effigy artifacts of the E/M Woodland were no longer in existence. Instead, technological advances marked the period. The first of these advances was the bow and arrow, indicated by the presence of small triangular projectile points. The bow and arrow likely made its way into the eastern woodlands via trade with Native groups to the west. This happened while the importation of exotic goods, such as copper from Michigan and obsidian from the Rocky Mountains, abated (Muller, 1986). Another technological advance, also from the west, was maize agriculture, which first took hold in Indiana at this time (Chapter 3).

The earliest group typically linked to the Late Woodland is the Allison-LaMotte. These people overlapped temporally with the E/M Woodland until about 1400 BP and their presence in Indiana is known through a number of sites in the west-central part of the state (Redmond and McCullough, 2000). My focus, however, is on the Albee aspect of the Late Woodland (e.g., MacLean, 1931; Winters, 1967). The LW Albee pottery was grit-tempered and cord-marked, although fabric impressed and plain shards occur in archeological assemblages (Kellar, 1983; McCord and Cochran, 1994; Redmond and McCullough, 2000). In addition to small triangular points, LW Albee artifacts included ceramic and limestone pipes, drills, cylindrical copper beads, bone beamers, turtle carapaces, gravers, perforators, antler tines, cut antler drifts, bone/antler hooks, large needles, raccoon baculum tools, and bird bone flutes (Winters, 1967; McCord and Cochran, 1994, 2003; Redmond and McCullough, 2000: 657).

The Albee people lived in nonnucleated, relatively small and widespread settlements primarily throughout central Indiana, but they expanded into northern and southern aspects of the state as well (Tomak, 1983; Redmond and McCullough, 2000). The Morell-Sheets from west-central Indiana is one of just a few studied Albee habitation sites (Bush, 2003, 2004). It overlooked a nearby creek and its Albee affinities included cord-marked pottery and arrow points (McCord and Cochran, 1994, 2003). It was seasonally occupied from late spring to early fall, based on the plant foods found there including nuts, seeds, and some maize (Bush, 2003).

Albee mortuary practices included mound and nonmound burials. Most Albee sites are known because of their mortuary component; mortuaries were commonly on natural knolls above wet lands or river valleys (Redmond and McCullough, 2000: 658). As noted earlier, the Albee

Mound site, located in the west-central part of the state, is the namesake for the LW Albee tradition. It was a large, natural mound containing numerous burials; the artifacts from the mound included shell beads, bone awls, antler flaking tools, and rectangular slate gorgets (MacLean, 1931). The Baker-Lowe burial mound in southern Indiana was a natural structure, too (Redmond and McCullough, 2000). Some Albee burials occurred in human-made mounds, including those at the Akers and Catlin sites (Anslinger, 1990; Redmond and McCullough, 2000). At the Shaffer and Shepherd sites in southern Indiana, interments were not in mounds and took place near habitation areas (Tomak, 1970).

A small site in northwestern Indiana, Ski Island, produced two intact adult graves placed in pits on the outskirts of the habitation area. The site eroded from a modest, sandy slope next to a large reservoir. Most of the year the site was submerged, but opening the dam to check for repairs ended up exposing the site in the early 1990s. A collector looking for artifacts found human bones sticking from the surface; I was part of the team that excavated the remains. The burials included an older adult female in a flexed position who had bone awls and pins made from turkey and small mammal bones underneath her. She also had a fist-sized stone next to her that may have held an animal hide in place over her. The other adult, also a flexed female, had a cord-marked vessel next to her.

It is likely the Ski Island burial artifacts reflect the lives of these women; perhaps the older woman used the tools found with her during her life; or, maybe she needed them for the afterlife. The same could be said about the younger woman and her accompanying ceramic vessel. Whatever the Albee cosmology was, it was important, to those who buried the women, to place these particular artifacts in their graves. I close the Albee section with this small, poorly known site to make a point before moving into larger and better-known precontact groups. Archaeology should not overlook small sites. Large sites are wonderful, but small sites tell important stories that may be absent among those who lived at the large localities.

Late Precontact

The Late Precontact followed the Late Woodland, starting around 750 years ago and continuing until Native people encountered Europeans.

In Indiana, French fur traders explored potential trade routes from the mid-1600s on, and the French founded their first sustained settlements in 1719 at Forts Philippe and Ouiatenon along the Wabash River in the northern third of the state (Glenn, 1992). Of course, European contact occurred at different times at different places, and brief encounters took place before settlements did. By the late 18th century, virtually all Native groups in Indiana had their lives impacted by Europeans, either through direct contact or through interactions with Native peoples displaced from the east (Glenn, 1992).

Here I discuss two of the several Late Precontact groups in Indiana because they are germane to the study at hand: the Fort Ancient and the Mississippian. The Indiana manifestation of the Fort Ancient is the Oliver tradition. It used to be that archeologists considered Oliver a distinct Late Precontact group, but over the decades, they realized its placement within Fort Ancient (McCullough, 2003). Here I use the informal moniker "Fort Ancient Oliver" to denote that the Fort Ancient people I studied are from Indiana.

Fort Ancient Oliver

Fort Ancient people lived in complex tribal-level societies; they had large villages that frequently had a central plaza surrounded by houses. They were maize horticulturists and made an extensive variety of ceramics, many of which had a diagnostic guilloche design (McCullough, 1992, 2003; Pollack and Henderson, 1992; Redmond, 2003). Lithics included arrow points and many Fort Ancient artifacts indicate influences from Mississippian people including ceramic styles and shell-tempering. There a number of sizable Fort Ancient sites in southeastern Indiana, western Ohio, and northern Kentucky. One of the more prominent was SunWatch in southwestern Ohio; the Fort Ancient people there occupied the site on at least two occasions between 800 and 500 BP (Cook, 2007). The apparent occupation and de-occupation of the site may relate to a swidden-like means of agriculture, where people farmed an area for years and then moved on to another site. After some time, perhaps many years, the people returned to their original village site where the long-fallow fields were ready again for planting (Henderson and Pollack, 2001).

The SunWatch cemetery produced 166 people, 103 subadults and 63 adults (Gosman and Ketcham, 2009). The burial population consisted of kin groups, indicated by "cluster analysis of burial, house, pit feature, and artifact characteristics and distributions" (Sciulli and Cook, 2016: 721). One of the kin groups buried in the northeast portion of the village had dog burials and people with dog and wolf adornments, including wolf jaw and wolf teeth pendants and headgear. Archeologists interpret this as evidence for a wolf clan or a male-oriented sodality (Heilman and Hoefer, 1981; Sciulli and Cook, 2016: 721). Evidence for similar clan or clan-like entities occur at other Fort Ancient sites including Anderson Village. Moreover, associations between the Wolf clan and the northeast corners of villages existed among historic groups related to the Fort Ancient (Sciulli and Cook, 2016).

The Fort Ancient Oliver tradition of Indiana extended from the southeastern to the northwestern aspects of the state, with concentrations along the East and West forks of the White River (McCullough, 2003; Redmond, 2003). Most Oliver sites were on river floodplains and terraces near major tributaries (Redmond, 2003). The Clampitt site in southern Indiana dates to around 600–700 BP. It is one of the most thoroughly documented Oliver tradition sites on record. Clampitt was about 0.41 hectares in size and had at least one stockade (and possibly a second) surrounding a central plaza. The Cox's Woods site, also from southern Indiana, had evidence for a stockade as well as a deep midden. Archeological work ceased before determining the extent and nature of the midden, but at 90 cm deep it indicates an intensive usage of the site. In addition, the site produced evidence of a sub-rectangular wall trench house, the only one of its kind known from Oliver sites (Redmond, 2000).

Clampitt had 39 pit features and Cox's Woods had 13. Several of these were cylindrical storage pits before they were used for refuse and are similar to Fort Ancient storage pits in the middle Ohio Valley (Redmond, 2000). The pits, post molds, and other indicators of domestic activity exist in a ring around the plaza; some of the pits produced charred maize, nutshell, and seeds from little barley, goosefoot, and maygrass (Redmond, 2000).

The largest Oliver cemetery in Indiana is that from Bowen (Dorwin, 1971). I discuss this site in more detail later, therefore, here I draw from other Fort Ancient contexts to describe their mortuary practices. Most Fort Ancient burials took place in areas between the village's central plaza and the houses and structures around it, although at times people buried infants and newborns in refuse pits. Mound burials took place as well (Pollack and Henderson, 1992). Funerary adornment was not common, but occasionally utilitarian objects and shells appeared in Fort Ancient burials. The aforementioned dog and wolf bone indicators of clan membership are infrequent finds, but, nonetheless, they make it clear that Fort Ancient people had mortuary differentiation likely related to social roles and identities linked to kinship (Pollack and Henderson, 1992; Sciulli and Cook, 2016).

Hardin Village had a large Fort Ancient cemetery. It was located in northern Kentucky on the south bank of the Ohio River (Osterholt, 2019). Occupied into the early historic period, Hardin lacked earthen mounds and its two settlements were organized into concentric rings; at the center of each settlement was a central plaza surrounded by a ring of burials. Beyond the burials was a ring of structures; Hardin had eight confirmed and 11 possible structures. One of the structures was a possible mortuary house; it was the only structure to have graves below it (Osterholt, 2019). Hardin's cemetery produced over 400 people. Around 86% of the burials were single inhumations although double and triple burials occurred. Two individuals had graves lined with limestone slabs. Fewer than half of the single interments had grave goods, and subadults were twice as likely to have grave goods as adults were (Osterholt, 2019). Thus, Fort Ancient cemeteries lacked much of the grave elaboration that is seen in their Mississippian contemporaries.

Mississippian

First used to describe a ceramic tradition, the term Mississippian applies to late precontact chiefdom-level populations primarily in the eastern woodlands. Historically, the traits of the Mississippian culture included large settlements exhibiting a stockade and central platform mound; maize-bean-squash agriculture; ornately decorated, shell-tempered pottery; triangular projectile points; shell and lithic hoes; and the presence of discoidals and other unique lithic and ceramic implements (Muller, 1986; Stoltman, 1978). Wide-ranging descriptions of the Mississippian culture appear periodically throughout the archeological literature; Griffin (1978) characterized Mississippians as people of the eastern deciduous woodlands who lived during the time period A.D. 800–1500. They had a ranked form of social organization, and had developed a specific complex adaptation to linear, environmentally circumscribed floodplain habitat zones. This adaptation involved maize horticulture and selective utilization of a limited number of wild plants and animals that represented dependable, seasonally abundant energy resources that could be exploited at a relatively low level of energy expenditure (Griffin, 1978: 486).

This definition is simplistic but it addresses some key points needed to understand the Mississippian as archeologists encountered it. This definition also does not inform us regarding what 'Mississippian' was. The Mississippian was not a particular culture so much as it was a realm of social and political influence based in large part on religious/mortuary beliefs (Pauketat, 2007). Starting from a site known as Cahokia in western Illinois around 1200 years ago, Mississippian ways spread to the north into Wisconsin and to the west into Missouri, and eventually into Oklahoma. By about 700 years ago it expanded east into Indiana and into the southeast through the gulf-states and over to Georgia. The spread of Mississippian ideas meant town construction followed a particular plan that included having a central plaza and at least one large platform mound. It also meant adopting maize, if a group had not done so already, because it was the staple underlying Mississippian expansion. Yet, amid the changes brought to the places where it spread, Mississippianization did not obviate local ways of life; it was not a hostile takeover, and it embraced several forms of sociopolitical organization and leadership (Pauketat, 2007). By incorporating a myriad of local cultural traditions, languages, and cosmologies, the Mississippian formed, in the words of Tim Pauketat, a "Transregional, spatio-cultural phenomenon ... an ethnoscape" (Pauketat, 2007: 85).

One of the best examples of Mississippian lifeways comes from Cahokia, which was the largest and most complex precontact city north of the Rio Grande (Alt, 2012). By any standard, Cahokia was a major site (Fowler, 1975, 1977; Gregg, 1975; Pauketat, 2007). It covered at least 1000 hectares and had over 120 earthen mounds. The largest mound, known today as Monks Mound, was over 30 m high and covered an area of 5 hectares at its base, which is larger than the base of the great pyramid at Giza, in Egypt. Monks Mound sat at the north end of a massive central plaza, which had around it platform and conical mounds and various other structures. Cahokia also had a ring of upright wooden posts, today known as 'woodhenge', which may have been a celestial calendar (Fowler, 1974). Population estimates usually range between 10,000 and 20,000 people, who included locals, pilgrims, and immigrants (Pauketat, 2007; Alt, 2012). It probably had some type of hierarchical social structure, although its means of sociopolitical organization and leadership is highly debated (e.g., Milner, 1998; Byers, 2006; Pauketat, 2007; Holt, 2009).

For decades archeologists saw Cahokia as a chiefdom or complex chiefdom (Fowler, 1974; Milner, 1998; Knight and Steponaitis, 1998; Fowler et al., 1999). It was a regional polity, but lacked some of the traits of state-level societies, such as writing and a standing army (Pauketat, 2007). Recently this view has undergone some reassessment as alternative views of statehood emerge (Holt, 2009). To Holt (2009), Cahokia could have been a state where people came to engage in public works and social exchanges not under duress or coercion, but rather via their own desire to be part of a social phenomenon. In this way, the state, called a theater state, was more like a stage for people to carry out social dramas they concocted within the political and social fabric (e.g., Holt, 2009). On the other hand, Byers (2006) does not see a hierarchical structure at Cahokia so much as a heterarchical one, where autonomous groups of people pooled their efforts to build monumental structures in order to participate in a world-renewal mortuary cult. No matter how archeologists ultimately decide to frame Cahokia's means of sociopolitical organization, it is clear that it was an extraordinary place laden with examples of technological, intellectual, and organizational achievement.

Mississippian settlement patterns generally consisted of two manifestations: nucleated and dispersed. Nucleated settlements had densely arranged living structures often surrounded by a fortification. These sites had hundreds or thousands of people, including some people having an elevated social status indicated by where they lived or their daily functions (see Pauketat, 2007). The dispersed pattern of settlement consisted of homesteads spread out along a floodplain. These settlements were largely autonomous but traded with and had other social connections with nucleated Mississippian towns; they were common in the lower Ohio River valley (Muller, 1986, 1997; Milner, 1991). Interestingly, settlement size had little effect on daily activities; those in the dispersed settlements had the same tools and performed the same functions as those in nucleated settlements; and, at both settlement types, nearly all economic functions took place at the domestic level (Muller, 1997).

Mississippian houses indicate sedentism for the Mississippian people (Smith, 1986). In the southeastern United States, houses had vertical poles set in trenches and covered with mud plaster and sticks (wattle-and-daub) and the roof was made of thatch. Houses were square and usually had a hearth at the center. This shape was the predominant design for all structures, including ceremonial structures, except that at times higher status people had larger domiciles on or near platform mounds (Muller, 1983; Pauketat, 2007).

Houses at Spiro, a large Mississippian site in Oklahoma, had cedar posts set into the ground. People wove cane and grasses between the wood posts and packed clay around the frame. These housed extended families, ranging from five to 15 people (Griffin, 1983; Muller, 1983). At Cahokia houses changed over time, from single and double post pit houses to rectangular wall trench houses. They increased in size too. By 900 BP, the area of an average house was approximately 18.6 m^2. By 500 BP, the average area approached 46.5 m^2. Moreover, house density was high; houses covered over 688 hectares. Two tracts of excavated area yielded 309 contemporaneous houses. There were approximately eight houses per 0.41 hectares at Cahokia, most of which were outside of the palisade (Muller, 1997), and older houses often had younger houses built over them (Gregg, 1975). Commonly, Mississippian people had a lightly-built summer house in addition to their wattle-and-daub home (Black, 1967; Muller, 1997).

Mississippian mortuary practices are varied and a thorough accounting is well-beyond the scope of this summary. In fact, there are so many they could fill entire books (see Goldstein, 1980; Sullivan and Mainfort, 2010). Briefly, Mississippian graves occurred in conical mounds, platform mounds, ridge-top mounds, low-round mounds, cemeteries having no mound, in stone boxes, and, at times, in caves (e.g., Goldstein, 1980; Simek and Cressler, 2010; Sullivan and Mainfort, 2010). Burial placements were in rows, in clusters, and in isolation (e.g., Black, 1967; Goldstein, 1980); positions included extended, flexed, and bundled. Some had copious artifactual inclusions while others had none. Some people were cremated, others had only parts of their bodies interred (e.g., Sullivan and Mainfort, 2010; Emerson et al., 2016). The variations in mortuary treatments stemmed from changes in mortuary customs over time as generations modified and adjusted practices they inherited from their ancestors, as well as from synchronic regional and local variants in belief, practice, and perceptions of the dead (e.g., Holt, 2009; Brown, 2010; Pauketat, 2010; Alt, 2012). The flow of immigrants into the Mississippian realm added to the belief system variability. There were, of course, religious themes throughout the Mississippianized eastern woodlands (e.g., Pauketat, 2010), but like widely-adopted religions of today, people internalized religious themes as independent actors and, as such, injected their own nuances into them.

One of the most elaborate Mississippian burials is that of Mound 72 at Cahokia, which produced over 20,000 shell beads, 800 projectile points, and hundreds of people. Earlier studies of the burial determined it housed two male leaders, at least one of which was placed on an elaborate bed of the aforementioned shell beads. Moreover, accompanying the men were hordes of sacrificed victims (Fowler et al., 1999). A recent reassessment of the skeletal remains from Mound 72, however, determined that one of the two individuals thought to be a male, was a female. Moreover, the bead bed was not intended for a single elite person, and the cluster of bones associated with the beads included several females and a child (Emerson et al., 2016). Mound 72 was a sacred mortuary place related to world creation, renewal, and fertility and not a grand burial of privileged males (Emerson et al., 2016). This interpretation, of course, does not make Mound 72 any less extraordinary. In fact, there does not seem to be any burial like it before or since (Pauketat, 2010). The reinterpretation helps us see Mound 72 from a new vantage point, where it was a persistent place for the living to interact with the dead.

Around 500 years ago, the Mississippian declined. Large social and political entities require a great deal of human input to keep them going; once they lose that effort the entity, be it a polity or a religious movement, fades. In Indiana, the post Mississippian people were the Caborn-Welborn. They lived in maize farming communities of up to a 100 rectangular houses or so. Some sites had central plazas, but none had earthen mounds or defensive walls (Pollack, 2004). These were the last of the precontact people in Indiana; the arrival of Europeans forever changed their Native lifeways.

CHAPTER 3

Subsistence and paleodietary reconstructions

Introduction

Bioarcheologists seek to understand ancient lives, therefore, we need a clear knowledge of diet and subsistence in order to understand certain aspects of the human experience including diseases, nutrition, and demography. For example, let us say that a group had evidence in their teeth of growth disruption during childhood, which we would see as hypoplastic lines across labial surfaces. What caused the disruption? Was it poor nutrition or something else? Because of its fundamental role in our health and ways of life, determining what people ate is at the heart of bioarchaeological analysis.

Subsistence is defined as the resources and behaviors associated with meeting a population's nutritional demands. Diet, on the other hand, is foods actually consumed (Hillson, 1979). There is usually a close link between diet and subsistence, but not always. For example, some groups rear plants or animals they do not eat, or eat sparingly. An example of this comes from the highlands of New Guinea, where people rear pigs for trade and only eat them on certain occasions (Strathern, 1975). Another comes from Arkansas about 1300 years ago. People there stored maize in a number of features, which from a subsistence standpoint indicated people farmed it. A study of bone chemistry determined, however, that only one person, a child, had evidence of maize consumption. Despite its archeological abundance, maize was not a dietary staple (Rose et al., 1991).

Archeological subsistence records derive from three primary sources, paleobotany, the study of plant remains at archeological sites, zooarcheology, the study of animal remains at archeological sites, and material culture indicative of cooking, storage, and processing. The paleobotanical record of ancient Indiana is a tremendous guide for understanding the foods people potentially consumed. It usually consists of charred seeds and nuts, but can include any part of a plant that happened to preserve including wood, rind, and cob fragments

Long 'on' the Tooth. DOI: https://doi.org/10.1016/B978-0-12-824306-0.00003-3

(Pearsall, 1989). Perhaps more than anyone, Leslie Bush has diligently uncovered Indiana's paleobotanical record, and archeologists and bioarcheologists appreciate the subsistence data she provides, much of which I draw from in this book. The zooarcheological record usually consists of animal bones that can range from nearly microscopic fish vertebrae to deer antlers half a meter long. Zooarcheologists are able to determine the environments where people hunted and the kinds of animals they preferred. The material culture record is the presence and distribution of artifacts used to harvest, carry, store, grind, boil, or cook foods such as ceramics, baskets, grinding stones, nutting stones, and hearths. Below are summaries of paleobotanical, zooarcheological, and material culture records from Indiana and surrounding areas for each archeological group.

Paleobotanical evidence for subsistence in Indiana

A glimpse of Early Archaic subsistence comes from southern Illinois. There archeologists found that black walnuts, pecans, and hazelnuts were staples (Styles et al., 1983: 284). Also present were seeds from grape, persimmon, wild bean, and wild goosefoot. Exploiting these particular resources must have been common throughout the area (Asch and Asch, 1976, 1980). Eventually, pecan and hazelnut declined in popularity and thick-shelled hickory increased (Asch and Asch, 1980; Styles et al., 1983). In addition to nuts, Early Archaic people collected wild seed plants growing in aquatic and alluvial soils including water shield, mint, dock, knotweed, and bedstraw (Johannessen, 1981: 172–174). In Kentucky, Early Archaic floral resources included hickory nuts, acorns, black walnuts, and berries (Cassidy, 1972). Specifically in the Green River area, hickory nuts constituted 80%–90%, by weight, of the recovered plant remains (Crawford, 1982: 219). The only domestication known from this time was the dog, which the Pre-Clovis people brought with them to the Americas when they first entered the continent (e.g., Erickson et al., 2005).

The M/L Archaic people lived as hunter/gatherers, some of whom experienced increased seasonal sedentism (e.g., Jefferies and Butler, 1982; Jefferies, 2008). Wild food resources included walnuts, hickory nuts, and acorns; underground storage organs like tubers and bulbs; grapes and berries; wild bean; wild greens and weedy plants; and aquatic plants (e.g., Crawford, 1982; Fritz, 2000; Simon, 2009). The wild weedy plants (perhaps sought for the starchy and oily seeds) underwent such intensive collection that it changed the anatomy of their seeds (Gremillion, 2015). Intentionally or not, the people harvesting these plants favored those that matured quickly. A seed with a thin shell, or testa, and a large embryo germinates more rapidly than those with thicker testa. An example of this is goosefoot (*Chenopodium berlandieri*), which over time experienced a decline in average testa thickness and an increase in average embryo size. Domestication occurred at the point goosefoot (or any species for that matter) became dependent upon humans to survive (Smith, 1985a,b; Smith and Cowan, 1987; Gremillion, 1993).

Some of the earliest paleobotanical evidence of plant domestication comes from the Cumberland Plateau in Kentucky, just beyond Indiana's border (e.g., Yarnell, 1993; Gremillion, 1996, 2015). Climatic fluctuations opened up forested areas that were excellent weedy plant habitats (Gremillion, 2015). In addition, anthropogenic changes to the forest, including burning, altered the landscape in ways that favored their growth (Fritz, 2000; Gremillion, 2015). The degree to which M/L Archaic people managed forests with fire is debated, but that they modified their environment in order to exercise their subsistence practices is certain (Gremillion, 2015). Not only did their management efforts favor the plants they eventually domesticated, they also favored certain nut-bearing trees (Gremillion, 2015). These efforts facilitated increased sedentism and food storage (e.g., Cowan, 1985).

Collectively, the domesticated starchy and oily seed-bearing plants are known as the eastern agricultural complex (EAC); the earliest of which were domesticated by 3000 BP; they were the aforementioned goosefoot, sumpweed (*Iva annua*), and sunflower (*Helianthus annuus*). Later, people added knotweed (*Polygonum erectum*), maygrass (*Phalaris caroliniana*), and little barley (*Hordeum pusillum*) (Fritz, 1993; Gremillion, 1996, 2015). Also domesticated were cucurbits (e.g., *Cucurbito pepo*); in fact, their domestication preceded that of the EAC (Simon, 2009), but their role in precontact diets is unclear. To date, there is no evidence of domestication during the M/L Archaic in Indiana. This indicates that domestication took place in particular areas of the eastern woodlands and gradually spread over time.

E/M Woodland subsistence strategies were extensions of those established during the M/L Archaic with continued exploitation of the

EAC (e.g., Buikstra, 1984; Johannessen, 1987; Smith and Cowan, 1987). Wild foods included hickory nut, walnut, amaranth, canary grass, smartweed, giant ragweed, marsh elder, butternut, acorn, chestnut, chinquapin, pawpaw, honey locust, green briar, raspberry, and ragweed (Cassidy, 1984). Goslin (1957) found hickory nuts, pumpkin, black walnut, goosefoot, and raspberry in 23 E/M Woodland mound sites in Indiana, Ohio, Kentucky, and West Virginia, and 10 E/M Woodland rockshelters in Kentucky. Rarely maize shows up in E/M Woodland botanical assemblages (Smith, 1986). It reached the eastern woodlands via trade with people from the southwest, where it entered the United States from Mexico (Benz, 2009); its infrequency in the E/M Woodland record indicates it was not a food resource (Fritz, 1993).

Late Woodland diets drew heavily from wild and domesticated resources (Conaty, 1983; Johannessen, 1987; Gremillion, 1996). During the Late Woodland in southern Illinois, starchy seeds made up 94% of the identifiable botanical remains (Johannessen, 1984a). At the Morell-Sheets site in east-central Indiana, little barley was the primary food, making up 65% of the seeds found there (Bush, 1994). Despite its popularity, it was not a domesticated variety (Bush, 2004). Other foods at Morell-Sheets were maize, raspberry, hickory nut, hazelnut, walnut, blueberry, maygrass, knotweed, elderberry, and verbena. Maize is far more common during the Late Woodland compared to the E/M Woodland. It made up about 17% of the botanicals at Morell-Sheets.

By the Late Precontact, maize was a staple throughout the eastern woodlands and throughout much of the temperate regions of North America (Bellwood, 2005). As maize became more popular, reaching perhaps 70% of the Late Precontact diet (Perzigian et al., 1984), the starchy and oily seeds became less so.

At the Fort Ancient Oliver tradition Clampitt site, hickory nut was most prevalent, followed by maize, walnut, hazelnut, acorn, blueberry, sumac, bramble, grape, grass, domesticated bean, and others. Goosefoot was present but not common (Bush, 1994). Maize accounted for 32% of the total botanical remains. At the contemporary Bowen site, maize comprised about 88% of the total botanical remains; the people of Bowen also exploited hickory nut and walnut.

Eventually, the introduction of kidney beans, originally from Mexico, gave people of the Mississippian the three domesticates (maize, beans, and squash/pumpkin) that anchored Native American agriculture until and throughout the period of European contact. Like their predecessors, however, the people of the Mississippian did not abandon collecting wild foods. Nuts and berries continued to be important (Kellar, 1967; Whalley, 1983).

Faunal evidence for subsistence

Although plant domestication increased over time, animal domestication did not. In fact, other than the dog, which arrived already domesticated, there were no other domesticated animals in the precontact New World. Thus, all animal foods required hunting. From the Early Archaic to the Late Precontact, whitetail deer was very important. Deer remains turn up at nearly every habitation site in Indiana (e.g. Tomak, 1970). Other animals that Native people hunted frequently included raccoon, beaver, muskrat, otter, wild turkey, box turtle, and fish (e.g. Cassidy, 1972). Mussels were incredibly popular during the M/L Archaic. This freshwater bivalve mollusk flourished in the shallows of the Ohio River and its tributaries. People harvested, steamed open, and consumed them before disposing of their shells in massive shell middens. One such midden in southern Indiana is 5–10 cm thick and extends for about one-half mile (Burdin, 2002).

Fishing must have been common during the M/L Archaic, too. Fish bones do not preserve as well as the hard, calcareous mussel shells. Nonetheless, bones from freshwater drum and catfish are frequent finds. In fact, many animals whose bones do not preserve well show up in faunal assemblages often enough to indicate that small animal hunting occured regularly; prey included small birds, reptiles, and amphibians (Cross, 1984). Preservation may not be the only factor that mitigates the likelihood of finding small animal bones at archeological sites; it is possible that people ate small animals whole, thus, keeping their bones from accumulating in features.

Like the M/L Archaic people, the E/M and Late Woodland people hunted a great deal of deer, along with turkey, raccoon, gray squirrel, and fox squirrel. Other animals were elk, cottontail, black bear, box turtle, frog, mole, bobcat, gray wolf, coyote, snapping turtle, passenger pigeon, Canada goose, bullfrog, badger, mountain lion, buffalo fish, red-shouldered hawk, woodchuck, muskrat, duck and striped skunk (Richards, 1988; Redmond, 1994). One might expect to see bison prominently on this list. However, modern bison (*Bison bison*) did not enter the state until about 500 years ago, around the beginning of the so-called "Little Ice Age" when average northern hemisphere temperatures dropped by about 2 degrees centigrade. They remained in the state until extirpation in 1800 (Tankersley and Adams, 1991). The only bison from an archeological context comes from southern Indiana and likely dates between 200 and 500 years ago (Tankersley and Adams, 1991).

Some of the best evidence for Late Precontact hunting comes from the sites of Angel and Cahokia. Angel produced over 500,000 animal bones (Kellar, 1967). These remains include 26 species of mammals, 32 species of birds, nine species of fishes, 31species of mussels, and five species of reptiles. Of this great assemblage, nearly 90% of the vertebrate remains came from whitetail deer (Neumann, 1961). Other important animals were gray squirrel, raccoon, fox squirrel, opossum, Adirondack cougar, Carolina beaver, rabbit, elk, and lynx (Adams, 1950). Finding large quantities of faunal remains at Mississippian sites is not uncommon (e.g. Parmalee, 1975; Cross, 1983, 1984; Kelly and Cross, 1984) but Angel's record is special.

Cahokia, too, boasts a large faunal collection. Analysts studied over 150,000 animal bone fragments. Like Angel, whitetail deer was very important at Cahokia. Likewise, birds and fish remains were common. Zooarcheologists identified 29 mammals, 72 birds, 29 fishes, nine reptiles and four amphibian species (Parmalee, 1975). The bird species included a large number of waterfowl such as great blue heron, common egret, American bittern, whistling swan, trumpeter swan, Canada goose, snow goose, mallard, black duck, wood duck, ring-necked duck, ruddy duck, and several others. Turkey, raptors, and the passenger pigeon also were common. Fishes included bullheads, sunfish, suckers, and a number of small species. One modestly sized feature yielded 21,000 fish bone fragments. None of the fishes from this feature exceeded two pounds, and most were under a quarter of a pound. To catch fish of this small size the people must have used a small-mesh seine (Parmalee, 1975). Incidentally, the fishes and water birds likely lived close to Mississippian villages. In order to build their enormous earthen mounds, the Mississippian people collected earth from huge barrow pits. As the pits filled with ground water, they became perfect habitat for waterfowl and fish. All told, Cahokia produced around 77,000 mammals, 52,000 fishes, 19,000 birds, 2900 turtles, 260 amphibians, and 221 snake bone fragments (Parmalee, 1975).

Material culture evidence for subsistence

It is intuitive to focus on the plant and animal remains for evidence of ancient subsistence; but artifacts are important as well. Their functions are usually intuitive based on their appearance. Nutting stones were broad and often flat-topped with small depressions carved into them. These depressions held nuts so they could be ground into a meal. Some nuts, like acorns, also required boiling to remove toxic tannins (Driver, 1952). When one finds nutting stones, it is a reasonable assumption that nut exploitation took place. Another subsistence technology that appears in the archeological record is the hoe. Hoes had a flat blade attached to the end of a handle. Archeologists tend to find them at sites where there also exists botanical evidence for horticulture or agriculture. A well-known Mississippian statuette, found near Cahokia, depicts a kneeling woman holding a short handled hoe. The intention of this particular art piece may have been to show a spiritual relationship between women and mother earth fertility rather than a historically accurate representation of farming behavior (Prentice, 1986). Nonetheless, it provides a unique view of Mississippian behavior and hoe usage in an agricultural population.

From the Early to the M/L Archaic, most indicators of subsistence (beyond projectile points used for hunting) were atlatls, nutting stones, hammer stones, and fishhooks. Atlatls would have given hunters a tremendous boost. Although their use in conflict is possible (e.g., Schmidt et al., 2010), it is surmised that their day-to-day application was for hunting terrestrial prey. Atlatls were frequent grave goods, particularly in the Green River area (Webb, 1946). A large nutting stone accompanied the grave of a M/L Archaic adult female and a possible preteen female in at the Wildcat site in north-central Indiana. Capping the grave with a nutting stone may have indicated an important link between food preparation and at least one of these females.

Fishhooks appear at many M/L Archaic sites throughout the Ohio and Green River valleys. There were numerous fishhook-manufacturing techniques, but, in general, making a hook involved incising bone or shell in a concentric pattern until a 'J'-shaped hook emerged (Moore, 2010). Moore found that variations in fishhook styles across the eastern woodlands reflected more than subsistence; they also reflected increasing cultural complexity and exchanges of cultural goods (Moore, 2010). Archeologists find fishhooks in a variety of archeological contexts, including graves. At the terminal M/L Archaic Menard's site in central Indiana, a fishhook accompanied a middle-to-old adult male (Schmidt and Hill, 2003). That was the only fishhook found at the site.

Another technology related to fishing is fish weirs. These are barriers placed across a shallow stream often made of stone but at times made of wood. The rocks form a 'V' shape, the tip of the 'V' being roughly in the middle and pointing downstream. Importantly, there are no rocks at the tip. The weir forces fish swimming downstream to the middle of the weir. There, the fish find an opening and, like cattle in a chute, are funneled through. On the other side of the opening there may have been a trap, or people ready to grab, net, or spear the fish (e.g., Lewis, 2006). Weirs are difficult to radiocarbon date and Native people continued to construct them after European contact. Thus, the use of weirs likely spanned thousands of years (e.g., Petersen et al., 1994). As a graduate student conducting fieldwork decades ago, I saw the remnants of a small weir in a northern Indiana stream. It was just a few centimeters under the water level and roughly in a V shape. Despite its condition at that time, it was easy to visualize its original effectiveness.

The Woodland period had grinding stones intended for milling seeds and, later, maize. Prior to the Late Woodland, grinding stone presence was modest. By the Late Woodland, their frequency increased and they were most prevalent during the Late Precontact. Late Woodland Albee sites in east-central Indiana had grinding stones, but no hoes. The Fort Ancient Oliver tradition Clampitt site had a grinding stone but no hoes (Schwartz, 1983; Cochran and McCord, 1988) and the Fort Ancient Oliver tradition Bowen site, had around 50 grinding stones (Dorwin, 1971). Wooden mortars and pestles debuted toward the end of the Late Woodland, but occur most often at Mississippian sites (Rose et al., 1991).

Like grinding stones, hoes reached their peak in the Late Precontact. Native people crafted hoe blades from shell and chert and the handles were wooden (Kellar, 1967). Shell hoes are present at numerous Mississippian sites from the Ohio River Valley. At Cahokia, chert hoes predominated. The Angel site in southern Indiana had 33 shells and 17 chert hoes, mortars and pestles, mullers, hundreds of hammer stones, celts, and anvils (Kellar, 1967). Eventually, hoe use was widespread in the eastern woodlands and it continued into European contact.

Diet

The goal of dietary reconstructions is to determine what foods people ate (e.g., Dennell, 1979; Hillson, 1979). To do this, it requires study of human remains. With one exception, all indicators of diet come from human tissues; usually it is the hard tissues, but on occasion soft tissues preserve and, as such, are suitable for analysis. The one indicator of diet that does not come directly from human remains is feces, called coprolites when recovered from ancient contexts. Because fecal compositions include plant and animal parts that passed through the body, most of what is in a coprolite is dietary (Reinhard and Bryant, 2008). Of course, nonfood items appear in them; but detailed coprolite studies can distinguish foods from non-foods (e.g., Reinhard et al., 1991).

The study of stable isotopes in human bones provides some of the best insights into ancient human diets (Schwarcz and Schoeninger, 2012). Isotopes are versions of an element that differ in their number of neutrons. Some are unstable and radioactive. Others are stable. The radioactive isotopes are useful for dating objects; as radioactive isotopes decay they indicate time since death. Stable isotopes do not decay, but, like their radioactive counterparts, they end up in our bones, particularly Carbon-12 (^{12}C) and Carbon-13 (^{13}C). Plants use carbon they collect from the atmosphere in the form of carbon dioxide. Most of the oxygen ends up released back into the air, while the carbon helps with photosynthesis. There are three primary photosynthesis pathways, two of which I discuss here; C_4 plants (so-called because they produce a four-carbon compound) live primarily in arid environments. They maximize water retention through a process that keeps heavier isotopes of carbon from escaping. Plants using a C_3 pathway live in areas with more water and/or sunlight than C_4 plants. They sequester water and carbon, less efficiently than do C_4 plants, leading to a lower ^{13}C to ^{12}C ratio. Carbon values are reported in parts per thousand and are always negative compared to the Pee Dee Belemnite reference standard (Schwarcz and Schoeninger, 1991). In North American archeology, the primary C_4 plant was maize; it was a tropical cultigen first domesticated in an arid region of Mexico around 9000 BP (Benz, 2009), hence, its C_4 pathway. Almost every other plant consumed in North America had a C_3 pathway, indicative of living in temperate climes.

Nitrogen (^{14}N and ^{15}N) are common stable isotopes found in the atmosphere and in living tissues. As animals eat, they concentrate nitrogen in their bodies. Herbivorous animals eat plants, which elevates the nitrogen values in those animals. Carnivorous animals then eat the herbivores, further elevating nitrogen values in their bodies. As one goes up the food chain, nitrogen values increase. Thus, animals like wolves have higher stable nitrogen isotope values than do whitetail deer. The comparison standard for stable nitrogen isotope values is atmospheric nitrogen. Because nitrogen concentrates as it moves from one trophic level to the next, the ratio of $^{14}N-^{15}N$ is higher than in the atmosphere. Like carbon, stable nitrogen isotope data are reported in parts per thousand (Schwarcz and Schoeninger, 1991).

In Indiana, a handful of isotope studies indicate that humans consumed primarily C_3 plants until the Late Woodland when C_4 plants became more common. From the M/L Archaic through the E/M Woodland, $^{13}C/^{12}C$ values hover around -20.0 or more, due to the consumption of local C_3 plants. During the Albee aspect of the Late Woodland, $^{13}C/^{12}C$ values were less negative but not fully indicative of a maize-based diet (Allegretto et al., 2006). By the latter half of the Late Woodland and into the Mississippian, however, C_4 plants dominated (Schurr, 1992; Cook and Price, 2017). At the Angel site, $^{13}C/^{12}C$ values averaged around -8.0 (Schurr, 1992). This is comparable to levels at other Mississippian sites in the Midwest including Cahokia (Buikstra, 1992; Cook and Price, 2017).

Stable isotope studies are tremendously valuable, but they have a few shortcomings. First, they are destructive. Bone and tooth samples are usually small, but the analysis process destroys them. Institutions in control of Native American remains, ranging from museums to extant tribes, tend to frown on destructive studies. Secondly, stable carbon isotopic studies are best at discerning dietary transitions between temperate and tropical species, which means not all dietary transitions are detectable.

Dental indicators of diet

The dental indicators of diet (DID) included here are those introduced in Chapter 1: Dental macrowear, microwear, and dental caries. Each of these has its history regarding human dietary reconstruction. As early as the late 19th century, researchers reported on the relationship between dental macrowear and diet, noting that indigenous peoples tended to have higher rates of macrowear than living people (e.g., Murphy, 1959; Molnar, 1968, 1971a,b). About the same time, researchers pointed out the relationship between caries and carbohydrate-rich foods. By the mid-1900s, people used microscopes to study dietary signals on teeth. Since then, researchers have used macrowear, microwear, and pathology to reconstruct diets of people from around the globe and through time (see Schmidt and Watson, 2019). Like all paleodietary approaches, dental-based studies have their limitations; but they provide information found via no other techniques.

Macrowear

Dental macrowear (also called enamel attrition) is the mechanical removal of dental hard tissues during mastication (Molnar, 1971a,b, 1972; Smith, 1972, 1984; Hillson, 1986; Williams and Woodhead, 1986; Watson and Schmidt, 2019). Macrowear is a normal dental function and occurs due to several factors including the abrasiveness of the diet, tooth-to-tooth contact during mastication, and bruxism (Molnar, 1972; Williams and Woodhead, 1986; Hillson, 1986). Another process that removes dental hard tissues is erosion, which is the chemical breakdown of teeth in an acidic environment (Williams and Woodhead, 1986; Watson and Schmidt, 2019). The rate of macrowear is not consistent across all human populations (e.g. Molnar, 1968, 1971, 1972; Lunt, 1974, 1978; van Reenan, 1982; Molnar et al., 1989; Fiorenza et al., 2019). Macrowear varies depending on the makeup of the diet and the environment within which people live. For example, people living in deserts may have sand contamination in their foods, which abrades their teeth and hastens macrowear (Smith, 1972). Hard diets, too, lead to heavy macrowear (Strait, 1991; Teaford, 1991).

Microwear

Dental microwear is macrowear but viewed microscopically. Scanning electron microscopes (SEM) were the state-of-the-art for microwear analysis in the 1970s (Walker et al., 1978; Ryan, 1979), and their use continued until the 2000s. SEMs provide high-resolution and high-magnification images of 3D surfaces. They use an electron beam fired down a tube to the specimen. The beam scans the specimen with the help of magnetic coils. Although they produce images that look like photographs, they use no light. Usually, the SEM generates micrographs from electrons kicked off the specimen by the electron beam. A collector in the specimen chamber picks up the electrons and converts them into images on a screen. To help with microwear data collection, Peter Ungar developed software designed to help analysts measure and count microwear pit and scratch features. Primarily, SEM-based microwear variables included pit and scratch frequencies, percentage of pits, mean pit and scratch lengths and widths and feature orientation.

The SEM-based approach provided a huge advance in dental microwear study, but it had its limitations. At the time, SEMs did not provide much in the way of 3D data; thus, SEM-based microwear analysis collected 2D data from 3D surfaces. To rectify this issue, Ungar and colleagues established dental microwear texture analysis (DMTA). It used a white-light confocal profiler, which provided the magnification and the 3D data sought by microwear analysts. To develop the data analysis software, Ungar and colleagues collaborated with Chris Brown at the Worcester Polytechnic Institute. They developed a new program called Toothfrax® that accompanied an existing program Brown co-developed called Sfrax®. These programs did not focus on individual features. Instead, they used scale-sensitive fractal analysis to characterize surface topography. No longer did analysts need to count or measure microwear features; instead they used Toothfrax® and Sfrax® to calculate surface texture characteristics. DMTA is the current state-of-the-art, and just a handful of archeology/paleontology programs in the world currently house profilers for the study of ancient teeth. I am fortunate that my Lab is among them.

Dental caries

Dental caries is a disease process caused by "the focal demineralization of dental hard tissues by organic acids produced by bacterial fermentation of dietary carbohydrates, especially sugars" (Larsen et al., 1991). Carious lesions occur as bacteria concentrate on teeth in an adherent gelatinous mat known as bacterial plaque. *Streptococcus mutans*, and other bacteria, process sugars such as glucose, sucrose, fructose, and lactose (Newbrun, 1982). The waste they produce is lactic acid. Enamel breaks down chemically at a pH of 4.0–5.5; the acid dissolves through the enamel causing cavitation (Hillson, 1986). Carious lesions occur in all teeth, but are usually most severe in the molars. Deep grooves between molar cusps are excellent places for sugary foods to lodge; they are also good places for bacteria to reside. Once food is stuck between the cusps, oral bacteria can easily metabolize it and deposit acidic waste (Goldstein, 1932; Anderson and Popovich, 1977; Walker and Erlandson, 1986).

Archeologists have noted a pattern in dental caries prevalence for nearly a century (e.g., Leigh, 1925). With few exceptions (e.g., Lukacs, 2016), dental caries are uncommon among foragers and extremely common in maize farmers, to an extent where nearly everyone in farming communities may have cavities. Cassidy (1984), for example, found a dental caries prevalence of 100% among Ohio River Valley Late Precontact agriculturists. The jump in dental caries associated with maize agriculture is widespread and found in groups throughout North America (e.g., Leigh, 1925, 1928; Stewart, 1931; Nelson, 1938; Greene, 1972; Behrend, 1978; Cook and Buikstra, 1979; Turner, 1979; Buikstra and Cook, 1980; Ortner and Putschar, 1985; Milner, 1984, 1985; Perzigian et al., 1984; Powell, 1985; Rose, 1984; Rose and Marks, 1985; Williams and Curzon, 1986; Larsen et al., 1991; Watson, 2008; Fields et al., 2009; Larsen, 2015).

Macrowear and microwear/DMTA studies infrequently report differences based on sex. It is far more common for bioarcheologists to report sex-based difference in dental caries. Larsen (1984) observed that along the Georgia coast, males suffered less from caries than females during the transition to agriculture. Larsen's study populations included precontact, nonagricultural groups; precontact, agricultural groups; early contact groups, and late contact groups. Contact groups were those Native Americans living after the Spanish arrived in the early 16th century (Larsen, 1984). Of the precontact, nonagricultural females, 10.7% had dental caries. By comparison, 69.4% of the precontact, agricultural females had dental caries. Early Contact females experienced a slight drop in caries frequency to 51.2%, but by the late contact, nearly nine out of 10 women had dental caries (87.0%). The males also had an increase through time in caries frequency. However, for the precontact, nonagricultural and precontact, agricultural groups, males had a lower caries frequency than the females (6.1% for precontact, preagricultural and 58.7% for precontact, agricultural).

Perzigian et al. (1984) noted a sex-based difference in caries prevalence in precontact Native Americans from Ohio for the nonagricultural and agricultural groups. In southwestern Ohio, 100% of an agricultural Fort Ancient population had dental caries. In contrast, only 13.3% of a Middle Woodland population had dental caries.

Another way to present dental caries data is by the average number of affected teeth per person. Using the same populations, 24.8% of the Fort Ancient teeth had caries, while only 13% of the Middle were carious. Among the Fort Ancient, more females had carious teeth than males, 27.1% versus 22.9%, respectively; this was true at the Mississippian Moundville site in Alabama, too. Among the female maxillary teeth, 6.7% of the anterior and 22.5% of the posterior teeth had dental caries. For the female mandibular teeth, 0.1% of the anterior and 27.2% of posterior teeth had caries. For the male maxillary teeth, 4.7% of the anterior and 23.1% of the posterior teeth had dental caries. For the male mandibular teeth, 2.3% of the anterior and 22.9% of the posterior teeth had carious lesions (Powell, 1981, 1988). Thus, sex-based dental caries prevalences are critical to explore.

Limits of this dental study: no meat

A stark limitation of the DID employed here is that they do a poor job of reflecting the consumption of meat. Meat is not cariogenic and not abrasive (e.g., Hua et al., 2015; Krueger et al., 2019). The closest any of these come to indicating meat is that some groups thought to eat large quantities of meat, like Neandertals and Bronze Age pastoralists, have distinct DMTA values; specifically, they have low surface complexities (e.g., El Zaatari and Hublin, 2014; El Zaatari et al., 2016; Karriger et al., 2016; Schmidt et al., 2016). This is congruent with experimental studies that determined meat creates almost no microwear features (e.g., Hua et al., 2015). Unfortunately, hard foods in the diet can mask meat signatures, so unless a population only consumed meat, I would not find clear evidence for it. A colleague, Kristin Krueger, is planning a series of experiments that may solve this problem in the near future (e.g., Krueger et al., 2019). There is a recently developed macrowear analysis technique, called dental fingerprinting, that is distinguishing meat-based diets (e.g., Kullmer et al., 2009; Fiorenza et al., 2019). It is not yet a routine approach to macrowear study, but it holds a great deal of promise and I hope it becomes more widely used. Unfortunately, the current study does not benefit from these ongoing developments and, as such, it avoids the question of meat consumption. Except for some discussion of people eating mussels during the M/L Archaic, I make no effort to explain the animal component of precontact diets.

CHAPTER 4

Addressing the problem

Introduction

This study reconstructs diets of precontact people from Indiana via dental macrowear, microwear/dental microwear texture analysis (DMTA), and pathology. There are several hypotheses tested here, but the overarching question is this: did precontact diets change from group to group before the shift to intensive maize agriculture during the Late Precontact? There are no expected differences based on age, except for macrowear and there are no expected differences based on sex, except for dental caries, where females should have more.

This study includes only adults. It excludes subadults, people under the age of 18, because deciduous teeth present certain challenges due to their thin enamel and temporary nature (Kelly et al., 2019). In addition, some groups had many children, while others had almost none available for study. Studies of subadult teeth are important and are becoming more commonplace (e.g., Mahoney et al., 2016; Williams et al., 2018; Kelly et al., 2019). Unfortunately, circumstances prevented their inclusion here.

Bioarcheological studies benefit from studying entire skeletons, even if the emphasis of a given study is on the teeth, because they offer a better opportunity to attain accurate age and sex estimates (Digangi and Moore, 2012). Yet, complete skeletons are not always available. For the current study, most skeletons were incomplete and for some all that remained were teeth and/or jaws.

Age, sex, and ancestry estimates followed osteological standards outlined in Buikstra and Ubelaker (1994). Age indicators included dental development and eruption, cranial suture closure, and pubic symphyseal face and auricular surface morphology. Age categories were young adult (18–35), middle adult (36–50), and old adult (50+). There ended up being very few old adults, which led to collapsing the middle and old adult categories into a single category (mid/old). Broad age categories

Long 'on' the Tooth. DOI: https://doi.org/10.1016/B978-0-12-824306-0.00001-X

like the ones used here are less than ideal, particularly given the value of transition analysis to provide probability- age estimates (e.g., Boldsen et al., 2002). Yet, given the state of the remains, their categorical age determinations will suffice. Moreover, I collected the age data many years ago and these specimens are no longer available for study.

Indicators of sex included cranial and post cranial robusticity, nuchal crest size, glabellar expression, supraorbital thickness, mastoid size, frontal bossing, malar expression, temporal line prominence, supramastoid crest prominence, mental eminence projection and shape, ascending ramus angle and width, inversion or eversion at gonion, sciatic notch width, pubic bone shape, ventral arc presence, subpubic concavity presence, medial pubic ridge morphology, subpubic angle, sacrum shape, and the overall relative size of the bones.

All individuals in the current study were of Native American ancestry. There is no evidence for historic era intrusions or admixture in any of the collections I studied. Ancestry determinations came from numerous dental indicators including tooth sizes and cusp number, and the presence of nonmetric traits indicative of Native Americans. Nondental indicators of ancestry included cranial, facial, and femoral morphology.

Materials: the study populations

This study included 334 people from 23 archeological sites representing five cultural entities which I will simply call "groups." Terminology for archeological populations varies tremendously; terms like "culture," "tradition," and "phase" mean different things to different scholars. In the archeology literature, some of the populations studied here represent temporal periods, like the Middle/Late Archaic, which existed for a particular period of time. Others, like the Mississippian, were regional phenomena and not a particular time or people. To avoid confusion, I have jettisoned standard archeological designations and I address each population I studied as a "group." The five groups are: the Middle/Late Archaic (M/L Archaic), the Early/Middle Woodland (E/M Woodland), the Albee tradition of the Late Woodland (LW Albee), the Fort Ancient Oliver tradition (FA Oliver), and the Mississippian. For each group, the total number of individuals studied is, M/L Archaic, 55 (+20 for DMTA); E/M Woodland, 55; LW Albee, 90; FA Oliver, 24 (+11 for DMTA); and Mississippian, 79.

The M/L Archaic sites include: Clark's Point, Elrod, Highrock Rockshelter, Little Pigeon Creek, and Bluegrass (for DMTA only). The E/M Woodland sites are: Anderson Mounds, Hr-6, New Castle, White, and Windsor. The LW Albee sites are: Albee Mound, Behem, Bucci, Commissary, Hesher, Shaffer, and Shepherd. The FA Oliver Tradition sites include: Bowen, Bundy-Voyles, Oliver Farm, and Bicycle Bridge (for DMTA only). The Mississippian sites are Angel and Wickliffe (Kentucky). I added Wickliffe to keep the Mississippian group from coming entirely from a single site (Fig. 4.1).

M/L Archaic

The Archaic sample for the macrowear, scanning electron microscope (SEM)-based microwear, and dental caries study included 784 teeth from 55 individuals, 27 males and 17 females. Additionally, 20 people from the Bluegrass site had a tooth studied via DMTA. Described below are the M/L Archaic sites used herein, all of which are from Indiana.

Bluegrass: The Bluegrass site (12-W-162) sits near the Ohio River in Warrick County, Indiana. It was a large mortuary site excavated in the 1980s as part of an effort to protect the remains from construction work. It produced around 80 people in extended, flexed, and tightly flexed positions. M/L Archaic lithics and radiocarbon dates place it near the end of the M/L Archaic (Stafford and Cantin, 2009). Most burials were on a ridge crest near pit features. The site also produced dog burials, but for the most part, they were away from the cemetery and habitation area. Included from this site were 20 individuals, seven males and seven females, exclusively for DMTA.

Clark's Point: Clark's Point (12-C1-3) is located in Clark County, Indiana in the Falls of the Ohio region in the southeast corner of the state. Excavated in the early half of the 20th century, the site is part of a series of well-known sites in the Falls area. The original number of individuals excavated and the original site size are largely unknown. Artifacts from Clark's Point site place it comfortably in the M/L Archaic. Twenty-one people were suitable for study, including 11 males and three females.

Elrod: Elrod (12-C1-1) is located in Clark County, Indiana near Clark's Point. The two sites were excavated about the same time, and they have similar artifacts. The current study included 20 people from Elrod, 11 males and seven females.

Figure 4.1 Locations for precontact sites used in this study. Blue = M/L Archaic; Green = E/M Woodland; Red = LW Albee; Orange = FAOliver; Yellow = Mississippian (for interpretation of the references to color in this figure legend, see the online version).

Highrock Rockshelter: Highrock rockshelter (12-Da-300), in Daviess County, Indiana was an accidentally discovered skeleton eroding from the riverbank overlooking the west fork of the White River. It was beneath a 10 m-high rock overhang. Much of the site had eroded down slope and it was dotted with looter holes. Lithics at the site dated it to the M/L Archaic. It contained a single person in a tightly flexed position.

Little Pigeon Creek: This site (12-W-340) is on Little Pigeon Creek, which is a small tributary of the Ohio River in Warrick County, Indiana. It sits on a multicomponent midden-mound; Archeologists recovered 31 individuals (Cook et al., 1986), 13 of which were suitable for study, including six males and five females.

E/M Woodland

The E/M Woodland sample includes 681 teeth from 55 individuals, including 25 males and 16 females. There are five E/M Woodland sites used in the current study, all of which are from Indiana.

Anderson Mounds: Anderson Mounds (12-Ma-2) is in Madison County, Indiana and is one of the most prominent sites in the state. It contains several large earthworks: seven circular enclosures, including a southern complex of circular enclosures, and a northern complex of subrectangular enclosures (Cochran, 1992: 30). The greatest earthwork is the Great Mound enclosure, which is nearly 100 m wide and formerly had a centrally located earthen platform. A plethora of artifacts and numerous radiocarbon dates place Anderson Mounds within the E/M Woodland. It held at least 10 individuals and a quantity of cremains at the time of excavation (Vickery, 1970). For the present study, however, only one Anderson Mounds individual was suitable for study, a middle adult male.

12-Hr-6: The 12-Hr-6 site is located in Harrison County, Indiana along the bank of the Ohio River. Many years ago, 12-Hr-6 began eroding out of the riverbank and, ever since, has been a popular site for looters. Because of the presence of Marion Thick pottery and some stemmed projectile points, it appears to date to the E/M Woodland. Erosion commingled the human remains. Of the 12 individuals present, 10 had dental remains suitable for study, three of which were male and one of which was female.

New Castle: The New Caste site (12-Hn-1) is in New Castle, Henry County, Indiana. The site is an earthwork complex located on a bluff overlooking the confluence of the Upper Big Blue and Little Blue rivers (Swartz, 1976). Excavated in the late 1960s and early 1970s, it consists of two mounds and ten circular enclosures arranged in a circular pattern. Human remains included cremains as well as bundle and primary inhumations. Nine individuals had dental remains suitable for study including six males and one female.

White: The White site (12-Hn-10) is in New Castle, Henry County, Indiana approximately a quarter mile west of the Upper Big Blue River. The site originally had three mounds, although only one remained at the time of excavation in 1967. The mound contained three log tombs and the remains of 18 people (Swartz, 1973). Radiocarbon dates place it the E/M Woodand period. Additionally, it had numerous Adena artifacts. Six individuals had teeth suitable for the current study, including one male and two females.

Windsor Mound: Windsor Mound (12-R-1) in Randolph County, Indiana is the largest prehistoric earthen mound located in the east-central part of the state. It is within the Upper White River West Fork drainage and occupies a ridge spur between the valleys of the White and Stony Creek rivers (McCord and Cochran, 1996: 4). Radiocarbon dates place Windsor to around 2000 years ago, and associated cultural elements support an association with the Adena culture. Local collectors damaged the site significantly. Between 1986 and 1988, two men, with landowner permission, tore through approximately 1/3 of the mound. Their efforts ceased just prior to the passage of a state law that protected Native American graves.

Most of the Windsor individuals used for the current study consisted of isolated crania and skulls. The location and nature of the mound leads archeologist to believe Windsor belongs to the Adena. There were a minimum of 44 individuals found at Windsor after the looting event ended (McCord and Cochran, 1996). Of those, 28 had dental remains suitable for study, including 14 males and 12 females.

LW Albee

The LW Albee sample consists of 1313 teeth representing 90 individuals, 34 males and 32 females from known Albee and Albee-like sites. There are seven LW Albee sites used here, all of which are from Indiana.

Albee Mound: The Albee Mound site (12-Su-1) is a large mortuary on a natural knoll adjacent to the Wabash River in Sullivan County, Indiana (Tomak, 1983). Excavations began in 1926, making it the first mound site professionally excavated in the state (MacLean, 1931). The site yielded 16 turtle shell bowls (found among 11 individuals), as well as shell beads, copper beads, projectile points, and an assortment of lithic and bone tools, and four ceramic jars. Of the 16 individuals with grave goods, four had accompanying artifact caches; archeologists also found an isolated artifact cache (Emerson et al., 2019; Maclean, 1931). A radiocarbon date from the nearby Cooke site (12-P-5) places Albee in western Indiana around 1200 BP (Redmond and McCullough 2000). Of the original 41 or so individuals found at Albee Mound, only 17 individuals were available for study, including seven males and six females.

Behem: The Behem site (12-Vi-688) is in Vigo County, Indiana. It is a single individual accidentally discovered by a landowner putting in a house foundation. Artifacts from the area place this person in the LW Albee.

Bucci: The Bucci cemetery (12-Gr-388) is in Greene County, Indiana on upland overlooking the Four Mile Marsh. Workers moving a house accidentally exposed the cemetery in 1968, and archeologists salvaged approximately 43 burials and artifacts including worked antler tine, cord marked pottery, and a turtle carapace (Tomak, 1970: 156). For the current study, only four individuals had teeth suitable for study, including two males.

Commissary: The Commissary site (12-Hn-2) is in east-central Indiana near the city of New Castle in Henry County. It sits on a promontory approximately 50 feet above the Big Blue River valley to the west and the Little Blue River valley to the south. Excavated during the late 1960s and early 1970s, Commissary is primarily a mortuary site (Houck and Swartz, 1972). The site had 104 burials, 65% of which were subadults (Glenn, 1982). Artifacts include a number of celts and at least one milling stone (Burkett and Cochran, 1985). It too had an isolated artifact cache like the Albee Mound site. The artifacts in it included triangular points, antler rods and tines, lithic drills, and chert flakes (Swartz, 1982:17; Emerson et al., 2019: 16). The current study included 36 Commissary adults, including 13 males and 13 females.

Hesher: The Hesher site (12-Hn-298) is near New Castle, Henry County, Indiana adjacent to several important archeological sites including the Commissary site. The physiographic zone and prehistoric vegetation profile are identical to Commissary. The site most likely dates to around 1100 BP, although at least one date from the site indicates it could have components about 1500 years old (Cochran and McCord, 1988). Like Albee Mound, Hesher had artifact caches associated with four burials as well as an isolated cache; it also produced triangular points (Cochran and McCord, 1988; Emerson et al., 2019). Archeologists found 12 individuals at Hesher, eight adults and four subadults. All of the adults had teeth suitable for study in this project, and they included four males and three females.

Shaffer: The Shaffer cemetery (12-Gr-109) is in Greene County, Indiana on upland that overlooks the White River flood plain (Tomak, 1970: 151). First excavated in the mid-20th century, originally it had 35 burials (and a cremation), although many were fragmentary. Subsequently, construction personnel accidentally discovered more remains, which archeologists recovered in the 1990s. Shaffer artifacts included two Albee jars, turtle shell bowls, antler drifts and tines, worked slate and limestone celt or celt-like artifact (Black, 1933; Tomak, 1970; Emerson et al., 2019). The current study included 10 Shaffer individuals, most of which had only dental elements available for study. Sex estimates indicate the presence of three males and three females.

Shepherd: The Shepherd Cemetery (12-Gr-60) is in Greene County, Indiana on upland overlooking the flood plain of the White River (Tomak, 1970: 153). First located in 1963, the site produced approximately 45 burials, although many were fragmentary and/or incomplete. The artifact assemblage of antler tines, shell beads, and projectile points placed Shepherd within the LW Albee. Only 14 individuals, seven males and two females, had dentitions suitable for study.

FA Oliver

The FA Oliver sample includes 451 teeth from 24 individuals, seven males and 12 females. There are four Oliver sites used here, all of which are from Indiana. In addition, 11 people from Bicycle Bridge contributed to the DMTA study.

Bicycle Bridge: The Bicycle Bridge site (12-C-259) is a Late Precontact site on a Bluff overlooking the Wabash River in Carroll County, Indiana; it serves here as a proxy for the FA Oliver for DMTA only. It is not demonstrably Oliver, meaning it lacks guilloche-pattern ceramics, but it is contemporaneous and in a part of the state occupied by FA Oliver people. A landowner discovered the human remains while putting in a wooden deck, which ended up commingling the remains. The Bicycle Bridge sample included 11 isolated teeth from young adults of unknown sex.

Bowen: The Bowen site (12-Ma-61) is a terminal Late Woodland site that dated to between 1200 and 500 BP (Dorwin, 1971). Bowen is in Marion County, Indiana within the city limits of Indianapolis, on a small rise about 3.7 m above the White River. Its cultural affiliation comes from its artifacts including guilloche-pattern ceramics (Dorwin, 1971). For the current study, 21 Bowen individuals, including six males and 10 females, had suitable teeth.

Bundy-Voyles: The Bundy-Voyles site (12-Mg-1) is in Morgan County, Indiana. It had a middle adult female burial, disturbed by modern farming activity. Its assignment to the FA Oliver comes from the presence of hundreds of large Oliver tradition ceramic vessel shards.

Oliver Farm: The Oliver Farm site (12-Ma-1) is the namesake for the Oliver ceramics. Located in Marion County, Indiana, not far from the Bowen site in Indianapolis, Oliver overlooks a bend in the White River (Householder, 1945). Of the three individuals found at Oliver, two, both estimated to be males, met the criteria for inclusion in the current study.

Mississippian

The Mississippian sample includes 1042 teeth from 79 individuals, including 32 males and 38 females. There are two Mississippian sites used herein. Angel is from Indiana and Wickliffe is from Kentucky.

Angel: The Angel site (12-Vg-1) is Indiana's largest precontact archeological site and its best representative of the Middle Mississippian culture (Black, 1943, 1967). Located on the Ohio River in Vanderburg County, Indiana, Angel covered approximately 100 acres. It had a central plaza surrounded by 11 large earthen mounds including a multilevel platform mound (Purdue, 1896; Black, 1967). This mound, called Mound A, is 196.29 by 126.49 m (644 × 415 feet) at its base. Additionally, a 1.25 mi long palisade surrounded the site. In total, Angel produced nearly 2.5 million artifacts, many of which indicate that Angel was independent of, but culturally linked to, other Mississippian sites in the American Bottoms (Schurr, 1992: 304–305).

Bioarcheological studies of the Angel human remains are ongoing, but there have been a number of studies over the years (e.g., Dragoo, 1949; Herrala, 1961; Cook, 1984; Hilgeman, 1988; Schurr, 1992; Schmidt, 1998). Herrala (1961) was the first to document that the people of Angel had a high level of dental caries. Hilgeman (1988) determined that cranial deformation was a relatively common practice for both males and females. A little more than half of the deformed crania had *cribra orbitalia* and *porotic hyperostosis*, which are pathological pitting of the orbital roofs and cranium that form as the body responds to anemia (Cook, 1984). I found that antemortem tooth loss was high among the people of Angel, likely due to maize consumption (Schmidt, 1998).

The most detailed study directly pertinent to diet was Schurr's (1992) study of stable nitrogen and carbon isotopes. Of the over 300 people excavated at the site, Schurr studied a sample of 50 individuals, among whom he found strong carbon signatures for maize consumption. In fact, Angel's level of maize consumption was comparable to other Mississippian sites in Illinois and the southeastern United States (Buikstra, 1992; Schurr, 1992). The nitrogen data indicate meat consumption typical for late precontact people (Schurr, 1992). The current study includes the same 50 people studied by Schurr, which had 24 males and 24 females. I focused on these individuals because of their excellent states of preservation, clear provenience, lack of commingling, and known isotopic signatures.

Wickliffe: The Wickliffe site (15-Ba-4), also known as the Wickliffe Mound Group, is a Mississippian site about 4 hectares in size. It is located in western Kentucky along bluffs that overlook the confluence of the Ohio and Mississippi rivers (Matternes, 1994: 3). I chose Wickliffe to join Angel because there are no other large Mississippian populations in Indiana, Wickliffe was comparable in size, and it was spatially and temporally close to Angel.

Like Angel, Wickliffe had a central plaza surrounded by platform mounds. In addition to several smaller mounds, it had a long, low mound that may had been an elite burial mound. Excavations began there in 1930s because of highway construction. Human remains from the site ended up being put on display for decades (Matternes, 1994), a tragic circumstance that should not have taken place. While human remains came from several mounds, Mound C contained the skeletal material studied in this project; a site chronology dates the Mound C cemetery to around 650 BP (Matternes, 1994). Additionally, none of the individuals from the cemetery had grave goods indicative of a higher social status (Matternes 1994). The Mound C cemetery had 231 people. Of these, 29 had dentitions suitable for the current study, including eight males and 13 females (Table 4.1, Fig. 4.1).

Methods

Macrowear scoring

Since the days of anatomist Paul Broca, several researchers have developed ordinal systems for documenting macrowear on human teeth, including Broca himself (e.g., Broca, 1879; Murphy, 1959; Miles, 1963; Molnar, 1968; Scott, 1979; Brothwell, 1981; Smith, 1984; Lovejoy, 1985). In keeping with Buikstra and Ubelaker (1994) guidelines, the current study followed the Smith (1984) method for the nonmolar teeth (incisors, canines, and premolars) and the Scott (1979) method for the molars. Each assigns a score based on enamel loss and dentin exposure. Teeth with little wear had lower scores; teeth showing greater wear received higher scores.

The Smith (1984) scores range from 1 to 8 and assesses entire crowns. A score of 1 indicates modest enamel loss and no dentin exposure. Scores of 2–5 indicate increasing dentin exposure, from a pinprick to most of the remaining crown surface. A score of 6 means all that remains is a thin enamel rim for premolars and canines, and some loss of the rim on the incisors. Scores of 7 and 8 indicate partial to complete enamel rim loss; a tooth that scores 8 has no enamel remaining. The Scott (1979) system ranges from 4 to 40. Each molar quadrant is scored independently on a scale of 1–10 (Fig. 4.2). Scores from 1–3 indicate no to modest dentin exposure and increased flattening of the cusp. Scores of 4–6 indicate the presence of distinct dentin patches from a pinprick to over 1/4th of the quadrant. A score of 7 means the dentin patch is large enough to coalesce with a neighboring dentin patch. Quadrants with a score of 8 have only thick enamel rims, and those with a score of 9 have only thin enamel rims remaining. A score of 10 means all enamel is gone from that quadrant. A sum of the four quadrants provides an overall tooth score. I scored all the teeth present

Table 4.1 Groups studied for the microwear, macrowear, and dental caries, their abbreviations used in the text, their approximate dates in years before the present (BP), and sample size (n).

Groups	Abbreviations used in some figures	Approximate dates	n
Middle/Late Archaic	M/L Archaic	5000–3000 BP	55 (+20 for DMTA)
Early/Middle Woodland	E/M Wood	2500–1500 BP	55
Late Woodland Albee	LW Albee	1300–800 BP	90
Fort Ancient Oliver	FA Oliver	800–500 BP	24 (+11 for DMTA)
Mississippian	Mississippian	750–550 BP	79

for each person. I did not score macrowear on teeth with large fractures or large carious lesions that obscured entire quadrants.

Dental microwear analysis

The SEM-based dental microwear analysis used predominantly mandibular, left, second molars (M2s). However, I used right M2 if the left was not present. Additionally, to bolster samples sizes, I included a few maxillary M2 and mandibular first molars (M1s) (e.g., Teaford, 1991; Pastor, 1993). Teaford (1991) reports no difference in microwear between maxillary and mandibular teeth.

It is not practical to study actual teeth. Instead, microwear analysts use high-resolution dental replicas usually made from epoxy resins. The casting procedure described below is a combination of several methods described in the literature (e.g., Waters and Savage, 1971; Scott, 1982; Rose, 1983; Gordon, 1984; Teaford, 1991; Buikstra and Ubelaker, 1994) as well as some procedures which I developed.

First, I washed teeth with tap water and a soft-bristled brush. Once dry, I again washed the teeth with a 95% ethanol solution (e.g., Pastor, 1993). Some teeth, however, had consolidant present, often in the form of polyvinyl acetate, which made preparing them for molding difficult. These teeth required soaking in acetone until they no longer felt 'tacky' to the touch (using a surgical glove for safety). This process was lengthy and often unsuccessful. Teeth that looked and felt clean often had microscopic strands of preservative present when eventually viewed with the SEM.

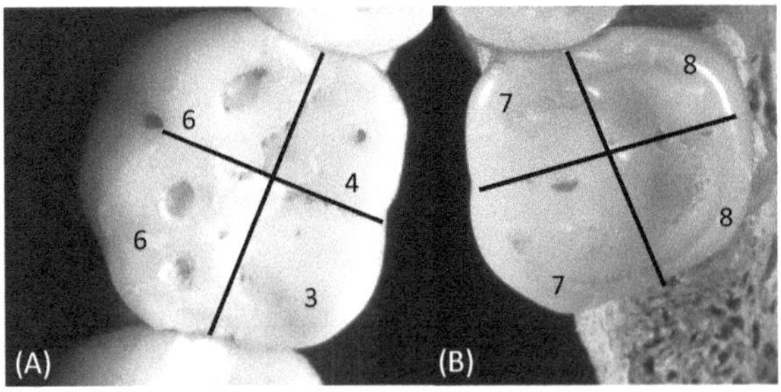

Figure 4.2 Examples of the Scott (1979) scoring system. (A) is a lower left first molar; each quadrant has its Scott score. The quadrant that scored 3 had no dentin exposure, while the quadrant with a score of 6 has a dentin patch larger than ¼ of the surface. (B) is a lower right first molar. It has more enamel missing and more dentin exposure than tooth (A). Notice the dentin patches have coalesced. These are not Native American teeth.

Molding took place at the facilities housing the remains; and commenced on clean teeth using a polyvinylsiloxane molding material, Coltene's President, light body. I placed the molding material on the occlusal surface first, using the cartridge mixing tip to work it into the occlusal grooves. I then worked down the sides of the crown in a circular motion until the molding material was at the widest part of the crown. After approximately 6–10 minutes, I removed the mold and placed the molds in labeled plastic bag (see Schmidt, 2001 for a more detailed explanation of dental molding).

In my lab, I made casts of the teeth by filling the molds with Super Hard Epoxy Resin® at a base-to-hardener ratio of 4:1. I rinsed the molds with ethanol, then used disposable pipettes to place the resin into the molds, being careful to avoid capturing air between the casting material and the mold. I placed the filled molds into a manual centrifuge for approximately 15–30 seconds. This forced the resin deeply into the relief of the molds and forced bubbles away from the area of contact between the two materials. The casts cured for 24 hours.

I affixed casts to aluminum stubs with conductive silver paint and, at times, copper tape. Each stub was sputter-coated with 200 Å of gold-palladium; the sputter-coating provides a very thin layer of metal, which improves the specimen's interaction with the electron beam. The scanning electron microscopy took place in the Electron Microscopy Laboratory in Agriculture at Purdue University using a JEOL JSM840 SEM in secondary electron emission mode. The standard kilovoltage was 15, the working distance was generally between 22 and 25 mm, the aperture setting was 3, and the probe current was standardized at 3×10^{10}.

Microscopy focused on phase II wear facets (as defined by Maier and Schneck, 1982) on the distal aspect of the mesio-buccal cusp (protoconid). Magnification was at 500×, which provided an area of study that was approximately 0.02 mm^2 (Teaford, 1991). I took micrographic images with a built-in polaroid camera (the SEM-based data collection took place in the 1990s) (Fig. 4.3). Feature counting and measuring employed the semi-automated Microware software, versions 2.2 and 4.0 (Ungar, 1995). To avoid observer bias in the classification of features, the software automatically distinguished pits and scratches using a length to width ratio of 4:1 (below four was a pit, above four was a scratch). The SEM-based microwear variables included percentage of pits (number of pits/total number of features), pit lengths (in microns [μm]), and scratch width (in μm).

DMTA used a Sensofar Plu 2300 white-light confocal profiler to study casts made in nearly the same way as they were for the SEM. The only difference is that more recently it has become standard to clean teeth before molding with a cotton swab rather than a soft brush. I used a 10× objective to find phase II facets and collected data with a 100× extra-long working distance objective lens. The resolution in the x-y plane was 0.17 and 0.20 μm in the z-plane. Data came from four automatically stitched contiguous areas that, together, created a data cloud from an area approximately 242 × 182 μm.

Data processing took place with SolarMap® (version 5.1.1), which I used to level the data (using the least squares leveling algorithm) and to "clean" areas unsuitable for study. Cleaning removed adherent particles and debris in the data cloud so that the software only computed true textural data. To keep sizes from each specimen similar, I only included those specimens where no more than 10% of the surface required cleaning. A tremendous strength of DMTA is the ability to inspect the data in many ways. I generated 2D photosimulations (which emulate SEM micrographs) and 3D representations in order to ensure that the surface features were genuine microwear (Fig. 4.4). I excluded any specimen with taphonomic pitting or areas obscured by consolidants or other fine films (e.g., Teaford, 1988a,b).

Texture calculations employed scale-sensitive fractal analysis software (see Scott et al., 2005, 2006). The texture variables addressed here included complexity (Asfc) and anisotropy (epLsar). Complexity and

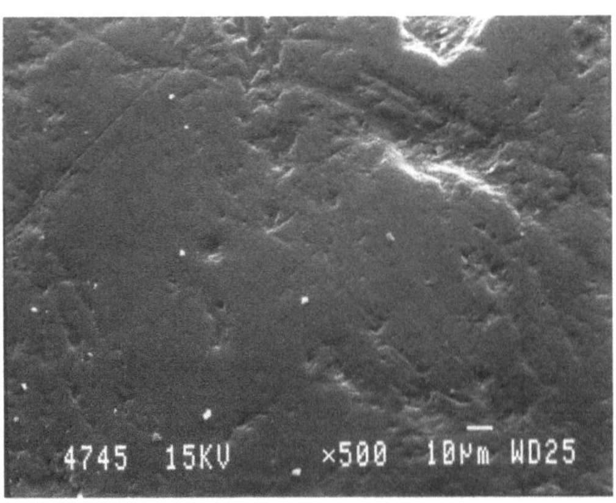

Figure 4.3 Representative scanning electron microscope micrograph of dental microwear. Magnification is 500×.

anisotropy calculations took place via Toothfrax® software. Surface complexity, more appropriately called area-scale fractal complexity (Asfc), is a measure of surface contours at very minute scales. Its output is the steepest slope of a curve on a log-log plot of relative surface area versus scale in μm^2, multiplied by -1000 (e.g., Scott et al., 2006). Surfaces with higher complexity values have a more uneven appearance; they look rough and pitted. This roughened appearance is associated with hard food diets (Scott et al., 2012). In humans from archeological contexts, surface complexities tend to range from 0.5 to 4 (e.g., El Zaatari, 2010; Chiu et al., 2012; Frazer, 2012; Mahoney et al., 2016; Remy et al., 2014; Van Sessen et al., 2013; Schmidt et al., 2019).

Anisotropy is a measure of feature orientation. The higher the anisotropy value, the more similar the orientations of microwear features. Known as exact-proportion length-scale anisotropy of relief (epLsar 1.8), anisotropy calculations involve dividing 36 length vectors, taken at 5° intervals, by the sum of all other vectors and then computing a mean for each individual (i.e., the exact-proportion method; see Scott et al., 2006). When calculated this way, anisotropy output values are very small and in humans tend to range between 0.0005 and

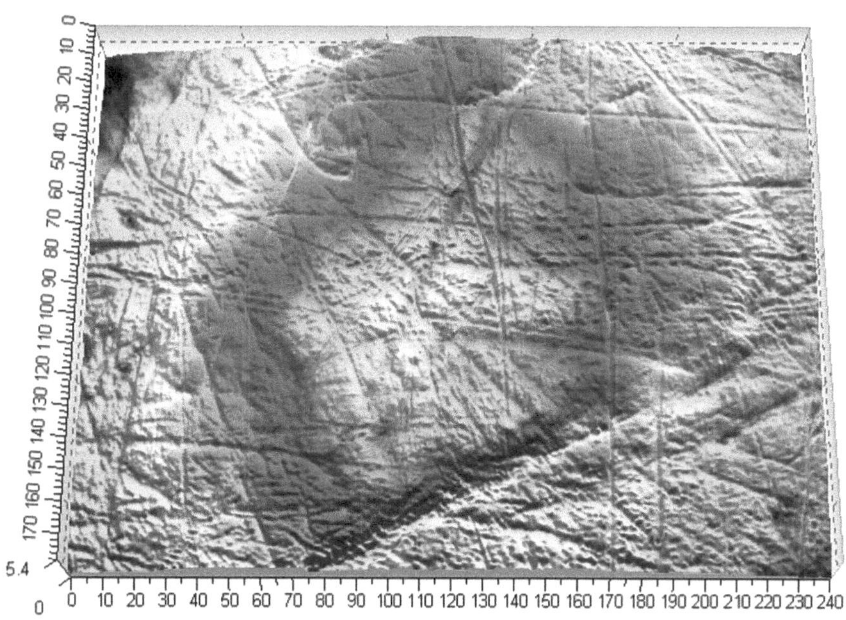

Figure 4.4 Three dimensional representation of dental microwear texture. The scale is in microns (μm) (Broca, 1879).

0.0090, with most populations averaging between 0.0020 and 0.0040. Anisotropy may be an indicator of the degree to which the jaw moves in a consistent direction. Tough fibrous foods, as well as homogenous foods, tend to generate higher anisotropy values, while harder diets tend to generate lower values (e.g., Chiu et al., 2012; El Zaatari, 2010; Frazer, 2012).

The DMTA procedures outlined here are standard among DMTA labs at this time, although they will likely change as technology changes. Profilers manufactured in the last few years calculate surfaces at finer data intervals than those made just a decade or so ago. That means the data from newer systems are denser with data points and, subsequently, their texture calculations differ from calculations made on data collected from older profilers. Fortunately, data filters and other means of standardizing data can overcome differences between profilers and standards will likely only improve as more labs engage in texture analysis (e.g., Arman et al., 2016).

Relationship of microwear and macrowear

In a previous study I compared second molar macrowear scores (because most microwear data came from second molars) to percentage of pit and scratch width data, using 78 people from the same groups in the current study. I found a correlation between scratch width and macrowear score (Pearson's $r = 0.411$; $r^2 = 0.169$; $n = 78$) (Figure 6.2); importantly age was only a factor for macrowear, not scratch width (Schmidt, 2010). By contrast, pit percentage and second molar macrowear were weakly inversely correlated (Pearson's $r = -0.233$; $r^2 = 0.055$; $n = 80$). Since scratches are long, linear abrasions, rather than ovoid pits, they remove dental hard tissues to a greater extent than pitting if the scratches are sufficiently wide (Schmidt, 2010). This is not to say that microwear pitting does not lead to high macrowear scores. It does (see Teaford, 1994). At least in humans, however, wide scratches are more effective at generating high degrees of macrowear. An analogy would be sandpaper with large-grit particles on it; large-grit particles create wider scratches and remove sanded surfaces more quickly than fine-grit sandpaper. Abrasive diets are like large-grit sandpaper on the teeth. Pushing or grinding sandpaper into a tooth would surely create macrowear, but moving the sandpaper back-and-forth would create long striae in the enamel and remove it more effectively.

Caries scoring

I scored dental caries following standard bioarcheological procedures that focus on visual appearance and do not use dental probes (Buikstra and Ubelaker, 1994). A lesion was present if a clearly defined pit (often outlined with a dark stain) was evident on the tooth. I grouped lesions into two categories: occlusal, which included any lesion on the occlusal surface of the tooth, and nonocclusal, which included any lesion forming cervically or interproximally (Fig. 4.5). Caries data represented two phenomena, prevalence and severity. Prevalence is the percentage of people affected per group. Severity is the number of teeth affected. I calculated severity only among those with at least one lesion because including people with no dental caries heavily skewed the data, making them unfit for statistical analysis (Sokal and Rohlf, 1995).

Dietary characteristics indicated by teeth

The dental indicators of diet (DID) are records of tooth use related to mastication manifest primarily as occlusal wear facets and carious pits. The DID data provide insight into particular characteristics of the foods people consumed. Macrowear reflects tooth use over a long period of time and is relative to age. All people experience macrowear, but some have their teeth wear much more quickly than others. Here, macrowear data reflects overall dietary abrasiveness. Highly abrasive diets are those that lead to high levels of macrowear, like the example I gave in Chapter 1; less abrasive diets lead to less macrowear over the course of a person's life. The SEM-based microwear variable percentage of pits indicates dietary hardness (e.g., Teaford and Walker, 1984; Walker and Teaford, 1989; Teaford, 1991; Ungar and Spencer, 1999; Teaford et al., 2001). Pit size is similar to pit percentage, in that larger pits tend to associate with harder diets. It provides a different view of hardness by indicating feature size rather than feature frequency. Scratch width is a good indicator of dietary abrasiveness, with wider scratches being associated with abrasive diets (e.g., Schmidt, 2001, 2010). The DMTA variable, complexity, indicates dietary hardness by measuring surface unevenness. In general, farming populations tend to have lower complexities and foragers tend to have higher complexities, although there are exceptions (e.g., El Zaatari, 2008, 2010; Da Gloria and Schmidt, 2019; Schmidt et al., 2019; Schmidt, El Zaatari, and Van Sessen, 2019). Anisotropy indicates dietary homogeneity. Diets that

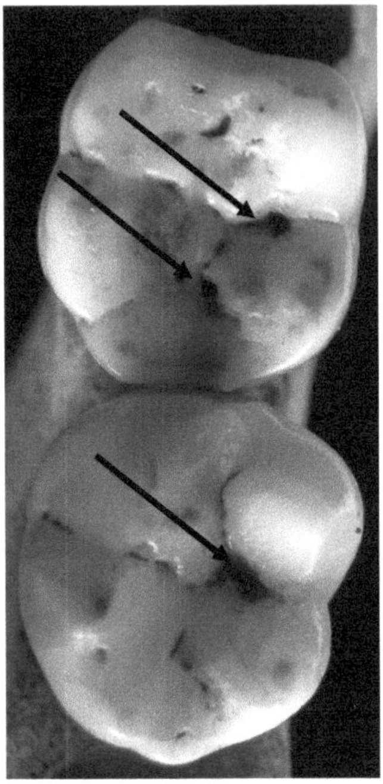

Figure 4.5 Arrows point to occlusal carious lesions in two lower left molars. These are not Native American teeth.

are similar in their overall makeup, like those of farmers, tend to have high anisotropy values; those with diverse constituents, like foragers, have lower values (e.g., Schmidt et al., 2019). Finally, dental caries data reflect the cariogenic nature of the diet. Diets leading to more people having dental caries are more cariogenic than those that do not. In the end, this study characterizes each group's diet as being abrasive or nonabrasive, hard or soft, homogeneous or heterogeneous, cariogenic or noncariogenic.

Statistical procedures

Null hypothesis statistical testing (NHST) has come under fire recently because of problems inherent with null conditions and the sensitivity p-values have to sample sizes (Smith, 2018, 2020). A concern with null hypotheses is that in many instances, particularly in bioarcheology, studies assume a null condition when, in reality, no such condition should be expected. For example, in most instances testing a null condition between male and female femur lengths is inappropriate because of human sexual dimorphism. Of course a sample of males and females could end up having the same average femur lengths, but that would be atypical, and not the default condition in humans. Therefore, instead of testing null hypotheses, researchers from a number of disciplines are emphasizing the use of effect indicators and their confidence intervals (CI) to determine practical, rather than statistical, significance (Smith, 2018). Indicators of effect size, like r^2, demonstrate strengths of relationships between variables. P-values do not. Effect indicator 95% CI indicate significance if they do not include zero. The current study does not employ traditional NHST, to the extent that I did not use p-values to determine significance except for tests of statistical assumptions and post hoc tests. Instead, I drew conclusions from the strength of the associations indicated by the effect indicators and their 95% CIs. My statistical outputs include p-values because at this time I feel more archeologists are comfortable with having them available, but they were ancillary to the interpretations I made.

The primary statistical tests were Model I analysis of variance (ANOVA) using the partial eta squared (η_p^2) effect indicator. I used an online calculator to compute 95% CI for η_p^2 (https://effect-size-calculator.herokuapp.com). Although the data allow for intra-*site* studies, the analyses here focus on intra- and inter-*group* comparisons (see Schmidt, 1998 for the intra-site tests). For all statistical procedures, the dependent variables were macrowear [anterior tooth macrowear (incisor/canine and premolar); molar macrowear (first, second, and third molar)], microwear (percentage of pits, pit length, scratch width), and dental caries [occlusal (anterior teeth and molars), and nonocclusal (anterior teeth and molars)]. The independent variables were group, (M/L Archaic, E/M Woodland, LW Albee, FA Oliver, Mississippian), age (young adult, mid/old adult), and sex (male, female). To ensure the data conformed to the assumptions of ANOVA, I conducted Kolmogorov-Smirnov and Levene's tests for normality and homogeneity of variance, respectively. Post Hoc tests were least significant difference.

CHAPTER 5

What did we learn?

Introduction

This chapter provides the results of the tests run for macrowear, microwear/dental microwear texture analysis (DMTA), and dental caries. The first part provides intragroup findings. For macrowear, age is the primary independent variable; for microwear/DMTA, age is controlled for by having all of the individuals being young adults. For dental caries, the ages are pooled. Dental caries is a continuous process, but due to antemortem tooth loss, the young and mid/old adults here have similar caries expressions (see Schmidt, 1998 for a detailed discussion of antemortem tooth loss in these groups). In addition, the number of young and mid/old adults is about the same for each group. The second part of this chapter focuses on intergroup comparisons.

Part I: intragroup findings

M/L Archaic

Macrowear: Male and female mean anterior teeth macrowear scores were nearly the same. Females averaged 6.00 and males 6.03. Based on the Smith (1984) scoring system, these scores indicated that the average Middle/Late Archaic (M/L Archaic) incisor, canine, and premolar each had a large dentin patch surrounded by a thin rim of enamel on a crown worn past its widest diameter. Standard deviations indicated the female variation was greater than that of the males. The mean female incisor/canine value (6.0) was nearly the same as that of the males (5.95). The male premolar value (6.29) was only slightly higher than that of the females (6.05) and there were no significant differences between the anterior teeth by sex. Differences by age were more stark. The young adult anterior tooth macrowear mean was 4.44; the mid/old adult mean was 6.32. The young adults averaged having a dentin patch of distinct size and a thick enamel rim, while the mid/old adults averaged having only a thin enamel rim remaining.

Long 'on' the Tooth. DOI: https://doi.org/10.1016/B978-0-12-824306-0.00002-1

The mean molar macrowear scores were 28.18 for the females and 31.97 for the males. Recall that the maximum possible score for molar macrowear via the Scott (1979) system is 40. To achieve scores around 30, each molar quadrant for the first, second, and third molars must have had, on average, large dentin patches that coalesced with neighboring quadrants. Like the anterior teeth, the standard deviation for the female molar macrowear was higher (6.96) than that for the males (5.67). Looking at each molar (i.e., first, second, and third) the female averages were 33.41, 29.42, and 21.95, respectively. For the males, the scores were 36.26, 32.60, and 22.29. For all three molars, the female standard deviation exceeded that of the males. Regarding age, the mean molar macrowear score for the young adults was 24.10 and for the mid/old adult it was 30.50. For young adults, their average molars had distinct dentin patches that had not yet coalesced. The mid/old adults averaged having coalesced dentin patches on every cusp and a thick enamel rim. Summaries of the M/L Archaic macrowear data are in Tables 5.1–5.4.

Table 5.1 M/L Archaic mean macrowear scores by sex for the anterior teeth and the molars.

Group	Sex		Anterior teeth mean macrowear scores	Molar mean macrowear scores
M/L Archaic	Female	Mean	6.00	28.18
		N	17	17
		SD	1.85	6.96
	Male	Mean	6.03	31.97
		N	25	25
		SD	1.28	5.67
	Total	Mean	6.02	30.43
		N	42	42
		SD	1.51	6.42

Table 5.2 M/L Archaic mean macrowear scores by sex for the anterior teeth only: incisors/canines and premolars.

Group	Sex		Incisor/Canine	Premolar
M/L Archaic	Female	Mean	6.00	6.05
		N	17	17
		SD	2.10	1.71
	Male	Mean	5.95	6.29
		N	24	23
		SD	1.49	1.21
	Total	Mean	5.97	6.19
		N	41	40
		SD	1.75	1.43

Table 5.3 M/L Archaic mean macrowear scores by sex for molars only: first, second, and third molars.

Group	Sex		First molar	Second molar	Third molar
M/L Archaic	Female	Mean	33.41	29.42	21.95
		N	16.00	16.00	16.00
		SD	6.31	8.31	10.73
	Male	Mean	36.26	32.60	22.29
		N	23.00	22.00	19.00
		SD	3.24	5.77	7.57
	Total	Mean	35.09	31.26	22.13
		N	39.00	38.00	35.00
		SD	4.88	7.03	9.01

Table 5.4 M/L Archaic mean anterior teeth and molar macrowear scores by age.

	Anterior teeth			Molars		
	Mean	SD	n	Mean	SD	n
Young adult	4.44	1.51	9	24.10	6.09	9
Mid/Old adult	6.32	1.51	10	30.50	6.04	10

Table 5.5 M/L Archaic scanning electron microscope-based microwear summary data by sex. Pit length and scratch width values are in μm. Sample sizes are in parentheses; the total includes those of unknown sex.

	Male (14)		Female (6)		Total (22)	
Features	Mean	SD	Mean	SD	Mean	SD
Percentage of pits	20.0	8.4	17.4	7.0	18.7	7.8
Pit length	10.2	4.4	8.5	1.5	10.1	4.1
Scratch width	1.8	0.50	1.7	0.71	1.8	0.53

Microwear: The M/L Archaic scanning electron microscope (SEM)-based microwear had a low percentage of pits, moderately sized pits, and very wide scratches (Table 5.5). The males had a higher percentage of pits (20.0% vs 17.4%), larger pits (mean = 10.2 vs 8.5 μm), and wider scratches (mean = 1.8 vs 1.7 μm) than the females, but there were no significant differences.

Among the M/L Archaic, the average DMTA complexity value was 1.49 and 0.0027 for anisotropy. The complexity value indicated some dietary hardness and the anisotropy pointed to jaw movement in many directions. The values for anisotropy and complexity were almost identical between the seven males and seven females suitable for study (Table 5.6).

Table 5.6 M/L Archaic DMTA data by sex.

M/L Archaic		Mean	SD	N
Anisotropy	Female	0.0028	0.0004	7
	Male	0.0026	0.0009	7
	Total	0.0027	0.0007	14
Complexity	Female	1.52	0.60	6
	Male	1.46	0.68	7
	Total	1.49	0.62	13

Table 5.7 M/L Archaic prevalence of dental caries among those of known-sex. Sample size is in parentheses.

Prevalence	Males (12)	Females (8)
Occlusal caries (all teeth)	25.0%	50.0%
Nonocclusal caries (all teeth)	25.0%	0
Carious anterior teeth	0	0
Carious molars	25.0%	50.0%

Dental caries: Overall, M/L Archaic dental caries prevalence (percentage of people affected) and severity (number of teeth affected per person with at least one lesion) were modest. Likewise, there were few differences among the sexes. One difference that stood out was that 25% of the males had at least one tooth expressing a nonocclusal lesion, while none of the females had nonocclusal lesions. Neither males nor females had carious anterior teeth, but more females had carious molars (Table 5.7). The percentages of males and females with caries was elevated relative to other M/L Archaic populations (e.g., Perzigian et al., 1984), which could be due to this study having a small sample of M/L Archaic people of known-sex.

In terms of severity, among those with at least one carious lesion, the average male had 8.5% of his total number of teeth and 18.4% of his molars affected by caries; for the average female 9.6% of all of her teeth and 23.0% of her molars had lesions. Except for nonocclusal lesion prevalence, the M/L Archaic caries data are similar between the males and females.

E/M Woodland

Macrowear: Early/Middle Woodland (E/M Woodland) male and female anterior teeth macrowear scores were similar; the females averaged 4.33 and the males averaged 4.73. The average E/M Woodland incisor, canine, and premolar had a distinct dentin patch surrounded

Table 5.8 E/M Woodland mean macrowear scores by sex for the anterior teeth and the molars.

Group	Sex		Anterior teeth mean macrowear score	Molar mean macrowear score
E/M Woodland	Female	Mean N SD	4.33 17 1.59	25.11 16 7.52
	Male	Mean N SD	4.73 24 1.75	25.07 25 8.12
	Total	Mean N SD	4.56 41 1.68	25.09 41 7.79

Table 5.9 E/M Woodland mean macrowear scores by sex for the anterior teeth only: incisors/canines and premolars.

Group	Sex		Incisor/Canine mean macrowear scores	Premolar mean macrowear scores
E/M Woodland	Female	Mean N SD	4.22 17 1.83	4.34 17 1.37
	Male	Mean N SD	4.87 21 1.85	4.86 24 1.73
	Total	Mean N SD	4.58 38 1.84	4.64 41 1.59

by a thick rim of enamel on a crown worn to a level just above its widest diameter. The male standard deviation slightly exceeded that of the females (Table 5.8). For the anterior tooth macrowear scores, the female incisor/canine and premolar means (4.22 and 4.34) were slightly lower than the male scores (4.87 and 4.86). These differences were not enough to be meaningful. Unlike sex, age is a factor. The young adult anterior tooth macrowear mean was 3.03; the mid/old adult mean was 5.60. The average young adult had a modest patch of dentin exposure, while the mid/old adults had large dentin patches surrounded by a distinct enamel rim (Table 5.9).

The mean molar macrowear scores were 25.11 for females and 25.07 for males. For both males and females, the average molar had distinct, but uncoalesced, dentin patches. Like the anterior teeth, the standard deviation for the female molar macrowear (7.52) was lower

Table 5.10 E/M Woodland mean macrowear scores by sex for molars only: first, second, and third molars.

Group	Sex		First molar	Second molar	Third molar
E/M Woodland	Female	Mean	29.99	25.04	18.34
		N	16	14	14
		SD	6.34	7.78	9.27
	Male	Mean	30.58	25.42	19.37
		N	23	21	22
		SD	7.50	8.11	7.67
	Total	Mean	30.34	25.26	18.97
		N	39	35	36
		SD	6.97	7.87	8.22

than that for the males (8.12). Looking at each molar (i.e., first, second, and third), the female average macrowear scores were 29.99, 25.04, and 18.34, respectively. For the males, the scores were 30.58, 25.42, and 19.37. For the first and second molars, the male standard deviation exceeded that of the females, but for the third molar, the female standard deviation was higher (Table 5.10). Regarding age, the mean molar macrowear score for the young adults was 18.20 and for the mid/old adult it was 31.17. The average young adult molars had small but distinct dentin patches that had not yet coalesced. The mid/old adults averaged having coalesced dentin patches and a little more than a 1 mm thick enamel rim (Table 5.11).

Microwear: The E/M Woodland SEM-based microwear had a high percentage of pits, large pits, and wide scratches (Table 5.12). The females had a higher percentage of pits (28.8% vs 24.9%), but the males had larger pits (mean = 14.0 vs 10.0 μm), and wider scratches (mean = 1.3 vs 1.2 μm). Overall, the male and female values were similar and there were no significant sex-based differences.

Among the E/M Woodland, those of known-sex had a DMTA complexity value of 1.54 (n = 11) and an anisotropy value of 0.0027 (n = 12). The complexity value was moderate and indicative of some dietary hardness. The anisotropy was low to moderate, indicating jaw movements in many directions. The male anisotropy (0.0031) was higher than that of the females (0.0025), as was the male complexity (1.65 vs 1.44); but these differences were not significant (Table 5.13).

Dental caries: The E/M Woodland dental caries prevalence and severity were low. Like the M/L Archaic, no one had anterior tooth

Table 5.11 E/M Woodland mean anterior teeth and molar macrowear scores by age.

E/M Woodland	Anterior teeth			Molars		
	Mean	SD	n	Mean	SD	n
Young adult	3.03	0.88	14	18.20	4.89	15
Mid/Old adult	5.60	1.37	20	31.17	4.13	20

Table 5.12 E/M Woodland scanning electron microscope-based microwear summary data by sex. Pit length and scratch width values are in μm. Sample sizes are in parentheses; the total includes those of unknown sex.

	Male (11)		Female (9)		Total (22)	
Features	Mean	SD	Mean	SD	Mean	SD
Percentage of pits	24.9	7.2	28.8	7.2	27.2	8.2
Pit length	14.0	9.9	10.0	3.8	12.8	8.0
Scratch width	1.2	0.42	1.3	0.45	1.4	0.66

Table 5.13 E/M Woodland DMTA data by sex.

E/M Woodland		Mean	SD	N
Anisotropy	Female	0.0025	0.0009	7
	Male	0.0031	0.0009	5
	Total	0.0027	0.0009	12
Complexity	Female	1.44	0.66	6
	Male	1.65	0.39	5
	Total	1.54	0.54	11

Table. 5.14 E/M Woodland dental caries prevalence among those of known-sex. Sample size is in parentheses.

Prevalence	Males (21)	Females (13) %
Occlusal caries	19.1%	46.2%
Nonocclusal caries	9.5%	0
Carious anterior teeth	0	0
Carious molars	14.3%	46.2%

dental caries, but both males and females had molar lesions. Also like the M/L Archaic, more males had nonocclusal lesions than females, although at 9.5% that number was low. The most distinct difference between males and females was in the posterior teeth; more than three times, as many females as males had carious molars (46.2% vs 14.3%).

In terms of severity, the percentage of teeth affected by caries (among those with at least one lesion) was relatively minuscule. For the percentage of all teeth affected by occlusal lesions, the means were 9.4 for males and 11.4 for females. The percentage of carious molars was almost identical for males and females (23.8 for males and 24.9 for females). Thus, while more females had dental caries, the percentage of affected teeth was the same for each sex (Table 5.14).

LW Albee

Macrowear: The Albee tradition of the Late Woodland (LW Albee) females mean was 4.54; for the males it was 5.39. These indicate the average LW Albee female incisor, canine, and premolar had wear similar to that of the E/M Woodland. However, for the males, the macrowear was greater and a typical male would have had a larger dentin patch than the average female. The male and female standard deviations were nearly the same (Table 5.15). The female incisor/canine and premolar means (4.76 and 4.18) were lower than the male means (5.66 and 5.01), which suggests some distinction between male and female anterior tooth use. The young adult anterior tooth macrowear mean was 3.41; the mid/old adult mean was 6.18. The average young adult had a modest patch of dentin exposure, while the mid/old adults had large dentin patches surrounded by a distinct enamel rim (Table 5.16).

The molar macrowear means were 19.39 for females and 25.03 for males. For the females, the average molar cusp was flat with a small dentin patch that was no greater than about one-fourth of the cusp. On average, the males had larger dentin patches that covered more than one-fourth of the cusp surface, but the dentin patches did not coalesce. The standard deviations for molar macrowear were around nine for both the females and males (Table 5.17). For each molar (i.e., first, second, and third), the female average macrowear scores were 22.46,

Table 5.15 LW Albee mean macrowear scores by sex for the anterior teeth and the molars.

Group	Sex		Anterior teeth mean macrowear score	Molar mean macrowear score
LW Albee	Female	Mean	4.54	19.39
		N	29	29
		SD	1.72	8.98
	Male	Mean	5.39	25.03
		N	29	27
		SD	1.73	9.31
	Total	Mean	4.96	22.11
		N	58	56
		SD	1.76	9.49

Table 5.16 LW Albee mean macrowear scores by sex for the anterior teeth only: incisors/canines and premolars.

Group	Sex		Incisor/canine mean macrowear scores	Premolar mean macrowear scores
LW Albee	Female	Mean	4.76	4.18
		N	28	28
		SD	1.80	1.77
	Male	Mean	5.66	5.01
		N	28	27
		SD	1.81	1.66
	Total	Mean	5.21	4.58
		N	56	55
		SD	1.85	1.75

Table 5.17 LW Albee mean macrowear scores by sex for molars only: first, second, and third molars.

Group	Sex		First molar	Second molar	Third molar
LW Albee	Female	Mean	22.46	17.48	14.32
		N	25.00	25.00	24.00
		SD	9.14	9.51	6.85
	Male	Mean	27.90	23.78	17.93
		N	25.00	25.00	22.00
		SD	7.71	10.42	10.13
	Total	Mean	25.18	20.63	16.05
		N	50.00	50.00	46.00
		SD	8.81	10.37	8.67

17.48, and 14.32, respectively. For the males, the scores were 27.90, 23.78, and 17.93. The male molar values were noticeably higher. In fact, sex-based statistically significant differences existed for molar score, first molar score, and second molar score, with η_p^2 values indicating medium-level effect sizes (Table 5.18).

For the first molar, the female standard deviation is larger, but for the second and third molars, the male standard deviations exceeded that of the females. Regarding age, the molar macrowear mean for the young adults was 14.48 and for the mid/old adult it was 29.62. For young adults, their average molar cusps were flat with almost no dentin exposed. For the mid/old adults, however, they averaged having coalesced dentin patches on every cusp and distinct enamel rims (Table 5.19).

Microwear: The LW Albee SEM-based microwear had a high percentage of pits, large pits, and moderate to wide scratches (Table 5.20). The LW Albee females had far more pits (31.9 vs 17.3), larger pits

Table. 5.18 ANOVA results for LW Albee female vs male molar macrowear scores.

		df	Mean Square	F	Sig.	η_p^2 (95% CI)
Molar	Between sexes Within sexes Total	1.00 54.00 55.00	445.10 83.55	5.33	0.025	0.090 (0.01–0.22)
First molar	Between sexes Within sexes Total	1.00 48.00 49.00	370.83 71.51	5.19	0.027	0.098 (0.01–0.24)
Second molar	Between sexes Within sexes Total	1.00 48.00 49.00	496.13 99.54	4.98	0.030	0.094 (0.01–0.23)
Third molar	Between sexes Within sexes Total	1.00 44.00 45.00	149.50 73.49	2.03	0.161	0.04 (0.0–0.17)

Table 5.19 LW Albee mean anterior teeth and molar macrowear scores by age.

LW Albee	Anterior teeth			Molars		
	Mean	SD	n	Mean	SD	n
Young adult	3.41	1.33	25	14.48	6.00	24
Mid/Old adult	6.18	0.94	25	29.62	6.14	24

Table 5.20 LW Albee scanning electron microscope-based microwear summary data by sex. Pit length and scratch width values are in μm. Sample sizes are in parentheses; the total includes those of unknown sex.

	Male (9)		Female (8)		Total (18)	
Features	Mean	SD	Mean	SD	Mean	SD
Percentage of pits	17.3	12.4	31.9	11.1	24.1	13.3
Pit length	10.4	6.0	11.1	2.9	10.5	4.6
Scratch width	1.1	0.4	1.4	0.4	1.3	0.4

(11.1 vs 10.4 μm), and wider scratches (1.4 vs 1.1 μm) than the males (Table 5.19). The male-female pit percentage disparity was statistically significant and the effect size was large (ANOVA, df = 1, F = 6.434, sig. = 0.023, $\eta_p{}^{2=}0.300$). In fact, LW Albee females had the highest percentage of pits compared to all groups in this study, and the LW Albee males had the lowest. Unfortunately, there were no DMTA data from LW Albee sites in this study.

Dental caries: The Late Woodland marked a noticeable jump in the percentage of people with dental caries. In the LW Albee, over half of the males and females had carious lesions. Approximately 61% of the

Table 5.21 LW Albee prevalence of dental caries among those of known-sex.

Prevalence	Males (27)	Females (28)
Occlusal caries	51.9%	60.7%
Nonocclusal caries	14.8%	25.0%
Carious anterior teeth	14.8%	21.4%
Carious molars	40.7%	57.7%

females and 52% of the males had carious lesions on at least one tooth. Both males and females had nonocclusal lesions, although nearly twice as many females than males had them. Likewise, both sexes had carious anterior teeth and, again, female values were higher. The most dramatic difference was in the molars where nearly 58% of the females had carious molars compared to 37% of the males (Table 5.21).

Unlike prevalence, the male and female dental caries severities were similar. Males had dental caries present on 16.7% of their teeth; the females had 17.8% affected. Among the males with dental caries, 33.3% of their molars had cavities, while for the females that number was 37.1%.

FA Oliver

Macrowear: The Fort Ancient Oliver tradition (FA Oliver) male and female anterior teeth macrowear means were high. The females mean was 4.18 and the males' was 5.19. The FA Oliver female incisors, canines, and premolars had distinct dentin patches; the males had larger dentin patches and distinct enamel rims. The male and female standard deviations differed noticeably, with the female standard deviation being greater. The female incisor/canine and premolar means (4.59 and 3.62) were lower than that of the males (5.45 and 4.82). Like the LW Albee, these scores may indicate differences between male and female anterior tooth use. The young and mid/old anterior tooth means were 3.22 and 5.34. The average young adult had rounded cusps and a minor patch of dentin exposure, while the mid/old adults had large dentin patches surrounded by a distinct enamel rim. The molar macrowear means were 14.66 for females and 19.38 for males. For the females, the average molar cusp was flat with a small pinpoint dentin patch. On average, the male dentin patches were about one-fourth of each cusp surface.

The standard deviations for molar macrowear were around five for both the females and males. For each molar (i.e., first, second, and third), the females averaged 18.02, 12.87, and 10.71, respectively. The male means were 22.08, 19.60, and 16.88 and noticeably higher than the female values, particularly for the second and third molars. However, the small FA Oliver samples sizes may have been exaggerated these differences.

For the first molar, the female standard deviation was larger, but for the second and third molars the male standard deviation exceeded that of the females. Regarding age, the young and mid/old adult molar means were 14.48 and 29.62, respectively. The young adults averaged having flat molar cusps with almost no dentin exposed. On average, the mid/old adults had coalesced dentin patches on every cusp and a distinct enamel rim (Tables 5.22–5.25).

Microwear: The FA Oliver SEM-based microwear had a moderate percentage of pits, small pits, and modest scratch widths (Table. 5.26). The males had more pits (19.4 vs 17.9) but the females had longer pits (6.4 vs 5.8). Both sexes had about the same average scratch widths, around 1 mm. In all, there were no meaningful sex-based microwear differences among the FA Oliver people.

The FA Oliver DMTA came exclusively from the Bicycle Bridge site; recall it lacked people of known-sex. The DMTA complexity value was 1.64 (n = 11) and the anisotropy was 0.0020 (Table 5.27). The complexity value indicated some dietary hardness. The anisotropy was low, indicating jaw movements in many directions.

Table 5.22 FA Oliver mean macrowear scores by sex for the anterior teeth and the molars.

Group	Sex		Anterior teeth mean macrowear score	Molar mean macrowear score
Oliver	Female	Mean	4.18	14.66
		N	12	11
		SD	1.70	5.37
	Male	Mean	5.19	19.38
		N	7	7
		SD	0.73	4.72
	Total	Mean	4.55	16.50
		N	19	18
		SD	1.48	5.52

Table 5.23 FA Oliver mean macrowear scores by sex for the anterior teeth only: incisors/canines and premolars.

Group	Sex		Incisor/canine mean macrowear scores	Premolar mean macrowear scores
FA Oliver	Female	Mean	4.59	3.62
		N	12	12
		SD	1.91	1.51
	Male	Mean	5.45	4.82
		N	7	7
		SD	0.81	0.69
	Total	Mean	4.91	4.06
		N	19	19
		SD	1.62	1.38

Table 5.24 FA Oliver mean macrowear scores by sex for molars only: first, second, and third molars.

Group	Sex		First molar	Second molar	Third molar
FA Oliver	Female	Mean	18.02	12.87	10.71
		N	11	9	7
		SD	4.41	7.06	7.65
	Male	Mean	22.08	19.60	16.88
		N	6	7	6
		SD	3.41	5.68	4.66
	Total	Mean	19.46	15.81	13.56
		N	17	16	13
		SD	4.45	7.17	6.97

Table 5.25 FA Oliver mean anterior teeth and molar macrowear scores by age.

FA Oliver	Anterior teeth			Molars		
	Mean	SD	n	Mean	SD	n
Young adult	3.22	1.32	11	13.51	5.05	11
Mid/Old adult	5.34	0.86	9	18.88	5.06	8

Table 5.26 FA Oliver scanning electron microscope-based microwear summary data by sex. Pit length and scratch width values are in μm. Sample sizes are in parentheses; the total includes those of unknown sex.

	Male (11)		Female (9)		Total (22)	
Features	Mean	SD	Mean	SD	Mean	SD
Percentage of pits	19.4	9.5	17.9	9.0	17.5	10.0
Pit length	5.8	2.5	6.4	3.7	6.7	4.5
Scratch width	1.0	0.21	1.1	0.3	1.1	0.2

Table 5.27 FA Oliver DMTA complexity and anisotropy values.

	Mean	SD	N
Complexity	1.64	0.70	11
Anisotropy	0.0020	0.0008	11

Table 5.28 FA Oliver prevalence of dental caries among those of known-sex. Sample size is in parentheses.

Prevalence	Males (7) %	Females (12) %
Occlusal caries	85.7%	100.0%
Nonocclusal caries	85.7%	66.6%
Carious anterior teeth	14.3%	25.0%
Carious molars	71.4%	58.3%

Caries: The FA Oliver people had a high prevalence and severity of dental caries. Every female and over 85% of the males had at least one carious lesion. Both occlusal and nonocclusal lesions were common. Anterior tooth lesions occurred in a quarter of the females and just under 15% of the males; however, about 70% of the males had carious molars but only 58.3% of the females did.

Regarding severity, 32.0% of male teeth and 25.2% of female teeth were carious. For the molars, those numbers become 33.1% and 53.7% for males and females, respectively. Thus, for the males about one-third of their dentition, including their molars, was carious. For the females, a smaller percentage of their anterior teeth had caries but a larger percentage of their molars were carious compared to the males (Table 5.28).

Mississippian

Macrowear: The Mississippian female anterior tooth macrowear mean was 3.52; for the males it was 4.75. The average female incisors, canines, and premolars had small dentin patches; the males had larger dentin patches and distinct enamel rims. The male and female standard deviations were similar (Tables 5.29 and 5.30). The female incisor/canine and premolar means (3.65 and 3.36) were lower than the male means (5.09 and 4.45). Like the Woodland groups, these differences may indicate meaningful differences between male and female anterior tooth use. A significant difference existed between the males and females for all anterior teeth, incisors/canines, and premolars (Table 5.31). The young adult anterior tooth macrowear mean was 2.98; the mid/old adult mean was

Table 5.29 Mississippian mean macrowear scores by sex for the anterior teeth and the molars.

Group	Sex		Anterior teeth mean macrowear score	Molar mean macrowear score
Mississippian	Female	Mean N SD	3.52 32 1.23	14.81 36 5.10
	Male	Mean N SD	4.75 28 1.45	19.99 30 7.07
	Total	Mean N SD	4.10 60 1.46	17.16 66 6.57

Table 5.30 Mississippian mean macrowear scores by sex for the anterior teeth only: incisors/canines and premolars.

Group	Sex		Incisor/canine mean macrowear scores	Premolar mean macrowear scores
Mississippian	Female	Mean N SD	3.65 27 1.23	3.36 32 1.23
	Male	Mean N SD	5.09 26 1.54	4.45 28 1.39
	Total	Mean N SD	4.35 53 1.56	3.87 60 1.41

Table 5.31 ANOVA results for Mississippian anterior tooth macrowear scores, male versus female. Comparisons are for anterior teeth only: all anterior teeth, incisors/canines, and premolars.

		df	Mean square	F	Sig.	η_p^2 (95% CI)
Anterior teeth	Between groups Within groups Total	1 58 59	22.605 1.781	12.692	0.001	0.180 (0.05–0.31)
Incisors/ canines	Between groups Within groups Total	1 51 52	27.393 1.933	14.17	0.000	0.217 (0.07–0.36)
Premolars	Between groups Within groups Total	1 58 59	17.835 1.703	10.471	0.002	0.153 (0.04–0.29)

5.16. The average young adult had rounded cusps and a minor patch of dentin exposure, while the mid/old adults had large dentin patches surrounded by a distinct enamel rim.

The mean molar macrowear scores were 14.81 for females and 19.99 for males. These scores indicated that the average female molar cusp was flat with a small pinpoint dentin patch; the males had small dentin patches that were no more than one-fourth of the cusp surface. The male standard deviations were larger than the females'. For each molar (i.e., first, second, and third), the female macrowear means were 17.59, 13.98, and 9.55, respectively. For the males, the scores were 22.34, 19.67, and 14.00. The male molar values were noticeably higher for all three molars and significantly different.

The young adult molar macrowear mean was 12.51; the mid/old adult mean was 22.47. Young adults averaged having molar cusps that were flat with almost no dentin exposed. The average mid/old adult had small pinpoint dentin patches on each molar cusp (Tables 5.32–5.34).

Table 5.32 Mississippian mean macrowear scores by sex for molars only: first, second, and third molars.

Group	Sex		First molar	Second molar	Third molar
Mississippian	Female	Mean N SD	17.59 31 5.44	13.98 31 4.81	9.55 20 5.57
	Male	Mean N SD	22.34 25 6.81	19.67 27 7.14	14.00 21 6.98
	Total	Mean N SD	19.71 56 6.48	16.63 58 6.60	11.83 41 6.64

Table 5.33 ANOVA results for Mississippian molar macrowear scores, male versus female. Comparisons are for molars only: all molars, first molar, second molar, and third molar.

		df	Mean square	F	Sig.	η_p^2 (95% CI)
Molars	Between groups Within groups Total	1 64 65	440.734 36.92	11.938	0.001	0.157 (0.04–0.29)
First molar	Between groups Within groups Total	1 54 55	312.772 37.012	8.45	0.005	0.135 (0.03–0.28)
Second molar	Between groups Within groups Total	1 56 57	466.986 36.052	12.953	0.001	0.188 (0.06–0.33)
Third molar	Between groups Within groups Total	1 39 40	202.493 40.088	5.051	0.030	0.115 (0.01–0.27)

Table 5.34 Mississipppian mean anterior teeth and molar macrowear scores by age.

Mississippian	Anterior teeth			Molars		
	Mean	SD	n	Mean	SD	n
Young adult	2.98	0.83	27	12.51	3.54	32
Mid/Old adult	5.16	1.23	28	22.47	5.85	28

Table 5.35 Mississippian scanning electron microscope-based microwear summary data by sex. Pit length and scratch width values are in μm. Sample sizes are in parentheses; the total includes those of unknown sex.

	Male (11)		Female (9)		Total (23)	
Features	Mean	SD	Mean	SD	Mean	SD
Percentage of pits	18.1	7.7	17.9	6.5	19.5	8.3
Pit length	8.4	4.2	10.7	5.3	9.7	4.9
Scratch width	1.0	0.2	1.0	0.3	1.0	0.2

Table 5.36 Mississippian DMTA data by sex.

		Mean	SD	n
Anisotropy	Female	0.0031	0.0018	8
	Male	0.0040	0.0012	6
	Total	0.0035	0.0016	14
Complexity	Female	1.11	0.28	7
	Male	0.96	0.28	5
	Total	1.05	0.27	12

Microwear: The Mississippian SEM-based microwear had a modest percentage of pits, moderate pit lengths, and small scratch widths (Table 5.35). The male and female percentages of pits were both around 18; but the female pit lengths were longer (10.7 vs 8.4 μm). Both sexes had the same average scratch width at 1 μm. All told, there were no meaningful sex-based microwear differences among the Mississippian.

The Mississippian DMTA came exclusively from the Angel site. The DMTA complexity value of 1.05 ($n = 12$) and an anisotropy value of 0.0035 (Table 5.36) indicated a diet low in hardness and similar in consistency, such that jaw movement was largely in the same direction. The male and female anisotropy values were different. The female anisotropy was 0.0031; the male mean was 0.0040. A difference of this magnitude can be significant (e.g., Schmidt et al., 2019). In this case, it was not perhaps because of the tremendous range of variation seen in the Mississippian females, some of whom had very low values (Fig. 5.1). Overall, the Mississippian DMTA anisotropy was higher and complexity was lower than that of the M/L Archaic, E/M Woodland, and the FA Oliver.

Caries: Mississippian caries data indicated high levels of infection for males and females. Both had an occlusal lesion prevalence over 80%. Likewise, nonocclusal lesions were common, they occurred in about half of the males and a third of the females. Around a quarter of the males and females had lesions in their anterior teeth. The male molar prevalence was 58.6%; for the females it was 77.1%.

Female severity was similar to that of the males. About 30% of the female teeth and 26% of the male teeth were carious. For the molars, over 60% of the female molars and about half of the male molars had carious lesions (Table 5.37).

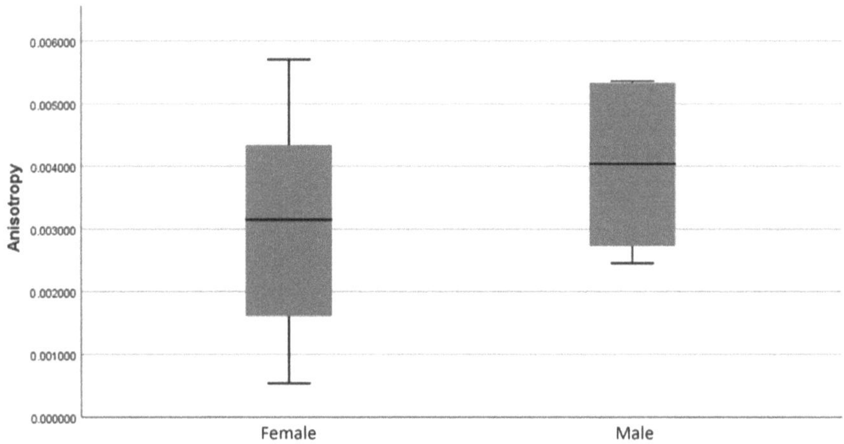

Figure 5.1 Box-and-whisker plots of Mississippian female and male anisotropy values. Note the wide range of female values, particularly toward the low end.

Table 5.37 Mississippian prevalence of dental caries among those of known-sex. Sample size is in parentheses.

Prevalence	Males (29)	Females (35)
Occlusal Caries	82.8%	80.0%
Nonocclusal caries	55.2%	34.3%
Carious anterior teeth	24.1%	28.6%
Carious molars	58.6%	77.1%

Part II: intergroup results

This section makes comparisons between groups. Included are 178 adults of known age and sex and 125 adults of unknown age and sex.

Macrowear: In general, macrowear declines over time. Starting with the anterior tooth macrowear, the M/L Archaic had the highest mean scores for both the young and old adults (Fig. 5.2, Table 5.38). The next highest was the LW Albee, followed by the E/M Woodland, FA Oliver, and the Mississippian. The differences between the groups for anterior tooth macrowear was significant ($\eta_p^2 = 0.119$; 95% CI = 0.037–0.173)

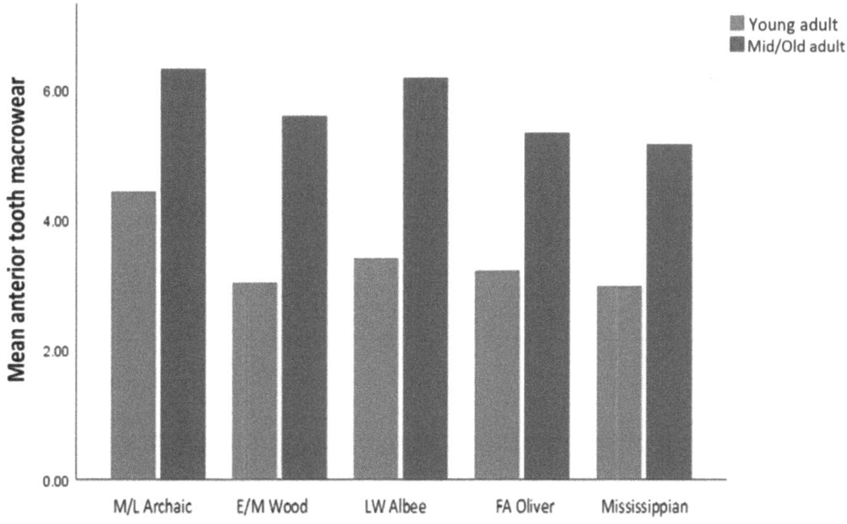

Figure 5.2 Mean anterior tooth macrowear scores by age and group.

Table 5.38 Mean anterior tooth macrowear scores by age and group.

	Group	Mean	SD	n
Young adult	M/L Archaic	4.44	1.51	9
	E/M Woodland	3.03	0.88	14
	LW Albee	3.41	1.3	25
	FA Oliver	3.22	1.32	11
	Mississippian	2.98	0.83	27
	Total	3.30	1.20	86
Mid/Old adult	M/L Archaic	6.32	1.51	10
	E/M Woodland	5.60	1.37	20
	LW Albee	6.18	0.94	25
	FA Oliver	5.34	0.86	9
	Mississippian	5.16	1.23	28
	Total	5.68	1.25	92

(Table 5.39). Post hoc results distinguished the M/L Archaic from the other groups, and the LW Albee differed from the FA Oliver and Mississippian (Table 5.40). As expected, age was highly significant (Table 5.39), and males and females had similar values for each group, and followed a similar pattern of decline through time (Fig. 5.3).

The molar macrowear decreased over time (Fig. 5.4). The M/L Archaic had the greatest molar macrowear for both young and mid/old adults. In fact, M/L Archaic young adult mean macrowear score exceeded the FA Oliver and Mississippian *mid/old* adult values. The next highest values were for the E/M Woodland, LW Albee, Mississippian, and FA Oliver (Fig. 5.5). The differences were significant ($\eta_p^2 = 0.341$,

Table 5.39 ANOVA results for anterior tooth macrowear score by age and group.

	df	Mean square	F	Sig.	η_p^2 (95% CI)
Corrected model	9	31.79	23.253	0.000	
Intercept	1	3034.727	2219.753	0.000	
Age	1	192.577	140.861	0.000	0.456 (0.44–0.58)
Group	4	7.782	5.692	0.000	0.119 (0.04–0.173)
Age* group	4	1.072	0.784	0.537	0.018
Error	168	1.367			
Total	178				
Corrected total	177				

R Squared = 0.555 (Adjusted R Squared = 0.531).

Table 5.40 LSD post hoc results for anterior tooth macrowear score for time.

Group	Group	Mean difference	Standard error	Sig.
M/L Archaic	E/M Woodland	0.8856*	0.33491	0.009
	LW Albee	0.6311*	0.31512	0.047
	FA Oliver	1.2552*	0.37458	0.001
	Mississippian	1.3356*	0.31115	0.000
E/M Woodland	M/L Archaic	−0.8856*	0.33491	0.009
	LW Albee	−0.2545	0.25991	0.329
	FA Oliver	0.3696	0.3295	0.264
	Mississippian	0.45	0.25508	0.080
LW Albee	M/L Archaic	−0.6311*	0.31512	0.047
	E/M Woodland	0.2545	0.25991	0.329
	FA Oliver	0.6242*	0.30935	0.045
	Mississippian	0.7046*	0.22847	0.002
FA Oliver	M/L Archaic	−1.2552*	0.37458	0.001
	E/M Woodland	−0.3696	0.3295	0.264
	LW Albee	−0.6242*	0.30935	0.045
	Mississippian	0.0804	0.30531	0.793
Mississippian	M/L Archaic	−1.3356*	0.31115	0.000
	E/M Woodland	−0.45	0.25508	0.080
	LW Albee	−0.7046*	0.22847	0.002
	FA Oliver	−0.0804	0.30531	0.793

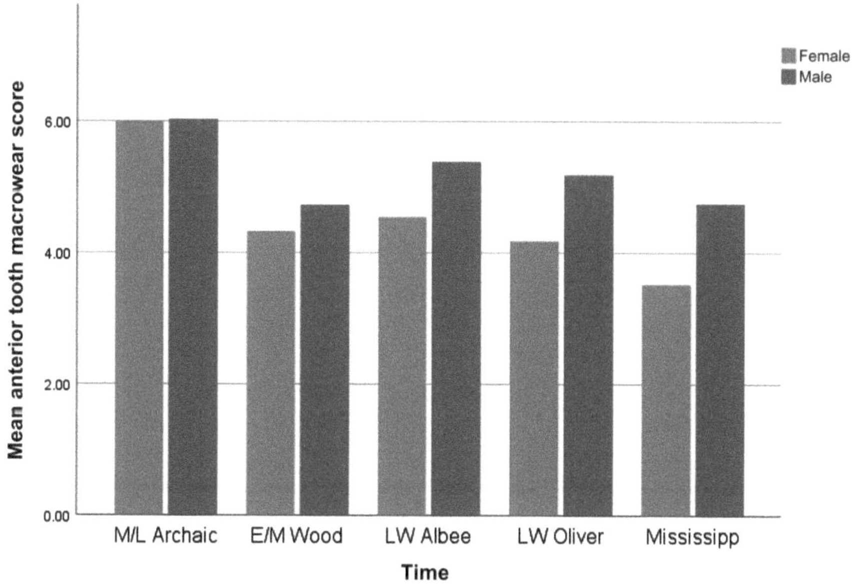

Figure 5.3 Mean anterior tooth macrowear score by sex and group.

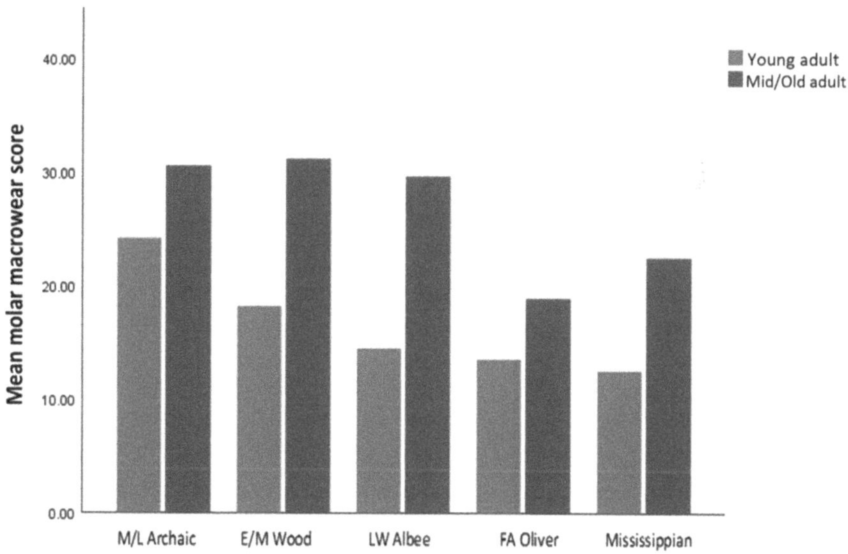

Figure 5.4 Mean molar macrowear scores by age and group.

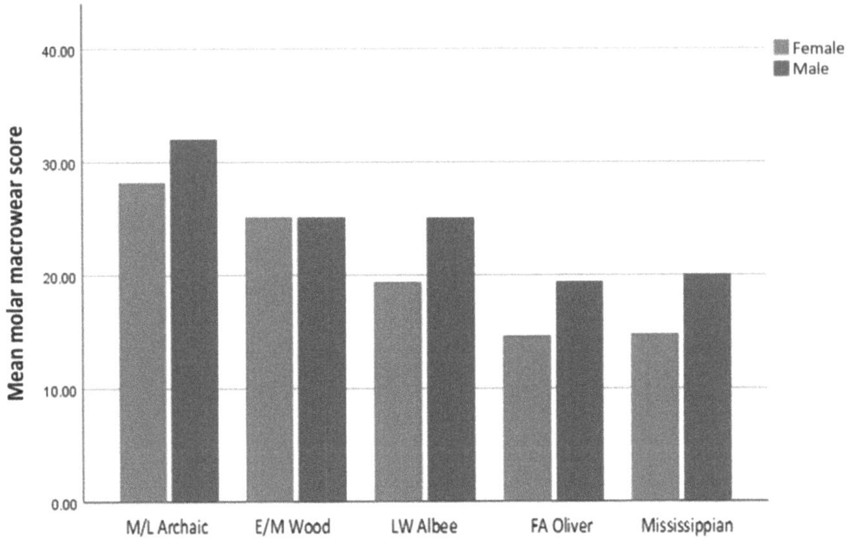

Figure 5.5 Mean molar macrowear scores by sex and group.

Table 5.41 Mean molar macrowear scores by age and group.

	Group	Mean	SD	n
Young adult	M/L Archaic	24.1	6.09	9
	E/M Woodland	18.20	4.89	15
	LW Albee	14.48	6.00	24
	FA Oliver	13.51	5.05	11
	Mississippian	12.51	3.54	32
	Total	15.24	6.00	91
Mid/Old adult	M/L Archaic	30.50	6.04	10
	E/M Woodland	31.17	4.13	20
	LW Albee	29.62	6.14	24
	FA Oliver	18.88	5.06	8
	Mississippian	22.47	5.85	28
	Total	26.89	7.00	90

95% CI = 0.23–0.40). Post hoc tests indicated multiple differences between groups. In fact, the only groups that did not differ were the FA Oliver–Mississippian and the M/L Archaic–E/M Woodland. In addition, the ANOVA results indicated a significant interaction for age by time. This was due primarily to the young adults from the M/L Archaic. The η_p^2 was moderate at 0.096 (see Tables 5.41–5.43). The declines in male and female mean scores were similar but not identical. Although described in detail in the intragroup comparison section, it is worth noting the biggest drop in female molar macrowear that came at the E/M Woodland to LW Albee; for the males, it came with the transition from the M/L Archaic to the E/M Woodland. From the M/L Archaic to the

Table 5.42 ANOVA results for molar macrowear score by age and group.

	df	Mean square	F	Sig.	η_p^2 (95% CI)
Corrected model	9	1001.63	36.254	0.000	
Intercept	1	66963.8	2423.729	0.000	
Age	1	3577.80	129.497	0.000	0.431 (0.33–0.49)
Group	4	612.314	22.162	0.000	0.341 (0.23–0.40)
Age*group	4	125.765	4.552	0.002	0.096 (0.04–0.15)
Error	171	27.628			
Total	181				
Corrected total	180				

R Squared = 0.656 (Adjusted R Squared = 0.638).

Table 5.43 LSD post hoc results of molar macrowear score for group.

Group	Group	Mean difference	Standard error	Sig.
M/L Archaic	E/M Woodland	1.9162	1.4978	0.203
	LW Albee	5.4808*	1.4246	0.000
	FA Oliver	11.7613*	1.7053	0.000
	Mississippian	10.3702*	1.3836	0.000
E/M Woodland	M/L Archaic	−1.9162	1.4978	0.203
	LW Albee	3.5645*	1.1683	0.003
	FA Oliver	9.8450*	1.4978	0.000
	Mississippian	8.4540*	1.1179	0.000
LW Albee	M/L Archaic	−5.4808*	1.4246	0.000
	E/M Woodland	−3.5645*	1.1683	0.003
	FA Oliver	6.2805*	1.4246	0.000
	Mississippian	4.8894*	1.0178	0.000
FA Oliver	M/L Archaic	−11.7613*	1.7053	0.000
	E/M Woodland	−9.8450*	1.4978	0.000
	LW Albee	−6.2805*	1.4246	0.000
	Mississippian	−1.3911	1.38369	0.316
Mississippian	M/L Archaic	−10.3702*	1.38369	0.000
	E/M Woodland	−8.4540*	1.11797	0.000
	LW Albee	−4.8894*	1.01787	0.000
	FA Oliver	1.3911	1.38369	0.316

FA Oliver, mean female microwear scores dropped around 46%, while for the males the drop was around 41%. Overall, males had greater molar macrowear than females, a difference that is significant, albeit with a modest to moderate effect size, when males and females from all groups are pooled (ANOVA, df = 1, n = 178, F = 21.530, η_p^2 = 0.088; 95% CI = 0.05–0.18).

Microwear: The SEM-based microwear indicated nuanced changes for each variable. Percentage of pits increased from M/L Archaic to the E/M Woodland and remained high for the LW Albee. It then dropped with the FA Oliver and Mississippian. For the M/L Archaic, the mean percentage of pits was 18.8%; for the E/M Woodland and the LW Albee the means were 26.4% and 24.1%, respectively. The FA

Oliver and Mississippian, mean percentage of pits were below 20 (Fig. 5.6). The ANOVA indicated significant differences between the E/M Woodland and the other groups except the LW Albee (Tables 5.44–5.46).

Pit length changed little through time (Fig. 5.7). Every group except the FA Oliver had mean pit lengths around 10 μm. The FA Oliver, however, had a mean pit length of 5.65 μm. This difference between the FA Oliver and the other groups was significant (Tables 5.47 and 5.48).

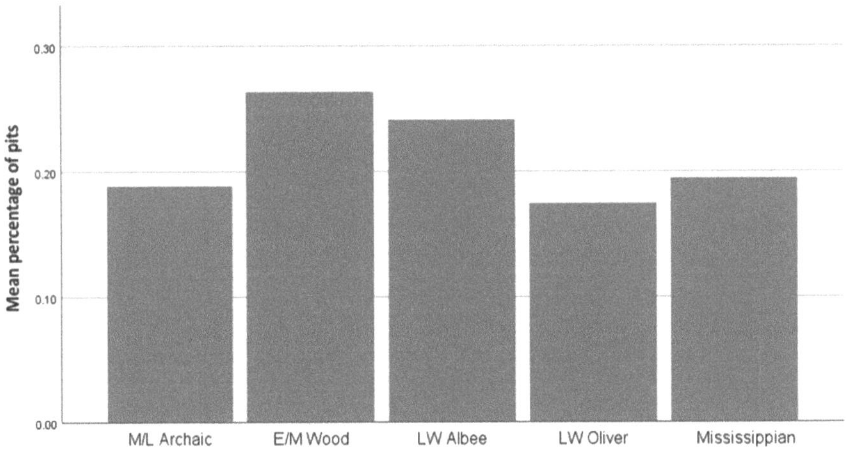

Figure 5.6 Mean percentage of pits by group.

Table 5.44 Summary of scanning electron microscope-based microwear data. Pit length are scratch width are in μm.

Group		Percentage of pits	Pit length	Scratch width
M/L Archaic	Mean	18.8	10.29	1.78
	N	21	21	21
	SD	0.08	4.12	0.54
E/M Woodland	Mean	26.4	10.83	1.21
	N	21	19	19
	SD	0.07	4.99	0.38
LW Albee	Mean	24.1	10.53	1.22
	N	18	18	17
	SD	0.13	4.55	0.35
FA Oliver	Mean	17.5	5.65	1.07
	N	12	11	12
	SD	0.10	2.92	0.22
Mississippian	Mean	19.5	9.14	1.00
	N	23	22	23
	SD	0.08	4.30	0.24

Table 5.45 ANOVA results for percentage of pits by group.					
Source	**df**	**Mean square**	**F**	**Sig.**	**η_p^2 (95% CI)**
Corrected model	4.000	0.03	3.04	0.021	
Intercept	1.000	4.06	465.42	0	
Group	4.000	0.03	3.04	0.021	0.119 (0.01–0.19)
Error	90.000	0.01			
Total	95.000				
Corrected total	94.000				

R Squared = 0.119 (Adjusted R Squared = 0.080).

Table 5.46 Post hoc tests for percentage of pits by group.				
Group	**Group**	**Mean difference**	**Standard error**	**Sig.**
M/L Archaic	E/M Wood	−0.0752*	0.029	0.011
	LW Albee	−0.053	0.030	0.081
	FA Oliver	0.014	0.034	0.684
	Mississippian	−0.006	0.028	0.826
E/M Woodland	M/L Archaic	0.0752*	0.029	0.011
	LW Albee	0.022	0.030	0.460
	FA Oliver	0.0890*	0.034	0.010
	Mississippian	0.0690*	0.028	0.016
LW Albee	M/L Archaic	0.053	0.030	0.081
	E/M Wood	−0.022	0.030	0.460
	FA Oliver	0.067	0.035	0.059
	Mississippian	0.047	0.029	0.116
FA Oliver	M/L Archaic	−0.014	0.034	0.684
	E/M Wood	−0.0890*	0.034	0.010
	LW Albee	−0.067	0.035	0.059
	Mississippian	−0.020	0.033	0.549
Mississippian	M/L Archaic	0.006	0.028	0.826
	E/M Wood	−0.0690*	0.028	0.016
	LW Albee	−0.047	0.029	0.116
	FA Oliver	0.020	0.033	0.549

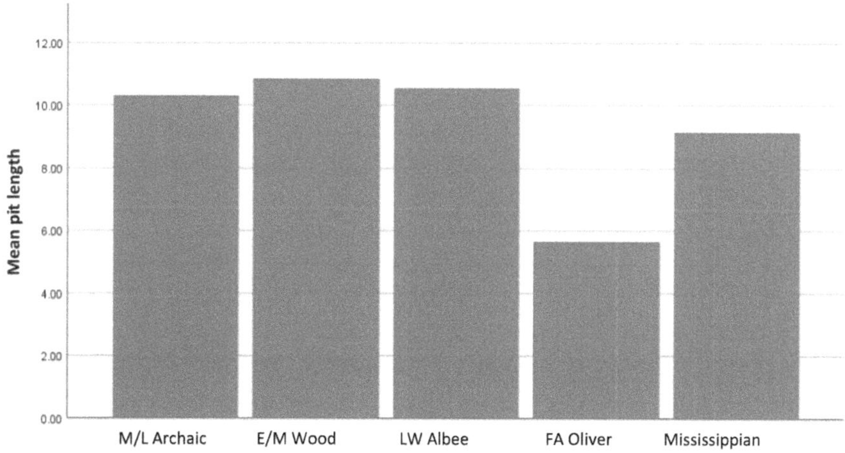

Figure 5.7 Mean pit length in μm by group.

Table 5.47 ANOVA results for pit length by group.

Source	df	Mean square	F	Sig.	η_p^2 (95% CI)
Corrected model	4.000	57.693	3.077	0.020	
Intercept	1.000	7383.219	393.779	0.000	
Group	4.000	57.693	3.077	0.020	0.125 (0.01–0.20)
Error	86.000	18.750			
Total	91.000				
Corrected total	90.000				

R Squared = 0.125 (Adjusted R Squared = 0.085).

Table 5.48 Post hoc results for pit length by group.

Group	Group	Mean difference	Standard error	Sig.
M/L Archaic	E/M Wood	−0.545	1.371	0.692
	LW Albee	−0.243	1.391	0.862
	FA Oliver	4.6396*	1.612	0.005
	Mississippian	1.146	1.321	0.388
E/M Woodland	M/L Archaic	0.545	1.371	0.692
	LW Albee	0.302	1.424	0.833
	FA Oliver	5.1842*	1.641	0.002
	Mississippian	1.690	1.356	0.216
LW Albee	M/L Archaic	0.243	1.391	0.862
	E/M Wood	−0.302	1.424	0.833
	FA Oliver	4.8827*	1.657	0.004
	Mississippian	1.389	1.376	0.316
FA Oliver	M/L Archaic	−4.6396*	1.612	0.005
	E/M Wood	−5.1842*	1.641	0.002
	LW Albee	−4.8827*	1.657	0.004
	Mississippian	−3.4938*	1.599	0.032
Mississippian	M/L Archaic	−1.146	1.321	0.388
	E/M Wood	−1.690	1.356	0.216
	LW Albee	−1.389	1.376	0.316
	FA Oliver	3.4938*	1.599	0.032

Scratch width declined over time. The widest scratch width was that of the M/L Archaic and was just under 1.8 μm; the narrowest was that of the Mississippian group at 1.0 μm (Fig. 5.8). Significant differences existed between the M/L Archaic and all other groups ($\eta_p^2 = 0.395$, 95% CI = 0.23–0.47) (Tables 5.49 and 5.50).

For the DMTA, the M/L Archaic and E/M Woodland complexity means were just below 1.5 and the FA Oliver was just above 1.6 (recall there were no LW Albee DMTA data). The Mississippian complexity was noticeably lower at 1.05. For anisotropy, the M/L Archaic, E/M Woodland, and the FA Oliver were all below 0.0030, while the Mississippian was above it at 0.0036 (Table 5.51).

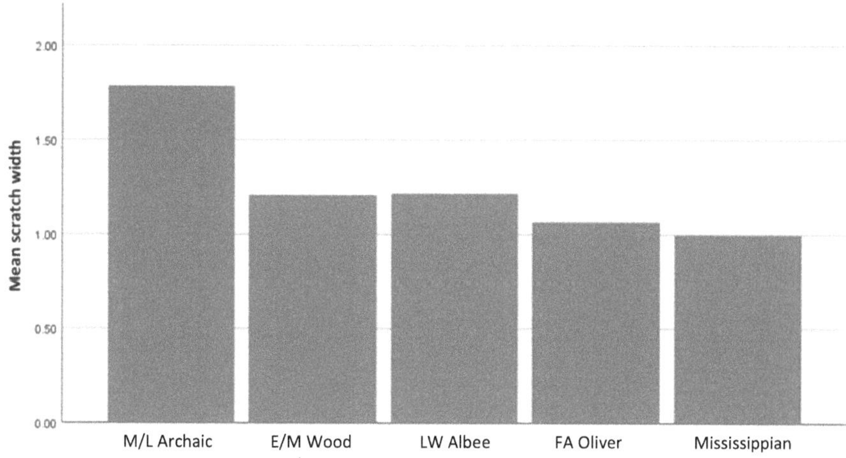

Figure 5.8 Mean scratch width in μm by group.

Table 5.49 ANOVA results for scratch width by group.

Source	df	Mean square	F	Sig.	η_p^2 (95% CI)
Corrected model	4	1.98	14.182	0.000	
Intercept	1	137.447	984.485	0.000	
Group	4	1.98	14.182	0.000	0.395 (0.23–0.47)
Error	87	0.14			
Total	92				
Corrected total	91				

R Squared = 0.395 (Adjusted R Squared = 0.367).

Table 5.50 Post hoc results for scratch width by group.

Group	Group	Mean difference	Standard error	Sig.
M/L Archaic	E/M Wood	0.5774*	0.11831	0.000
	LW Albee	0.5695*	0.1219	0.000
	FA Oliver	0.7198*	0.13521	0.000
	Mississippian	0.7887*	0.11278	0.000
E/M Woodland	M/L Archaic	−0.5774*	0.11831	0.000
	LW Albee	−0.0079	0.12474	0.949
	FA Oliver	0.1424	0.13778	0.304
	Mississippian	0.2113	0.11584	0.072
LW Albee	M/L Archaic	−0.5695*	0.1219	0.000
	E/M Wood	0.0079	0.12474	0.949
	FA Oliver	0.1503	0.14088	0.289
	Mississippian	0.2192	0.11951	0.070
FA Oliver	M/L Archaic	−0.7198*	0.13521	0.000
	E/M Wood	−0.1424	0.13778	0.304
	LW Albee	−0.1503	0.14088	0.289
	Mississippian	0.0689	0.13306	0.606
Mississippian	M/L Archaic	−0.7887*	0.11278	0.000
	E/M Wood	−0.2113	0.11584	0.072
	LW Albee	−0.2192	0.11951	0.070
	FA Oliver	−0.0689	0.13306	0.606

Table 5.51 Complexity and anisotropy summary data by group.

	Complexity			Anisotropy		
Group	Mean	SD	n	Mean	SD	n
M/L Archaic	1.46	0.65	18	0.0026	0.0009	19
E/M Woodland	1.48	0.55	12	0.0026	0.0010	13
FA Oliver	1.64	0.69	11	0.0020	0.0008	11
Mississippian	1.05	0.27	12	0.0036	0.0015	14
Total			53			57

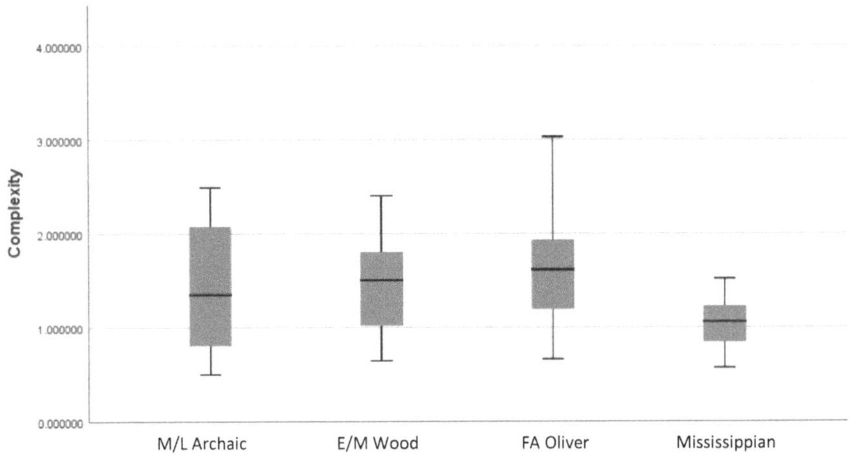

Figure 5.9 Box-and-whisker plots for complexity, n = 56.

Table 5.52 ANOVA results for anisotropy.

	df	Mean square	F	Sig.	Partial eta squared (95% CI)
Corrected model	3	4.50E-06	3.594	0.019	
Intercept	1	0	309.127	0.000	
Group	3	4.50E-06	3.594	0.019	0.169 (0.02–0.21)
Error	53	1.25E-06			
Total	57				
Corrected total	56				

R Squared = 0.169 (Adjusted R Squared = 0.122).

There were no significant differences for complexity. Fig. 5.9 is a box-and-whisker plot depicting the ranges of variation in each group; all groups had individuals with high and low complexity values. The Mississippian had the smallest range, but it fit within the ranges of the other groups.

There was a significant difference among the groups for anisotropy ($\eta_p^2 = 0.169$; 95% CI = 0.02–0.21) (Table 5.52). Post hoc tests revealed

Table 5.53 LSD post hoc tests for anisotropy. All groups differ from Angel.

Group 1	Group 2	Sig.
M/L Archaic	E/M Wood FA Oliver Mississippian	0.932 0.191 0.032*
E/M Woodland	M/L Archaic FA Oliver Mississippian	0.932 0.256 0.041*
FA Oliver	M/L Archaic E/M Wood Mississippian	0.191 0.256 0.003*
Mississippian	M/L Archaic E/M Wood FA Oliver	0.032* 0.041* 0.003*

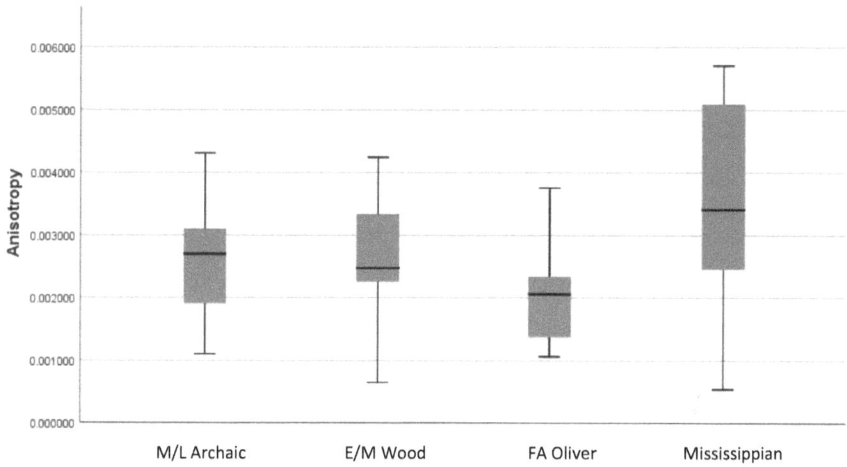

Figure 5.10 Box-and-whisker plots for anisotropy, n = 57.

the Angel site differed from all other sites (Table 5.53). Fig. 5.10 is a box-and-whisker plot for anisotropy. Unlike complexity, the Mississippian group had the greatest range of variation; a few individuals had anisotropies well below the rest. The M/L Archaic, E/M Woodland, and the FA Oliver had similar ranges and medians.

Dental caries: Prior to the LW Albee, no group exceeded a 50% prevalence. After the LW Albee, the average prevalence jumped to 81.3%. The LW Albee had a sizable prevalence disparity between males and females that is not in the preceding M/L Archaic and E/M Woodland groups. After the LW Albee, male and female values resumed being similar to each other. The FA Oliver had a spike in male anterior tooth prevalence, although this difference could be an exaggeration due to the small known-sex sample sizes.

The group with the highest prevalence overall was the FA Oliver, where nearly everyone had at least one carious tooth. The Mississippian population had a similarly high prevalence, around 82%. The E/M Woodland had the lowest prevalence at 29%. The M/L Archaic prevalence was 35%, which is unusually high for people of that time (e.g., Cassidy, 1984).

The highest prevalence of nonocclusal dental caries was among the FA Oliver group; 70% had nonocclusal caries. In contrast, the LW Albee had a nonocclusal prevalence of 20% and the Mississippian had a nonocclusal prevalence of 43.8% (Tables 5.54–5.56; Figs. 5.11–5.15).

Table 5.54 Occlusal and nonocclusal dental caries prevalence for anterior teeth by sex and group.

Group	Anterior tooth prevalence		
	All	Male	Female
M/L Archaic (20)	0	0	0
E/M Woodland (34)	0	0	0
LW Albee (55)	18.2%	14.8%	21.4%
FA Oliver (19)	21.1%	14.3%	25.0%
Mississippian (64)	26.6%	24.1%	28.6%

Table 5.55 Occlusal and nonocclusal dental caries prevalence for molars by sex and group.

Group	Molar prevalence		
	All	Male	Female
M/L Archaic (20)	35.0%	25.0%	50.0%
E/M Woodland (34)	29.4%	19.1%	46.2%
LW Albee (55)	56.4%	51.9%	60.7%
FA Oliver (19)	94.7%	85.7%	100.0%
Mississippian (64)	81.3%	82.8%	80.0%

Table 5.56 Nonocclusal dental caries prevalence for all teeth (anterior and molars).

Group	Prevalence
M/L Archaic	15%
E/M Woodland	8%
LW Albee	20%
FA Oliver	70%
Mississippian	44%

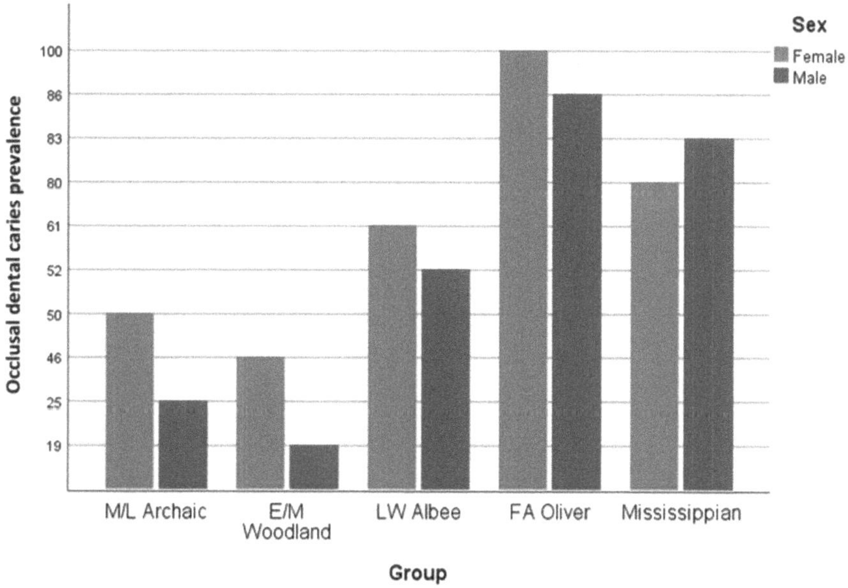

Figure 5.11 Occlusal dental caries prevalence by group and sex.

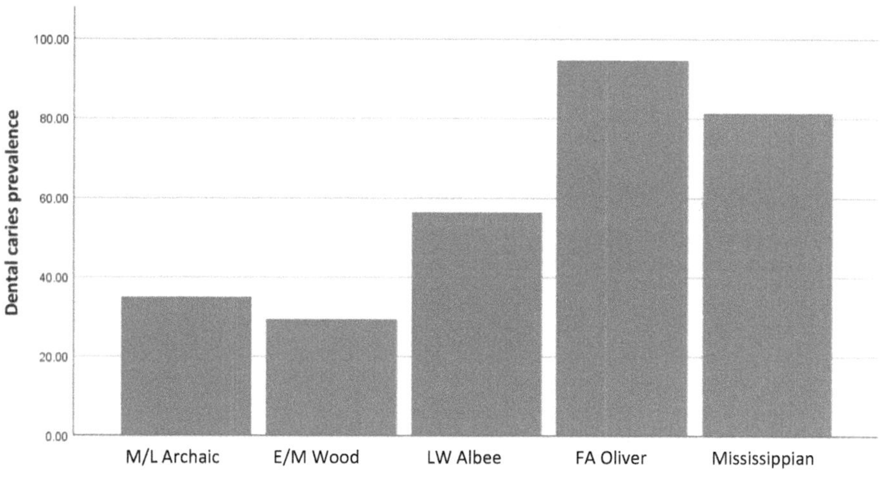

Figure 5.12 Prevalence of occlusal and nonocclusal dental caries on all teeth (anterior and molars) by group.

A hierarchical cluster analysis of caries summary data yielded a dendrogram that sorted groups by their prevalence of occlusal and nonocclusal molar dental caries, young adult molar dental caries, mid/old adult molar dental caries, and anterior tooth caries. The analysis

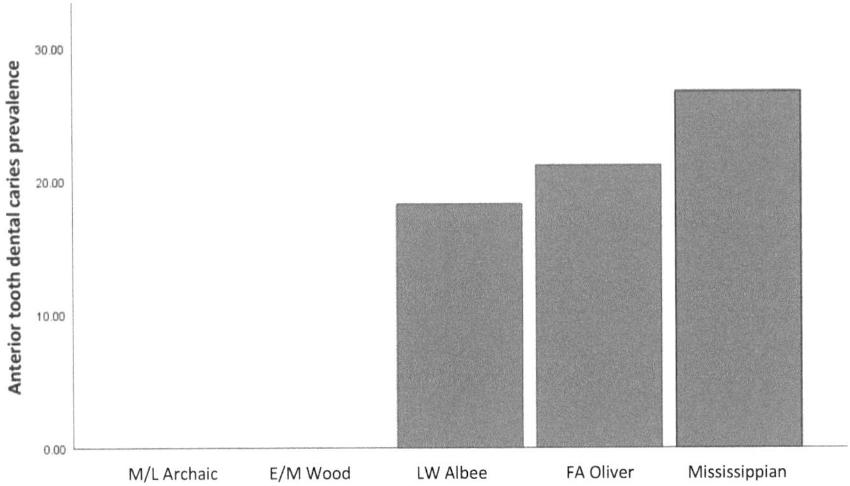

Figure 5.13 Prevalence of occlusal and nonocclusal anterior tooth dental caries by group.

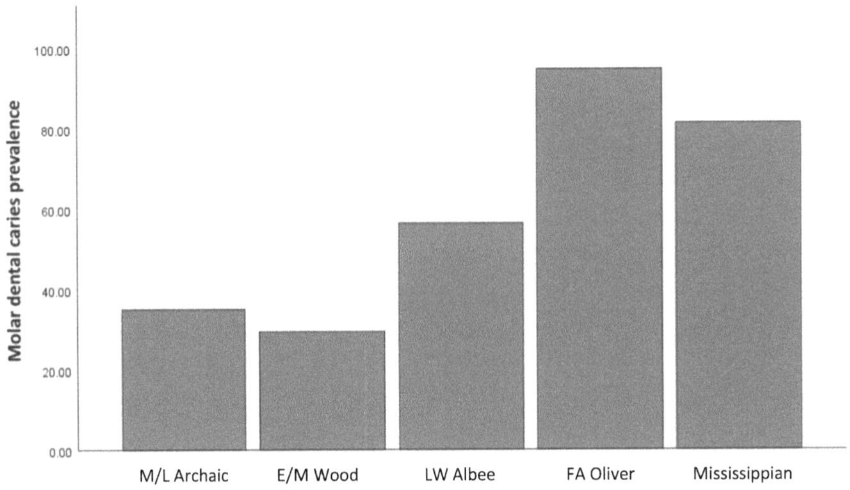

Figure 5.14 Prevalence of occlusal and nonocclusal molar dental caries by group.

generated four clusters; the first cluster had both the M/L Archaic and the E/M Woodland; the other groups formed their own clusters. The analysis then linked the LW Albee to the FA Oliver and Mississippian clusters. The M/L Archaic and E/M Woodland clusters did not connect to the others (Table 5.57; Fig. 5.16). Thus, in terms of dental caries prevalence, the LW Albee shared more with the FA Oliver and Mississippian than the M/L Archaic and E/M Woodland.

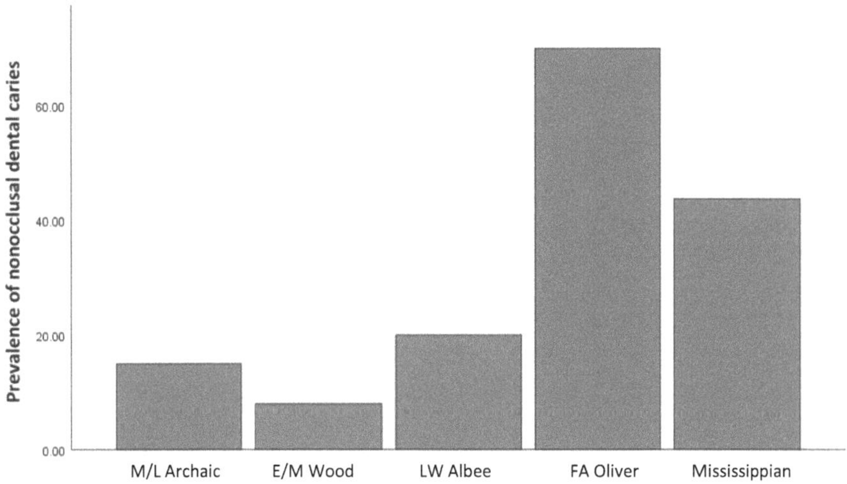

Figure 5.15 Prevalence of nonocclusal dental caries by group.

Table 5.57 Cluster memberships based on hierarchical cluster analysis of dental caries data.

Cluster membership	
Case	**Clusters**
1:M/L Archaic	1.00
2:E/M Woodland	1.00
3:LW Albee	2.00
4:FA Oliver	3.00
5:Mississippian	4.00

Prior to the LW Albee, people averaged having dental caries in around 10% of their teeth. From the LW Albee on, the average person had dental caries in about 25% of their teeth. Looking just at molar severity, the pre-LW Albee average was about 22%, while it was about 46% from the LW Albee and after. Overall, females had more cavities per mouth. The FA Oliver had the greatest severity of dental caries, including nonocclusal lesions, followed by the Mississippian group (Table 5.58).

ANOVA results for molar severity found that nearly all groups differed from each other. The LW Albee and the FA Oliver did not differ and the FA Oliver and the Mississippian did not differ, although the LW Albee and the Mississippian did ($\eta_p^2 = 0.320$, 95% CI = 0.24–0.048) (Tables 5.59 and 5.60).

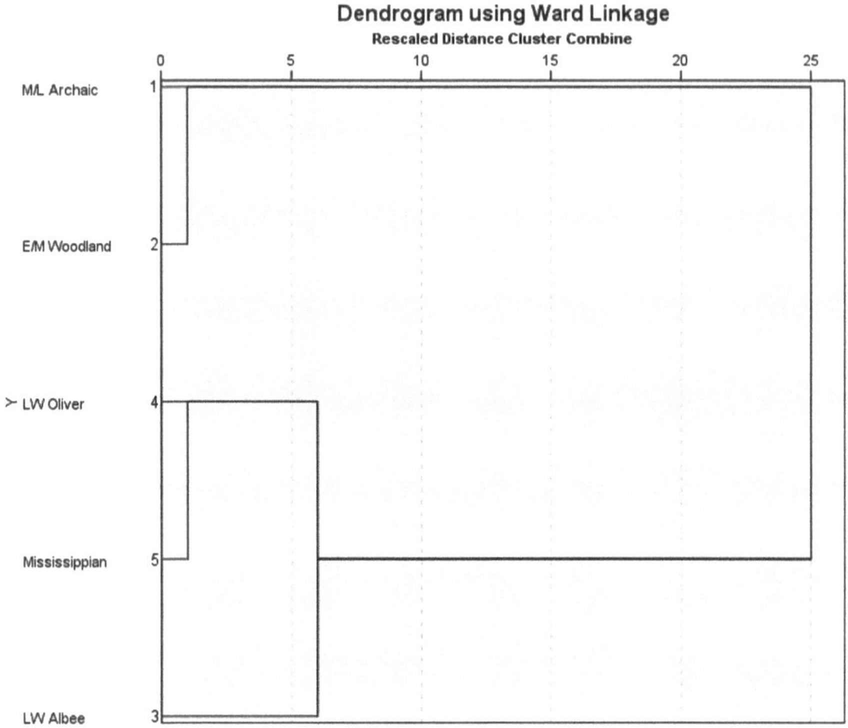

Figure 5.16 Hierarchical cluster analysis dendrogram based on group prevalences of molar, young adult molar, mid/old adult molar, and anterior tooth dental caries.

Table 5.58 Dental caries severity by sex and group.

Group	Anterior teeth and molar severity			Molar severity		
	All	Male	Female	All	Male	Female
M/L Archaic	9.1%	8.5%	9.6%	20.7%	18.4%	23.0%
E/M Woodland	10.4%	9.4%	11.4%	24.4%	23.8.%	24.9%
LW Albee	17.3%	16.7%	17.8%	35.2%	33.3%	37.1%
FA Oliver	28.6%	32.0%	25.2%	43.4%	33.1%	53.7%
Mississippian	28.1%	25.5%	30.6%	58.5%	53.0%	64.0%

Table 5.59 ANOVA results for molar dental caries severity.

Source	df	Mean square	F	Sig.	η_p^2 (95% CI)
Corrected model	4.00	0.59	14.91	0.000	
Intercept	1.00	13.28	333.99	0.000	
Group	4.00	0.59	14.91	0.000	0.320 (0.24–0.48)
Error	127.00	0.04			
Total	132.00				
Corrected total	131.00				

R Squared = 0.320 (Adjusted R Squared = 0.298).

Table 5.60 Post hoc for molar dental caries severity.

Group	Group	Mean difference	Standard error	Sig.
M/L Archaic	E/M Wood	−0.04	0.08	0.657
	LW Albee	−0.1760*	0.06	0.004
	FA Oliver	−0.2792*	0.07	0.000
	Mississippian	−0.3705*	0.06	0.000
E/M Woodland	M/L Archaic	0.04	0.08	0.657
	LW Albee	−0.1407*	0.07	0.040
	FA Oliver	−0.2439*	0.08	0.003
	Mississippian	−0.3352*	0.07	0.000
LW Albee	M/L Archaic	0.1760*	0.06	0.004
	E/M Wood	0.1407*	0.07	0.040
	FA Oliver	−0.10	0.06	0.097
	Mississippian	−0.1945*	0.04	0.000
FA Oliver	M/L Archaic	0.2792*	0.07	0.000
	E/M Wood	0.2439*	0.08	0.003
	LW Albee	0.10	0.06	0.097
	Mississippian	−0.09	0.06	0.132
Mississippian	M/L Archaic	0.3705*	0.06	0.000
	E/M Wood	0.3352*	0.07	0.000
	LW Albee	0.1945*	0.04	0.000
	FA Oliver	0.09	0.06	0.132

There is a linear relationship between prevalence and severity. A scatterplot of molar dental caries severity and prevalence shows that the M/L Archaic and the E/M Woodland had low prevalences and low severity. On the other end, the Mississippian and FA Oliver groups had high prevalences and severity. Between the low and high groups was the LW Albee, which had intermediate prevalence and severity. The sequence of groups, however, does not match their order in time. The M/L Archaic exceeded the E/M Woodland group and the FA Oliver exceeded the Mississippian group (Fig. 5.17).

A final assessment considered data from each of the dental indicators of diet. At first using just caries data, but then using macrowear, microwear, and dental caries summary data, I constructed a hierarchical cluster analysis using Ward's linkage with all values converted to Z-scores. The variables were anterior tooth macrowear, young adult molar macrowear, mid/old adult molar macrowear, nonocclusal dental caries prevalence, anterior teeth dental caries prevalence, molar dental caries prevalence, molar dental caries severity, all teeth dental caries

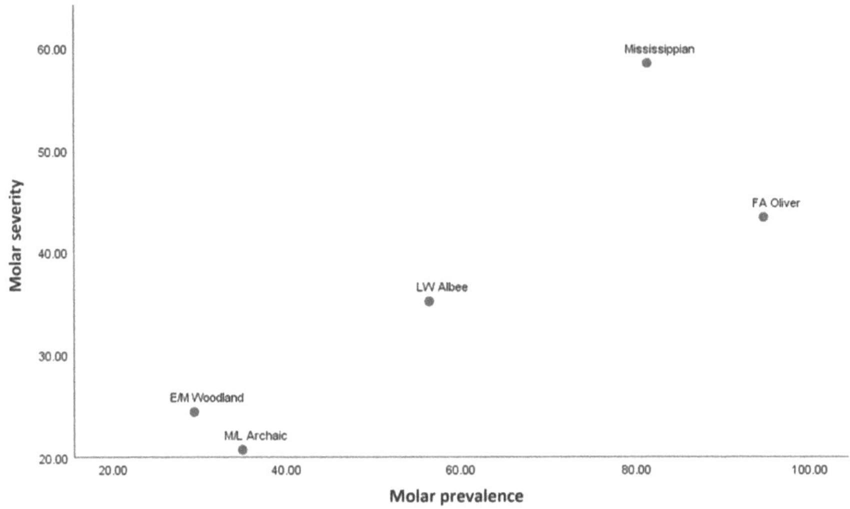

Figure 5.17 Scatterplot of molar dental caries severity and prevalence, n = 275.

Table 5.61 Hierarchical cluster analysis dissimilarity matrix based on anterior tooth macrowear, young adult molar macrowear, mid/old adult molar macrowear, macrowear score, anterior teeth dental caries prevalence, molar dental caries prevalence, molar dental caries severity, all teeth dental caries prevalence, percentage of pits, pit width, and scratch width data.

Case	Squared Euclidean distance				
	1:M/L Archaic	2:E/M Wood	3:LW Albee	4:FA Oliver	5:Mississippian
1:M/L Archaic	0	16.844	16.715	46.094	43.346
2:E/M Woodland	16.844	0	7.461	38.844	27.32
3:LW Albee	16.715	7.461	0	22.967	13.961
4:FA Oliver	46.094	38.844	22.967	0	6.449
5:Mississippian	43.346	27.32	13.961	6.449	0

prevalence, percentage of pits, pit width, and scratch width. I was unable to include DMTA variables because of the missing LW Albee data.

The resulting dendrogram linked the LW Albee and E/M Woodland; it also linked the FA Oliver and the Mississippian. The LW Albee–E/M Woodland cluster then linked to the M/L Archaic (see Table 5.61 for a dissimilarity matrix). The LW Albee, therefore,

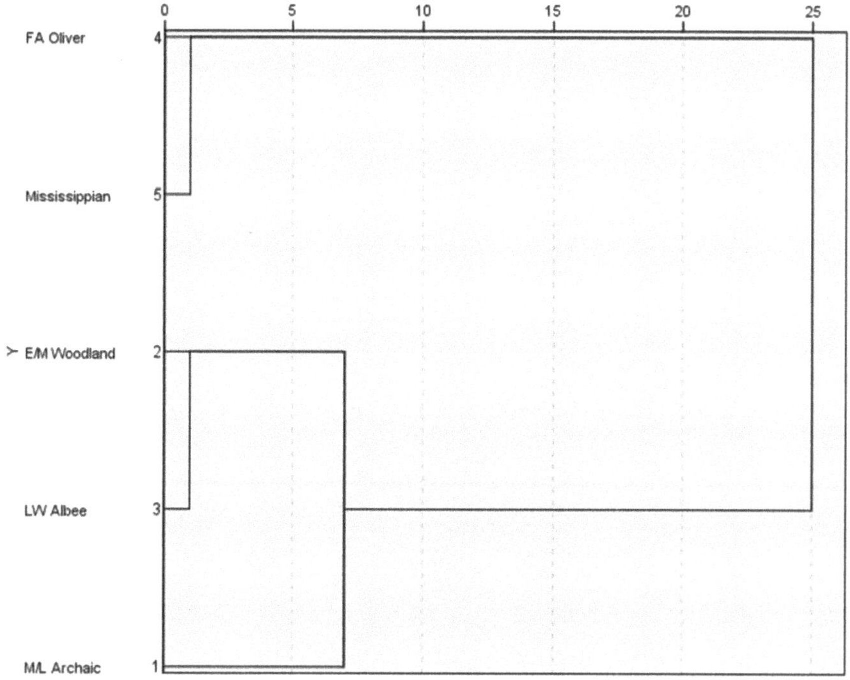

Figure 5.18 Dendrogram of group relationships based on summary young adult anterior tooth macrowear, mid/old adult anterior tooth macrowear, young adult molar macrowear, mid/old adult molar macrowear, macrowear score, anterior teeth dental caries prevalence, molar dental caries prevalence, molar dental caries severity, all teeth dental caries prevalence, percentage of pits, pit width, and scratch width data. Notice the LW Albee link with the E/M Woodland and not with the other maize agriculturists.

did not cluster with the other maize consumers, as it did in the cluster analysis based solely on the caries data; including the macrowear and SEM-based microwear data changed the LW Albee placement (Fig 5.18).

CHAPTER 6

Discussion: what does it all mean?

Introduction

Recall from Chapters 3 and 4 that reconstructing diets relies on inferences drawn from skeletal indicators. For example, ^{13}C output informs analysts of its presence in the bone relative to a standard. Through diligent testing of C_3 and C_4 plants, ^{13}C values from precontact North America are likely to be from maize (Tykot, 2009). Similarly, dental indicators provide characteristics of the diet, such as its abrasiveness, hardness, textural complexity and cariosity. For the most part, however, they do not yield signatures of particular foods, in part, because relatively few researchers engage in this kind of study and establishing food-specific wear features has proven to be very time consuming. Until such time that we have reliable tooth-based signatures to determine the specific foods people ate, dental analysts draw from the subsistence record to find the most common resources having the characteristics indicated by the teeth. For example, in populations having dental evidence for a hard diet and a subsistence record replete with walnuts and hickory nuts, the interpretation of the diet would be the consumption of nuts (e.g., Talalay et al., 1984). If on the other hand, a subsistence record included nuts but there was no evidence of hard food consumption on the teeth, the dietary interpretation would exclude them.

The first section of this chapter explores the *characteristics* of the foods consumed by each group, based on the dental indicators; following it is a summary of the *interpretations* of these characteristics based on the subsistence evidence from each group. Together, the dietary characteristics and their interpretations make up the dietary reconstructions. The second part of this chapter explores the individual contributions of each dental indicators of diet (DID) as well as their archeological implications.

Dietary reconstructions

Dietary characteristics based on the dental indicators of diet

M/L Archaic: The M/L Archaic people had a very abrasive diet that wore both the anterior teeth and the molars to great degrees.

Long 'on' the Tooth. DOI: https://doi.org/10.1016/B978-0-12-824306-0.00006-9

The premolars wore to an extent that surpassed that of the incisors and canines, likely because of their role in mastication. The scanning electron microscope (SEM)-based microwear indicated a poorly processed diet for the M/L Archaic compared to the diets of later groups. It must have included large amounts of exogenous grit to produce the large features it did, particularly scratch widths. The dental microwear texture analysis (DMTA) data pointed to diverse feature orientations indicative of hunter-gatherers (e.g., Schmidt et al., 2019); the diet was sufficiently heterogeneous to necessitate jaw movement in many directions. Lastly, the diet was not very cariogenic and those with dental caries likely had them secondary to extreme macrowear that exposed pulp chambers. Relatively few individuals had carious lesions and those that did had relatively few cavities in their mouths. Overall, male and female diets were similar and did not differ significantly, although about twice as many females had carious lesions than males.

In sum, the M/L Archaic diet was abrasive, moderately hard, heterogeneous, weakly cariogenic, and similar for the sexes.

E/M Woodland: The E/M Woodland diet led to a slight reduction in anterior tooth and molar macrowear compared to the preceding M/L Archaic; but it was still high compared to the later groups. The SEM-based microwear indicated the diet was harder and less abrasive than that of the M/L Archaic. In fact, the E/M Woodland percentage of pits was the highest in this study. A significant decline in scratch width compared to the M/L Archaic indicated a reduction in the size of dietary abrasives and the DMTA data indicated a somewhat coarse and heterogeneous diet. The E/M Woodland diet was low in cariosity; few individuals had carious lesions and those who did had only a few present. Like the M/L Archaic, more females had carious lesions. In sum, the E/M Woodland diet was abrasive, hard, heterogeneous, weakly cariogenic, and similar for the sexes.

LW Albee: The LW Albee diet was less abrasive than the M/L Archaic and the E/M Woodland diets, but it was more abrasive than the FA Oliver and Mississippian diets. The premolar macrowear was lower than the incisor macrowear, which, along with a reduction in molar macrowear, indicated an overall reduction in dietary abrasiveness. The LW Albee SEM-based microwear indicated a hard diet, comparable to that of the E/M Woodland. The cariogenic nature of the LW Albee diet was well above that of E/M Woodland. About half of the LW Albee people had dental caries, although the severity was modest compared to the FA Oliver and Mississippian. This indicated that a cariogenic food was widely available to LW Albee people, but it made up a smaller portion of the diet than it did in subsequent groups. Males had significantly more macrowear, while females had more pitting on their teeth and more had carious lesions. In sum, the LW Albee diet was moderately abrasive, hard, moderately cariogenic, and had sex-based differences.

FA Oliver: The FA Oliver diet was nonabrasive; its anterior macrowear scores were low and the incisor macrowear exceeded the premolar macrowear. Likewise, the molar macrowear scores were low. The SEM-based microwear indicated a diet that had little grit, and was likely highly processed. It had the lowest percentage of pits and the smallest pit lengths. The DMTA data, however, indicated a somewhat coarse, heterogenous, diet. Not surprsingly, the diet was very cariogenic. Nearly every person from this group had at least one occlusal or nonocclusal lesion. The FA Oliver diet also had a high level of nonocclusal and anterior teeth caries. Males tended to have more macrowear but overall males and females had similar DID scores. In sum, the FA Oliver diet was nonabrasive, had some hard elements, heterogenous, highly cariogenic, and similar for the sexes.

Mississippian: The Mississippian diet was not abrasive and had few hard elements. The premolar and molar macrowear both indicated modest masticatory demand. The SEM-based microwear indicated a nonabrasive, soft diet that was highly processed. The DMTA indicated a soft, homogeneous diet. The dental caries data indicated a very cariogenic diet; most individuals had dental caries and those with lesions had several carious lesions per mouth. Other than males having more macrowear, the diets for males and females differed little. In sum, the Mississippian diet was nonabrasive, soft, homogenous, highly cariogenic, and similar for the sexes.

Dietary interpretations of the dental indicators of diet characteristics via the subsistence record

M/L Archaic: The best candidates for M/L Archaic abrasive foods were terrestrial plants including roots, tubers, and bulbs contaminated with grit and/or rich in phytoliths. Examples available in the eastern woodlands include American lotus, cattail, groundnut, hog peanut, and Jerusalem artichoke (e.g., Scarry, 2003:56). Another resource from a grit-rich environment was the mussel (e.g., Webb, 1946; Emerson and McElrath, 1983: 238; Patch, 2005; Claassen, 2005). Being filter feeders, sand and other grit can contaminate mussels and archeologists in California have documented extreme macrowear among presumed precontact shellfish consumers (e.g., Leigh, 1928; Walker, 1978; Schmucker, 1985). Although, a study of M/L Archaic people from the Indian Knoll and Black Earth sites complicates the link between macrowear and mussels. Indian Knoll sits on the Green River, while Black Earth, in southern Illinois, is well away from the Ohio River Valley mussel beds. Despite their different environments, and presumably differing access to mussels, there were no differences in their macrowear scores (Nealis and Seeman, 2015). This could mean that mussels were not the primary abrasive agent in M/L Archaic diets. It also could mean that M/L Archaic people ate mussels regardless of where they lived and/or died. It is hard to imagine that mussel consumption did not affect M/L Archaic macrowear, but, wild plant remains are common at M/L Archaic sites and they are probably an important contributor to M/L Archaic macrowear.

The hard foods indicated by the pit percentage are likely nuts; no other food type in M/L Archaic botanical assemblages are as hard or as common (e.g., Emerson and McElrath, 1983; Chapman and Watson, 1993; Schmidt and Tomak, 1999; Simon, 2009). The M/L Archaic percentage of pits was moderate and its DMTA complexity was similar to that of the Woodland groups. Together, these indicate that nuts were important but that other foods were, too. It is possible that nut consumption increased when nuts were available and diminished during other times of the year.

The severe macrowear also indicates that food processing was minimal; the lack of ceramics and the relatively small number of M/L Archaic grinding stones in Indiana probably reflects the reality of the time (e.g., Winters, 1969; Fortier, 1983; Stafford and Cantin, 2009). Had the M/L Archaic macrowear indicated a nonabrasive diet, then the low numbers of grinding stones and ceramic vessels would have been perplexing. As it is, the dental data and the archeological record agree.

Incidentally, it is possible that processing foods with stones of a very coarse nature increased macrowear by introducing exogenous grit from the stone itself. Thus, some of the contamination in the M/L

Archaic diet could have come from the tools they used; however, since processing foods with grinding stones was relatively uncommon, it is unlikely that they were major factors in generating macrowear. In all, the M/L Archaic dental dietary indicators point to a diet based on wild, poorly or unprocessed foods including terrestrial plants, nuts, seeds, and possibly (probably?) mussels. People ate some cariogenic wild foods, like grape, too.

E/M Woodland: The E/M Woodland diet focused on hard food items like nuts, which are ubiquitous in E/M Woodland paleobotanical assemblages (e.g., Fritz, 1993). At the same time, the dietary abrasives declined. This could have happened if the increased nut consumption limited exposure to contaminated or phytolith-rich plants. It also could have resulted from an increase in food processing. Both of these probably played a role, but in this case the microwear data indicate that the bigger change was the food and to a lesser extent the food processing. I say this because the scratch widths, although smaller than the M/L Archaic, are still larger than the other groups, and the DMTA complexity is similar to the other groups. If food processing was the major factor, then I would expect the E/M Woodland macrowear and the pit percentage to be lower. The added dependence on nuts was probably all that was needed to decrease the scratch widths.

Thus, the E/M Woodland diet marked a dietary transition from the M/L Archaic. This change, like most in precontact Indiana, was not about a revolutionary change in foods, but changes to the proportions certain foods contributed. I suspect nuts were important to the people of the M/L Archaic; but, they were more important to the people of the E/M Woodland (Schmidt, 2001). Interestingly, this dietary shift would be undetectable to other means of dietary reconstruction, like stable isotopes, because the change did not go from a C_3 to a C_4 food. Finally, despite sporadic reports of maize appearing during the E/M Woodland, there was no dental evidence for its consumption. The low level of dental caries was consistent with macrowear-related caries and the consumption of modestly cariogenic wild foods like berries and grapes.

LW Albee: The reconstruction of the LW Albee diet was perhaps the most intriguing. It was with the LW Albee that a noticeable increase in cariosity occurred, indicating the consumption of maize. In fact, isotopic, subsistence, and oral pathology data all point to maize consumption increasing during the Late Woodland period of the eastern woodlands (see Cohen and Armelagos, 1984; Kelley and Larsen, 1991; Larsen, 2015). It is reasonable to infer, then, that maize was the cariogenic food of the LW Albee diet. Furthermore, the DID indicated that maize was not the primary LW Albee food, which echoes Allegretto et al.'s (2006) LW Albee stable isotope findings. The agreement between the LW Albee dental and isotopic data is important because the intermediate isotope values may have been unconvincing on their own. The agreement goes even further when we consider that at the LW Albee Morell-Sheets site, maize made up 17% of all recovered botanical remains, which made it the second most abundant resource behind little barley (Bush, 2004). All indications are that maize was in the LW Albee diet, but not the main food.

For the first time in precontact Indiana, maize was a meaningful dietary constituent. Importantly, the LW Albee diet included hard foods, too; its dietary hardness was second only to that of the E/M Woodland, and, like the E/M Woodland, nuts are a common Late Woodland subsistence component (e.g., Johannessen, 1984a; King, 1985; Wymer, 1993). The LW Albee dietary hardness could be due, in part, to consuming starchy and oily seeds (including little barley), but the role of nuts is difficult to deny. All told, the evidence points to the LW Albee diet consisting of maize and nuts and at least some abrasive wild foods.

FA Oliver: Going into this study, there was little doubt the FA Oliver people consumed maize given the subsistence and carbon isotope data (e.g., Cook and Schurr, 2009; Cook and Price, 2017). The dental caries data backed this up as did some of the SEM-based microwear data. What stood out, however, was the DMTA signature, which indicated some dietary hardness; something I have seen in other Late Precontact groups (e.g., Stone and Krueger, 2015; Schmidt and Remy, 2016; Lagan et al., 2018). The subsistence record indicates nuts appear in large quantities at Fort Ancient sites (e.g., Wagner, 1987; Bush, 2004). Not all of my archeology colleagues are onboard with the idea that FA Oliver people consumed sizable quantities of nuts, but as more Fort Ancient people express DMTA evidence for hard food consumption, it gets harder to ignore the significance of nuts in FA Oliver diets. The dietary evidence

Table 6.1 Summary of dental indicators of diet and presumptive foods they indicate by group.

Group	Characteristics of diet	Interpretations of diet
M/L Archaic	• Abrasive • Moderately hard • Heterogenous • Weakly cariogenic	• Grit-contaminated riverine and terrestrial foods (underground storage organs and mussels?) • Nuts • Sugary wild foods (e.g., berries, grapes) • No maize
E/M Woodland	• Abrasive • Hard • Heterogenous • Weakly cariogenic	• Some grit-contaminated foods • Nuts (starchy/oily seeds?) • Sugary wild foods • No maize
LW Albee	• Moderately abrasive • Hard • Moderately cariogenic	• Few grit-contaminated foods • Nuts (starchy/oily seeds?) • Some maize
FA Oliver	• Nonabrasive • Some hard elements • Heterogenous • Highly cariogenic	• No grit-contaminated foods • Some nuts (starchy/oily seeds?) • Primarily maize
Mississippian	• Nonabrasive • Soft • Homogeneous • Highly cariogenic	• No grit-contaminated foods • Few nuts (starchy/oily seeds?) • Primarily maize

indicates the FA Oliver committed to intensive maize agriculture, but they did not entirely abandon the collecting ways of the preceding LW Albee. In essence, they flipped the LW Albee diet such that maize became the staple and the wild foods became secondary. Beyond the hard food signatures, the rest of the FA Oliver dental indicators tell a consistent story; the diet was highly processed and nonabrasive, likely due to improved pottery and food grinding technology.

Mississippian: Like the FA Oliver, the Mississippian diet was not abrasive and highly cariogenic. Unlike the FA Oliver, there were few signs of hard foods. Of all the populations, the Mississippian had the highest percentage of teeth per mouth affected by caries attesting to their highly cariogenic diet. Evidence for maize consumption was not a surprise; archeologists have found maize at nearly every Mississippian site, including the Angel site (Kellar, 1967; Schurr, 1992). Mississippians exhibited the smallest scratch widths and the lowest evidence for dietary abrasiveness. The pit percentage and mean pit lengths indicated the Mississippian folks had some hard foods in their diet, but, overall, these were less important than maize (Table 6.1).

Contributions of the individual dental indicators

In this section, I discuss the individual contributions of the dental indicators to each of the dietary reconstructions and to the archeological contexts of each group. Its intention is to explore the nuances of each variable, particularly as they pertain to age and sex, as well as their relationships to related variables. This section concludes with a discussion of archeologically relevant interpretations I have made based on these nuances and relationships.

Macrowear

Age was a significant factor affecting macrowear score. For most groups the mean young adult anterior tooth score was about 50–60% that of the mid/old adults. An exception was the M/L Archaic young adults, whose anterior tooth scores were 70.3% of the mid/old adults. Like the anterior teeth, for most groups young adult molar scores were about 50–60% that of the mid/old adults. Exception swere the M/L Archaic and the FA Oliver, whose young adults' scores were 79.0% and 71.4% of their respective mid/old adults. These exceptions are tied to the extremely rapid rate of macrowear for the M/L Archaic people and the slow rate of macrowear for the FA Oliver; their mid/old adults had the lowest molar macrowear scores of all groups. At only 18.9, the FA Oliver mid/old adult mean molar macrowear score was well below the means of the other groups. Returning to the M/L Archaic, their macrowear scores are so high that, he ordinal nature of the macrowear scoring could have exaggerated the M/L Archaic young adult-to-mid/old adult ratio. The maximum score any person could get was 40, which kept the M/L Archaic mean in the low 30s. However, if the scale had scores above 40, meaning it scored macrowear as it reduced the roots, then several M/L Archaic people would have had scored over 40. These are the people I mentioned in Chapter 1 who had several individuals with molars reduced to root nubs. A restructured or wider-ranging scoring system would have allowed the mid/old adults to score higher and have a more typical relationship between their scores and those of the young adults.

From the M/L Archaic to the Late Precontact, males equaled or exceeded the female means for macrowear; this was true for anterior teeth and molars. The male-female anterior tooth disparity emerged during the E/M Woodland, and reached its greatest extent during the Mississippian. For the molars, the difference between the sexes became more apparent after the E/M Woodland (refer to Figure 5.5).

Explanations for males having more macrowear range from different forms of extramasticatory functions to males having greater bite forces (e.g., Gorka et al., 2016). The increase in disparity over time, however, indicates behavioral differences; the males continued to introduce abrasives into their mouths (through the diet or extramasticatory tooth use) even as the females moved to eating less abrasive foods. Importantly, none of the sex-based differences described here are based on intergroup age differences. Although addressed in more detail elsewhere, there are no age imbalances in these comparisons (see Schmidt, 1998).

Another way to view the macrowear decline is to calculate the percentage drop from group to group. After the M/L Archaic, macrowear declined after each group an average of 14% for the females and about 12% for the males. The biggest decline in female anterior tooth macrowear was 28%, from the M/L Archaic to the E/M Woodland. The next biggest drop was around 15% between the FA Oliver and the Mississippian. The biggest decline for the female molar macrowear was 24%, which took place between the LW Albee and the FA Oliver. The next largest decline was the E/M Woodland to LW Albee at nearly 23%. The E/M Woodland women used their anterior less than the M/L Archaic women, but the biggest decline in female dietary abrasiveness, indicated by their molar macrowear, came just before and after the LW Albee.

Like the females, the biggest decline in male anterior tooth macrowear took place from the M/L Archaic to the E/M Woodland. At around 22%, it was not as great as the females' largest decline, but it was sizable nonetheless. The second highest change in male anterior tooth macrowear was actually a 12% increase between the E/M Woodland and the LW Albee. The biggest decline in male molar macrowear was between the LW Albee and the FA Oliver at 23%, although at 22%, the decline from the M/L Archaic to the E/M Woodland was about the same. Together, the males and females had significant changes in anterior tooth use after the M/L Archaic, and in masticatory habits around the time of the LW Albee. The E/M Woodland widespread use of pottery could be responsible for the reduction in dietary abrasiveness after the M/L Archaic, but the anterior teeth versus molar macrowear data indicate it affected the anterior teeth more. Perhaps at first, pottery reduced the processing demands placed on E/M Woodland anterior teeth more than it affected the abrasiveness of what the people ate.

The transition to maize agriculture during the LW Albee brought about a major decline in molar macrowear for the females, but the LW Albee males had the same macrowear scores as E/M Woodland males. After the LW Albee, both male and female molar macrowear scores dropped appreciably, but the female scores dropped more. Prior to the LW Albee, male and female molar scores were similar, differing by an average of about 6%; after the LW Albee, their molar scores differed by about 25% (recall Figure 5.3). Interestingly, during the LW Albee the male and female values differed by around 24%, like those during the Late Precontact; yet, their overall molar means were high, like their predecessors. Thus, the LW Albee version of maize agriculture led to the female diet losing its abrasiveness faster than the male diet did, although overall the LW Albee diet was more abrasive than that of the Late Precontact farmers.

By the FA Oliver, anterior tooth and molar macrowear scores declined to about the same level as that of the Mississippians. Both of these groups exploited maize and they overlapped temporally making their similarity in macrowear understandable. By comparing the Late Precontact groups to the LW Albee, it is clear a major shift to intensive maize reliance took place that reduced overall macrowear on all of the teeth. There were many technological advances during the Late Precontact, thus it is difficult to determine what specifically led to the macrowear decrease. It is likely related to many improvements, including well-made pottery and wooden grinding tools.

The incisor/canine and the premolar macrowear scores were roughly the same for the M/L Archaic and the E/M Woodland. The LW Albee incisor/canine scores remained high but their premolar scores were lower. This condition was true for the FA Oliver and the Mississippian as well. The average incisor/canine macrowear score for the LW Albee through the Mississippian was 4.8. The average for the premolars was 4.2. The biggest disparity was among the FA Oliver people, whose incisor/canine mean was 4.9 and its premolar mean was 4.1. Since premolars can take on some chewing, it is possible that as dietary abrasiveness declined with maize agriculture, the macrowear on the premolars dropped. The incisor/canine scores also declined through time, but not to the same extent as the premolars, indicating their functions changed less.

The relative constancy of the anterior tooth macrowear may be due to extramasticatory uses of the incisors and canines. This would not be unusual, humans have used their teeth as tools for hundreds of thousands of years (e.g., Krueger and Ungar, 2010, 2012, 2017). If extramasticatory uses of the anterior teeth explain the incisor/canine—premolar divergence in macrowear scores, then the ways in which people used their teeth as tools changed less over time than did their diets. Typically, extramasticatory macrowear has distinctive macroscopic and microscopic features including chipping, grooving, and unusual wear angles (Hylander, 1977; Larsen, 1985; Hillson, 1997). The anterior teeth I studied lacked obvious macroscopic evidence of extramasticatory wear, but I did not examine anterior teeth microscopically for signs of it.

The first, second, and third molar macrowear data indicate that macrowear decreased from the earlier to the later groups for all three molars. Not surprisingly, first molars had the highest mean wear scores; they are the first molars to erupt. The second molars had the next highest macrowear scores and they erupt around age 12 or so. The third molars had the lowest macrowear scores and they erupt around ages 18 to 21 (e.g., Liversidge, 2009). For the M/L Archaic, the third molar value was about 63% of the first molar (22.1 vs 35.1). The E/M Woodland and the LW Albee had about the same percentage. The FA Oliver, however, had third molar macrowear that was 70% of the first molar value. The Mississippian third molar was 60% of the first molar score. Except for the FA Oliver, the groups had roughly the same relationship between first and third molar wear, despite having disparate overall macrowear scores. The FA Oliver first-to-third molar macrowear ratio relates to that group's overall low rate of macrowear; the first molars had little wear by the time the third molars erupted.

The second molar macrowear scores support the extreme nature of the M/L Archaic macrowear. For most of the groups, the second molar macrowear was roughly equidistant from the first and third molar macrowear scores. For the M/L Archaic, it was closer to the first molar value and, itself, was a high score. The M/L Archaic first molar mean was 35.09 and the second molar was 31.26. To put that second molar value into perspective, no other group had a first molar macrowear score that was as high as the M/L Archaic's second molar score. The closest was the E/M Woodland first molar mean at 30.34.

Scanning electron microsope-based microwear

Percentage of pits: The pit percentage for the M/L Archaic was just below 20%; After the M/L Archaic there was a significant increase in dietary hardness; for the E/M Woodland, the percentage of pit was closer to 25%. Recall that both the Indiana M/L Archaic and the E/M Woodland were hunter-gatherers with the latter having some level of eastern agricultural complex (EAC) horticulture. Percentage of pits is sensitive to dietary hardness (e.g., Teaford, 1991, 1994; Ungar, 1994) and an increase in pit percentage indicates the E/M and LW Albee diets included more hard objects than the M/L Archaic diet. It is possible the E/M Woodland EAC crops added to their dietary hardness because small grains are challenging to fully mill or grind (Gremillion, 2004) and researchers have found sizable EAC seed fragments in coprolites (Gremillion, 1996). Nonetheless, there is evidence that through cooking and grinding people were able to remove chaff and harvest EAC starches and oils (Gremillion, 2004). Gremillion (2004) also points out that EAC foods did not offer a great return on energy investment in environments where nuts were abundant, and they may have served primarily as wintertime foods when processing them did not distract from cultivation and food collecting activities (Gremillion, 2004). Typically, starchy foods reduce dietary hardness rather than exacerbate it (e.g., Schmidt et al., 2019). In contrast, there is evidence for nut-related pitting from contextual and experimental studies (e.g., Harmon and Rose, 1988). For these reasons, I see the percentage of pit data supporting the consumption of nuts during the E/M Woodland.

The LW Albee pit percentage was statistically indistinguishable from the E/M Woodland's despite having people whose diet included maize. Like the E/M Woodland, the LW Albee had access to the EAC and nuts. The addition of maize did not mitigate the LW Albee dietary hardness, despite being a relatively soft food. Moreover, the food processing capabilities of the LW Albee indicated by their well-made pottery and grinding stones, did not reduce their dietary hardness. Unless the LW Albee people were keen to eating raw or barely ground EAC seeds and maize, nuts remain a culprit for the LW Albee dietary hardness.

After the LW Albee, there was a drop in dietary hardness to levels comparable to that of the M/L Archaic. The Late Precontact farmers, therefore, had a dietary hardness that was similar to some hunter-gatherers. Clearly, people of the Late Precontact supplemented their maize diet with other foods. How often that happened is unclear, but they must have eaten foods in addition to maize, otherwise their pit percentage would have been well below that of the M/L Archaic people.

In fact, it appears all groups had some level of hard foods in their diets regardless of their subsistence strategies.

Pit length: The pit length data are largely static. For the most part, pit lengths did not change through time. The only population to differ from the others was the FA Oliver, which had pit lengths that were only about half the length of those from the other groups. The smaller sizes may indicate that they consumed foods that broke into unusually sized fragments, but that seems unlikely. I address this issue again in the DMTA complexity section.

Scratch width: The results indicated a significant difference between the M/L Archaic and the E/M Woodland groups; mean scratch widths fell from around 1.8–1.4 μm. This was the largest scratch width decline and it likely related to a decrease in the sizes of dietary abrasives (e.g., Schmidt, 2001). Any one dietary particle can pit or scratch a tooth; but certain foods, like those contaminated with exogenous grit, tend to generate linear scratches (Teaford, 1991). Additionally, the larger the grit, the wider the scratch (see Calandra et al., 2012; Winkler et al., 2020b). The loss of the large contaminants during the E/M Woodland may have been due to consuming fewer mussels and/or underground storage organs (USOs). As I noted earlier, improvements in pottery may have removed some of the larger contaminants, but dietary abrasives persisted. The E/M Woodland and the LW Albee scratch widths did not differ from each other, but they both differed from the Mississippian group. By the Late Precontact, the diet included only minor abrasives and grit contamination was nominal.

Another possibility is that the reduction in scratch widths had more to do with the endogenous nature of the plants people ate and less with exogenous contamination. Phytoliths are silica deposits within plants used for support and protection against herbivorous animals. They vary in size, but have roughly the same diameters as sand and silt particles (e.g., Piperno, 2006; Massey et al., 2007). Phytoliths are abundant in stems and leaves, and rarer in seeds and nuts (e.g., Piperno, 1984, 1985; Tsartsidou et al., 2007). Studies have shown that phytolith-bearing plants generate dental microwear features (Kay and Covert, 1983; Fox et al., 1994, 1996; Gügel et al., 2001; Calandra et al., 2016), although perhaps not to the same extent as grit and endogenous hard elements of the food (e.g., Sanson et al., 2007). Precontact people encountered phytoliths in the wild and domesticated foods they consumed, but their exposure may have declined over time as they intensified their consumption of plant parts having fewer phytoliths (e.g., nuts and domesticated seeds including maize). In instances where phytolith-rich foods remained important parts of the diet, their effects on microwear would have remained more constant. For example, in the southwest United States, Danielson and Reinhard (1998) and Reinhard and Danielson (2005) found sizable microwear features on precontact forager and farmer teeth that they suspected were due to consuming desert succulents. They followed up on their suspicion by examining coprolites representative of their study groups and found within them succulent phytoliths. We have no such coprolite confirmation among the populations studied here, nonetheless, I see no reason to ignore the potential role phytoliths played as a dietary abrasive. In the end, we simply need more research in this area.

Dental microwear texture analysis

Complexity: That the complexity did not significantly differ across the groups was a surprise. Usually, populations with means around 1.0 are significantly different from groups having means around 1.5 (Schmidt et al., 2019). The Mississippian group had the lowest and most distinctive complexity average at 1.0. The rest were at or just above 1.5, so why no significant difference? The issue was the variation. The M/L Archaic, E/M Woodland, and the FA Oliver groups all had large standard deviations compared to the Mississippian group. The reasons for intra-group variations were many, but a relationship between season of death and storage is something to consider. People who died in the fall or winter may have consumed different foods than those who died in the spring or summer, particularly in those groups who had limited storage capabilities, or who only stored certain types of foods at certain sites. The box and whisker plot in Figure 5.9 shows within group variation diminishing over time with the exception of the FA Oliver. In the FA Oliver data, there is a single individual with a complexity value over 3. It was not a statistical outlier, but it was the only person in the study to exceed 2.5, let alone 3. If I remove that person, a new boxplot shows a diachronic decrease in variation (Fig. 6.1). The reduced variation in the E/M Woodland and the Mississippian may indicate that foods were more season-specific for the M/L Archaic and became less season-specific over time. The Mississippian people had many ways to store maize for year-round consumption. The FA Oliver

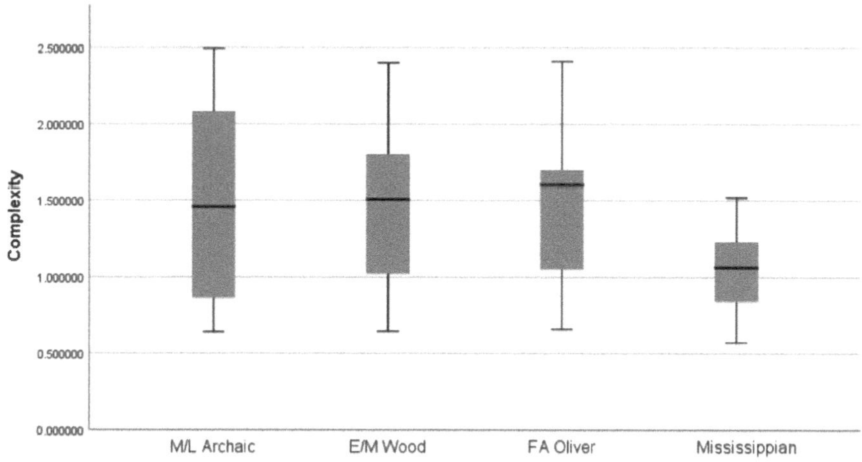

Figure 6.1 Box and whisker plot of complexity by group. FA Oliver is missing a single individual with a complexity over 3.0.

did too, but since the FA Oliver people studied here came from sites that were far smaller and less permanent than Angel or Wickliffe, it stands to reason their maize storage was more ephemeral leaving some people to die during seasons when maize was not as abundantly available (i.e., the individual with very high complexity). In the end, the overlapping ranges of variation obviated the mean differences. Not finding a significant difference for the most highly regarded variable of the latest microwear technology is somewhat disconcerting. However, as I consider other DMTA data sets I am finding that it is, in fact, the range of variation between groups, rather than their averages, that best distinguish populations. For example, in a study of people from Herculaneum who died due to the eruption of Mount Vesuvius in AD 79, mean differences among the old and young, male and female are modest at best. But, major distinctions existed in the ranges of variation for each demographic group (e.g., Remy and Schmidt, 2016).

Unpacking the Mississippian complexity range a bit more, their stark decrease in variation may be indicating that the Mississippian means for storing, processing, and distributing foods led to more similar diets for their people compared to the other groups, including the FA Oliver. This is not to say that the Mississippian diet was not altered seasonally. But the diet was consistently soft to an extent that the hardest and softest diets barely differed. In contrast, even without the individual with the very high complexity value, the FA Oliver range of variation was more like that of the preceding Woodland groups than the Mississippians. I do not expect the Mississippian complexity values here to represent all Mississippian groups; I suspect they are on the low end of the Late Precontact spectrum based on previous research of farming peoples (Schmidt et al., 2019). I am curious to see, however, if other Mississippian groups have the same modest range of variation as the group studied here.

There is another issue with complexity needing attention. The FA Oliver complexity value was comparable to the nonagricultural L/M Archaic and the E/M Woodland. That contrasts with the SEM-based macrowear data, which indicated the FA Oliver had fewer pits and distinctly smaller pits than the nonagriculturists. This contradiction may be a matter of scale. The SEM-based microwear data represent an area about 1/10th that of the DMTA data. When an observer looks at a surface at that scale it is important to find representative areas. If a surface has pit features that are so large they do not fully fit in the image, analysts will look for another spot where it is possible to measure features in their entirety. This means that large pits can be missed using SEM-based microwear. With DMTA, analysts survey larger areas and instead of manually counting features, the entire surface geometry is calculated. Therefore, it appears the FA Oliver people did have a hard food component to their diet, which led to a complexity similar to that of the M/L Archaic and E/M Woodland people, but it was at a scale better detected by DMTA complexity.

Anisotropy: Anisotropy distinguished the Mississippian group from the rest. The Mississippians had the highest anisotropy, indicating their jaw movement was in a consistent direction. The FA Oliver anisotropy, however, was not like that of the Mississippian people and looks more like nonagricultural groups (e.g., Schmidt et al., 2019). This was unexpected given their clear indications of agriculture. The anisotropy data indicate the jaw moved in many directions, perhaps to masticate a variety of foods having a variety of mechanical properties. It also reinforces the FA Oliver complexity value that indicated the presence of some hard foods. The overall FA Oliver DMTA signature indicates they ate more wild foods than did the Mississippians and, together with the SEM-based microwear, they reveal that the FA Oliver and the Mississippians were not dietary clones.

Dental caries

Occlusal lesions: The M/L Archaic occlusal prevalence was high relative to other precontact M/L Archaic populations from the eastern woodlands (e.g., Perzigian et al., 1984). The reasons for this are not clear. It is possible that the current study included more lesion types than other studies. It also is possible that dental caries related to extreme macrowear elevated the number of people bearing caries. Unlike prevalence, the M/L Archaic severity was similar to findings among other Archaic groups (e.g., Perzigian et al., 1984). Thus, I do not feel that the elevated M/L Archaic dental caries prevalence found here indicates a unique Indiana diet. In any event, the M/L Archaic caries prevalence was relatively low, the second lowest of the groups next to the E/M Woodland.

The E/M Woodland occlusal caries prevalence and severity were strikingly similar to that of the M/L Archaic. Both lacked anterior tooth lesions and both had a molar lesion prevalence around 30%; and, like the M/L Archaic, the E/M Woodland had twice as many females with dental caries compared to the males. Sample size was not as problematic with the E/M Woodland, which had 34 skeletons suitable for sex estimation. The dichotomy between the sexes likely owes to a behavioral phenomenon that had more females exposed to cariogenic foods. A division of labor where females collected wild grapes, berries, and fruit could have led to the caries disparity. Equally likely, there were differences in food preference and females sought sweeter foods more often than males. It is also possible that some pregnant females experienced dental caries at elevated rates due to changes in oral chemistry (Lukacs, 2010). It is difficult to isolate a single cause, but the caries difference between the E/M Woodland males and females is not spurious.

The LW Albee was the first population to have had anterior tooth dental caries. The anterior teeth are excellent indicators of caries severity because they are not involved with mastication; if they are carious, the level of cariogenic foods in the diet must be sizable. The LW Albee also was the first group to have a dental caries prevalence that reached 50% of the population. Their dental caries data indicate a distinct change in *foodways* (i.e., food production, preparation, presentation, and consumption [Welch and Scarry, 1995: 397]); but incipient maize agriculture may not have marked a major shift in LW Albee *lifeways*.

Maize cultivation affected where people put their agricultural efforts, but in terms of day-to-day activities, maize may have been just another form of food production to go along with already existing squash and EAC cultivation methods. It is plausible that to the LW Albee people, maize did little more than add another element to existing subsistence strategies that collectively minimized the risk of a subsistence failure (e.g., Schoeninger, 2009). It is not until after the LW Albee that maize is associated with more profound changes in precontact lifeways, including population nucleation, social stratification, and increased warfare (e.g., Milner et al., 1991; Dye, 2006; Alt, 2012).

At 94.7% and 81.3%, the FA Oliver and Mississippian groups exhibited the highest prevalences of dental caries. Having this many people with dental caries is congruent with the isotopic evidence for both groups relying heavily on maize (e.g., Buikstra, 1992; Schurr, 1992; Cook and Schurr, 2009). These Late Precontact groups had the highest prevalence of anterior tooth dental caries and the highest severities. In all, the FA Oliver and Mississippian males and females must have consumed copious amounts of maize. The Mississippian prevalence was somewhat lower than that of the FA Oliver, but the difference was minor. Both groups had the vast majority of their people affected by caries and of those people with dental caries, most had numerous cavities at the time of their deaths.

The prevalence-based hierarchical cluster analysis described in Chapter 5 linked the M/L Archaic and the E/M Woodland into a common cluster. It then linked the FA Oliver and the Mississippian; secondarily, it linked the LW Albee to the two Late Precontact groups. Based solely on dental caries data, then, the LW Albee was more similar to the Late Precontact groups than to the M/L Archaic and E/M Woodland. Its dental caries prevalence was only about half that of the Late Precontact groups, but that was well above its predecessors.

Nonocclusal lesions: Nonocclusal lesion prevalence was lower than occlusal prevalence for all groups and males had more nonocclusal lesions than their female counter parts, although sex-based differences were not significant. The LW Albee females had more than the males, and together they had more than double the nonocclusal lesions as the E/M Woodland. The FA Oliver had the highest overall nonocclusal prevalence at 70%; for the Mississippian people, around half of the males and about a third of the females had nonocclusal lesions. In addition to consuming a more cariogenic diet, the Late Precontact people may have ritually consumed cariogenic beverages associated with feasting, religious practices, kinship, etc. (see Goldstein, 2003; Tykot, 2006 for discussions regarding of maize beer in precontact Andean and Mesoamerican groups).

Additional archeological and bioarcheological implications of the dental indicators of diet

The following discusses additional, perhaps less explicit, implications of the dietary reconstructions for each group. I suspect there are other implications of this study that I have yet to consider, but these have drawn my attention and I am sharing them here. Primarily, these implications address particular cultural and, in a few cases, biological phenomena dependent upon dietary information.

The M/L Archaic and the E/M Woodland males and females shared what they hunted and gathered with each other. Their diets were diverse and, in terms of macrowear and microwear/DMTA, they were indiscernible. The only dental indicator that differed by sex was caries; females had a higher prevalence of occlusal lesions. The difference between males and females was minor from a statistical standpoint, perhaps because of the small sample of sexable adults, but in a practical sense, the differences may have been important since for both groups about twice as many females had lesions. The higher prevalence of female dental caries may have been due to more females foraging for and eating sugary foods, although dental caries related to gestation and fertility should not be ignored (Lukacs, 2008). What is important is that the M/L Archaic and the E/M Woodland shared nearly identical, low-level, sex-based caries prevalence disparities. Despite the passing of centuries and changes in dietary hardness, the relationships males and females had to wild cariogenic foods remained static. The implication is that male and female subsistence roles and/or dietary preferences did not change as the overall diet became harder, and other cultural practices related to the Adena and Hopewell phenomena came about.

An implication of the E/M Woodland increase in hard food consumption is that it may lend support to hypotheses regarding M/L Archaic to E/M Woodland changes in forest maintenance. Kristin Gremillion (2015) points out that forest management via fire and selective harvesting associated with EAC cultivation favored certain nut producing trees, including walnut, hickory, and chestnut. She is not convinced that burning was a means to manage the nut trees, themselves, and she argues the degree of anthropogenic changes to ancient forests at the time was not enough to equate to a fully developed agroforestry. Nonetheless, efforts to manage the forest after the M/L Archaic may be the underlying reason for the increase in E/M Woodland nut consumption as their behaviors actively promoted the availability of nearby nut resources (e.g., Delcourt et al., 1998; Fritz, 2000; Gremillion, 2015).

A bioarcheologically relevant implication of the E/M Woodland dietary reconstruction concerns the relationship between reductions in macrowear and the widespread use of ceramics (e.g., Hinton et al., 1980). Changes in food processing can lead to decreases in occlusal macrowear (e.g., Watson, 2008). For the people of the E/M Woodland the addition of ceramics may have aided their reduction in macrowear and decrease in scratch width. However, their macrowear and scratch widths were still higher than all later groups, and the E/M Woodland diet was harder than that of the M/L Archaic. Any role ceramics played in reducing mechanical demands on teeth, therefore, was relatively modest as people continued to consume hard and abrasive foods. This is important since some researchers implicate pottery as a catalyst for Holocene dental reduction because, in their view, ceramics led to a diet that was easier to chew (see Hill, 2004 for a review of dental reduction). Ceramics did impact dietary abrasiveness by the Late Woodland, but during the E/M Woodland, the DID data indicate the diet remained mechanically demanding. Thus, it is unlikely that ceramics played an exclusive role in dental reduction and other factors need consideration (see Detty, 2019).

An archeological/bioarcheological implication associated with the LW Albee concerns the divergence that took place between male and female diets indicated by macrowear. LW Albee males and females experienced dramatic increases in caries prevalence and severity compared to the previous groups. Yet the males had a diet that was similar in abrasiveness to that of the E/M Woodland. Perhaps their subsistence roles changed less than did the females' as maize entered the diet. Males continued carrying out hunting tasks and other behaviors that exposed them to unprocessed foods. On the other hand, the females' macrowear indicates they consumed more of the processed foods. The implication is that the incipient maize agriculture of the LW Albee had a larger effect on female diets, and perhaps their subsistence behaviors, than it did on the male diets and behaviors.

I did not anticipate finding DMTA evidence for hard food consumption among the FA Oliver. To contextualize their dental textures, I compared the FA Oliver data to data from 450 North American, European, Asian, and African farmers from 31 archeological sites that were part of a previous study (e.g., Schmidt et al., 2019). The FA Oliver surface complexity of 1.64 was higher than the average for the farming groups (mean = 1.36, 95% CI of the mean = 1.29–1.40), and its anisotropy of 0.0020 was far lower than both the average farmer (0.0035), and forager (0.0027) (Schmidt et al., 2019). Compared to farmers and foragers from around the globe, the FA Oliver DMTA data point to a forager-like diet. The evidence for hard food consumption does not obviate the dental caries, macrowear, and isotopic data that collectively indicate a sizable dependence upon maize; it, however, does echo findings of their periodic increases in the exploitation of wild and, perhaps, EAC foods (e.g., King, 1993). In her study, Martin reasoned that there might have been an increased demand for wild foods when crops failed, or when planting was restricted due to social or environmental circumstances (Martin, 2009). The implication of finding evidence of FA Oliver hard food consumption is that the long-standing ethnobotanical subsistence record indicating that nuts made up an important component of Late Precontact foodways (e.g., King, 1993; Bush, 2004; Emerson et al., 2005) has additional support from the bioarcheological record.

Intergroup dietary relationships

I have described the dietary reconstructions largely as they pertained to each group. In reality, these diets, and their variations, were fluid over time. The cultural labels are devices of archeology, and fail to convey adequately the influences any group had from the people that came before them. For example, the steps M/L Archaic people took regarding sedentism and domestication set the stage for the diet of the E/M Woodland people. Nearly all of the resources exploited during the E/M Woodland were part of the M/L Archaic subsistence spectrum. The E/M Woodland shift in emphasis toward hard foods was important for that group and evident in their teeth, but they ate the same hard foods that were available to their M/L Archaic predecessors.

Despite shedding the Adena/Hopewell phenomenon, the LW Albee continued the EAC domestication that started before them and they likely benefited from some of the preceding exchange and trade networks that eventually brought little barley, maize, and the bow-and-arrow into Indiana (e.g., Emerson and Titelbaum, 2000; McElrath et al., 2000; Bush, 2004; Benz, 2009). The subsequent people of the Late Precontact continued the same foraging, EAC horticulture, and maize agriculture of their ancestors; their nuance was to intensify maize production.

There is through all of these diets a thread of continuity that began over 5000 years ago. The dental data suggest that even the introduction of maize did not revolutionize precontact lifeways. Initially, people folded it into their existing horticultural paradigm and for the most part, life went on as usual. It took centuries before maize became the iconic food it did and the foundation of Late Precontac regional polities (e.g., Alt, 2012).

The dietary transitions described here, therefore, were episodes where people adjusted their foodways to address their nutritional needs given their sociocultural and/or environmental circumstances; they were not orthogenetic stages. Each episode marked an adjustment, but not necessarily an improvement. This is not to say that technology did not improve over time or that people's understanding of plant husbandry did not improve. Rather, it is to say that the LW Albee diet, for example, was *not* an improvement over the E/M Woodland diet. Both diets had their advantages and disadvantages. Each precontact group had the benefit of the knowledge they inherited from their forebears, but each also faced new situations that required novel solutions. Thus, precontact diets were not a progression, but a sequence of strategies drawn from a line of histories and applied to the situations of the day.

CHAPTER 7

Something to chew on

Introduction

This book set out to answer the following question: based on dental evidence, did diets in Indiana change prior to intensive maize agriculture during the Late Precontact? Keeping in mind the vagaries of labeling archeological groups discussed in Chapter 6, the answer is, yes: the dental indicators of diet (DID) data were consistent with dietary shifts prior to the Late Precontact based on the determination that each group had a unique dietary signature. Some groups differed little from each other while others diverged profoundly; nonetheless, all groups were distinct. The E/M Woodland diet was harder than that of the M/L Archaic; the LW Albee diet was less abrasive and more cariogenic than the E/M Woodland diet; the FA Oliver diet was less abrasive and more cariogenic than the LW Albee diet; and the Mississippian diet was softer than that of the FA Oliver. Each group adjusted the diet it inherited by altering the species that were most commonly collected or grown. Overall, diets became less abrasive and more cariogenic, and males and females experienced these changes in different ways.

The DID reconstructions provide insights into the persistent adjustments in diet precontact people made, although the motivations for these changes remain elusive. It is tempting to tie dietary shifts to the continuous restructuring of sociopolitical organization, religious beliefs, leadership, commerce, etc. Diets likely played roles in forming and ending some cultural practices. For instance, it is hard to imagine the rise and spread of the Mississippians without maize, yet I cannot argue that maize caused the Mississippian emergence. Thus, one should view the shifts in diet described here as accompanying certain cultural transitions, but not necessarily eliciting them. In the end, this book exposed *what* changes in diet took place, but not *why* they happened or how they related to cultural practices beyond subsistence and foodways. As tempting as it might be to speculate, we need more research before meaningful attempts at "*why*" questions are feasible. Contemplating "*why*" diets changed is nonetheless worthwhile because it can lead to new ideas to

Long 'on' the Tooth. DOI: https://doi.org/10.1016/B978-0-12-824306-0.00005-7

test. In science, speculations give us ideas, but tests give us the answers. New questions based on this study will lead to new hypotheses and experiments that should help us get closer to understanding how the changing diets of precontact Indiana came to be.

There's something in the teeth

I did not anticipate some of the new questions that this book generates; such findings are exciting parts of empirical analyses, providing new information and leading us down unanticipated paths of inquiry. Here are brief summaries of those unexpected findings.

- Males and females experienced macrowear declines at different times. Females had a steeper decline with agriculture during the LW Albee while males had a steeper decline after the M/L Archaic, and a similarly steep decline after the LW Albee. The female decline with agriculture indicates that the LW Albee diet led to starkly less macrowear compared to that of their E/M Woodland predecessors. Macrowear results from a lifetime of tooth wear, so LW Albee females must have had a very different diet than the E/M Woodland females. The LW Albee males, however, did not. Perhaps an intimate relationship existed between females, and agriculture's origin, and its eventual importance in the Indiana diet (e.g., Watson and Kennedy, 1991).
- Incisor/canine and premolar macrowear scores were more similar in hunter/gatherers than in farmers. It appears that, as diets soften, the demands on premolars diminish more than on incisors. This could relate to a continued need to use the incisors as tools or, it may be an artifact of the edge-to-edge bite common in the New World's Native peoples. Clearly more study is necessary in other populations but it may be that this relationship is a predictor of diet.
- The DMTA complexity variation decreased over time, an unexpected result because population sizes increased over time. It is plausible that the proportion of people consuming hard foods rather than the hardness of foods declined. In contrast, anisotropy variation increased over time. In the Late Precontact, numerous people had anisotropy values well above and well below the mean. The relationship between complexity and anisotropy here may indicate that harder diets, more often than not, lead to low anisotropies, while softer diets might lead to either high or low anisotropies.

- Many more females had carious lesions when groups had a low prevalence, and had only somewhat more when group prevalence was high. Again, more females' having lesions is not unusual; but the reasons for the sex-based differences in these particular groups is poorly understood. As noted earlier, teasing out causes of cariogenesis is difficult, but in this case is worth pursuing because it shines additional light on females as initiators of dietary transitions (e.g., Watson and Kennedy, 1991; Roth, 2006).

Another surprise was the overall DID signature found among LW Albee people. To me, they had the most intriguing teeth because they bore characteristics of their ancestors and descendants and reflected a truly mixed economy. They exploited local foods and a tropical cultigen; they had macrowear and microwear like their forebears and dental caries more on par with later groups. By adding maize to their diets, females changed their tooth use more than did the males, although both experienced dental caries similarly. In addition, the agreement among the DID, subsistence, and isotopic data regarding maize's supplemental role is exciting. In all, the LW Albee diet beautifully encapsulated what came before and what was to come for precontact people.

Dental Indicators of Diet now and later

The macrowear, SEM-based microwear/DMTA, and dental caries components of the DID complemented each other and provided a broad interpretative platform; losing any one of the indicators would have made reconstructions less valuable. For example, without the microwear data, I would have missed, or misunderstood, the M/L Archaic-to-E/M Woodland transition. The scanning electron microscope (SEM)-based microwear study and the DMTA were particularly valuable indicators of dietary hardness and heterogeneity. Studies of microwear and microwear texture are less common than macrowear and dental caries, in large part because of the technology they require, but their ability to expose researchers to fine-scale changes of dental surfaces makes them promising avenues of human dental study.

While this study has generated new data and included some relatively novel approaches to reconstructing human diets, its shortcomings will be easy to identify. For instance, how do beans and squash figure into these diets? Right now, I do not know. Archeologists, like other scientists, have to accept that, despite their best efforts, their studies rarely solve the entire puzzle; they simply add pieces to it. In the words of my doctoral committee member and colleague Gregory A. Reinhardt (who passed them to me from his advisor), any scientific study is never the last word, only the next word. I assembled a few pieces of the puzzle here, but there are many more to go and I am excited to see what that next word is.

My suspicion is that few people have read entire books on dietary reconstructions based solely on teeth. While this is likely true, the number of researchers' applying DID to ancient peoples is growing (see Schmidt and Watson, 2019). Keep an eye out for Luca Fiorenza, Stefano Benazzi, and Ottmar Kullmer, whose work concerns macrowear and dental fingerprinting, as well as people such as Kristin Krueger, Sireen El Zaatari, Almudena Estalrrich, Peter Ungar, Ivan Calandra, and Mark Teaford, who continue to develop and improve DMTA. Although I characterize DMTA as being relatively new to bioarcheology, researchers in other disciplines have used it widely and developed numerous insightful dietary models (e.g., Ungar, 2012).

One way analysts develop texture-based diet models is to study the microwear texture of living animals with known diets (e.g., Delezene et al., 2013; El Zaatari et al., 2016; Grine et al., 2013; Karriger et al., 2016; Scott et al., 2005; Ungar, 2012; Ungar et al., 2008, 2012, 2016; Ungar and Scott, 2009; Ungar and Sponheimer, 2011). In turn, researchers apply these animal models to human ancestors, which serve as another experimental setting where enamel thickness, tooth size, cusp shape, and so on, contextualize textural characteristics (e.g., Calandra et al., 2012; Delezene et al., 2016; DeSantis et al., 2012; El Zaatari, 2008, 2010; Estalrrich and Rosas, 2015; Purnell and Darras, 2016; Ragni et al., 2017; Schmidt et al., 2011, 2016, 2019; Schmidt and Remy, 2016; Schulz et al., 2013; Scott et al., 2005, 2006, 2012, 2016; Shearer et al., 2015; Spengler et al., 2018; Teaford and Ungar, 2014; Teaford et al., 2017; Ungar et al., 2008; Willman et al., 2018).

Beyond the field-collected data, lab-based experiments that use chewing simulators are elucidating relationships between bite force, food properties, and dental texture (Daegling et al. Ungar, 2016; Hua et al., 2015; Xia et al., 2015, 2017; Krueger et al., 2018). As our models improve, so, too, will our dietary reconstructions of archeological populations, our hope being that we will uncover particular textural indicators for particular diets, what Ungar (2017) calls "foodprints." We have more work to do, but, as it is, DMTA has a very bright future.

Once living people

In the course of uncovering the lives and lifeways of precontact people, it is important not to romanticize them. They did not live in perfect harmony with nature. Over the millennia, they suffered through periodic deforestation, over-hunting, warfare, food scarcity, and disease. They were not magical beings or wildlings in some kind of Eden. They were not noble savages. They faced their challenges, and they flourished. Having had the privilege of studying precontact people of North America, I feel it is critical to state what should be obvious: Native peoples are also living people with cultural practices, identities, and heritages that maintain and nurture millions. Their greatness did not end in 1492. To this day, Native peoples in the Americas are diverse and vital, and they deserve dignity and respect.

I think of human cultural and biological diversity like pages in a grand book of knowledge. Each group, living and deceased, contributes pages, and everyone benefits from reading that book. When ancient sites are bulldozed, or indigenous groups forcibly acculturated, pages vanish and the book of human knowledge shrinks. My hope is that the book of human knowledge not only remains large but also expands and I hope archeologists can play at least a small, but meaningful, role in that.

Control of the dead

So, who decides when, where, in what ways archeologists study ancient people? Early in my career, the answer was simple. Working in Indiana, I followed the guidelines and requirements for being an archeologist as outlined by the state, which provided excavation permits to qualified professionals, including me. Easy, the law decided. Today, I see archeology differently and better recognize how excluded Native people have felt by archeologists and the public alike. Most of my professional career I did not seek or include Native American input. That was a mistake, because while I was out there envisioning myself as an ally, a friend to Native people because of the information I was salvaging, they saw me as something quite different.

Over the last several years, I have benefitted from learning Native viewpoints through a series of consultation meetings with Native representatives who are seeking to claim remains at my institution and elsewhere. At first, the consultation process was difficult and humbling.

I was embarrassed to hear bold criticisms of my career; and it stunned me when a tribal member stated during a meeting that the tribe's initial perception of me, in essence, was that I was a colonialist bent on stealing from Native people. He said nothing about my being an ally. Or a friend. This was a devastating dose of reality, one I would have gotten years prior had I been more inclusive of Native voices. Today, I am far more aware of those voices, and my work benefits tremendously from insights gained from Native peoples.

Thus, control of the dead is an evolving concept, which includes ever-increasing Native input and updated burial protection laws. In United States federal law, the Native American Graves Protection and Repatriation Act allows tribes to make claims and assume legal control over ancestral remains. It is a powerful tool, but, in the end, changes in sensibilities will be what leads to cooperation among all vested parties. Of course, changing sensibilities requires sincere and ongoing dialog. Listening to Native concerns directly from Native Americans has had the biggest effect on me.

Because of this exposure, I hope archeologists are learning early in their careers the importance of heeding Native concerns and engaging with Native peoples. All perceptions that archeology is associated with colonialism must dissolve, but for that to happen we must embrace Native perspectives. I see changes in the profession and I am optimistic about our future, but challenges ahead will require compromise and understanding. If we truly wish to preserve ancient histories for a greater good, we need to make sure that good is for everyone.

Who cares?

Let us return to Greg Reinhardt. In addition to being a mentor to me, a role he continues even in his retirement, he is a mentor to the archeology and bioarcheology graduate students at our institution. Our graduate program is modest in size and all of the graduate faculty, including our retiree, help with theses and oral defenses. At the end of each graduate student's hour-long presentation, he asks a simple question: "who cares?" His intention is not to criticize, and he asks it respectfully. A fair question, it could, and should, be asked of any scientist. When students write up their thesis proposals a year before their defense we ask them to consider the significance of what they are doing. Nonetheless, "who cares?" bears a certain sobriety that can be unsettling.

At this point, I ask that question of my own work. Who cares about this study? Why did I bother? Why does any study of ancient people matter, and why should anyone care about people of the past? I have many possible responses to these questions, but I focus on two avenues of consideration. The first concerns the value of the DID. Recall from Chapter 3 that in all of bioarcheology, there are just a few ways that people can determine ancient diets, and each has its limitations. By coupling traditional and state-of-the-art approaches, the DID shed light on behaviors that were formerly either unknown or unconfirmed. We now have far greater awareness of the foods that entered precontact people's bodies and the ways those foods differed within and between groups. It may be a modest step, but it is a step, nonetheless, toward an empirically based representation of ancient diets. Furthermore, what we learned came from the people of Indiana, whose under-studied lifeways we now understand a little better.

The second avenue of consideration is the foundation of all cross-cultural study. I feel that people of the past are relevant because they deepen our appreciation of humanity. If we look around the world today, much of its strife and violence comes from cross-cultural conflict that stems primarily from ignorance—ignorance of humanity's roots: its variation, biology, and culture. The basis for some of this ignorance is a misunderstanding of humans in the past. Archeology is one way, and I want to emphasize it is just *one* way, that humans can explore their biological and cultural heritages. Our shared, yet diverse, history informs us regarding the natures of being human. Therefore, I see my bioarcheological studies – like all anthropological works – providing a practical service, one that offers a comprehension of humanity's vastness and better informs us about those around us—an all-encompassing comprehension capable of reducing cross-cultural conflict and, in doing so, saving lives.

Last bite

This book has covered quite a bit of ground; I have cited studies ranging from *Archeopteryx* to architecture, from dental wear to wolf cults. Such is the nature of bioarcheology and its nexus of biology and behavior. To explore the science of human teeth, it takes this kind of sweeping effort if we are going to understand dental shapes, functions, and changes. Despite the breadth of study they require, to me teeth are the best aspects of our bodies to explore the intersection of what we are and what we do. I hope my enthusiasm for teeth is evident and bolsters your curiosity, if only for the choppers in your own mouth. Perhaps you can give them one more look, but this time thinking about the stories they tell and the history they preserve, like the time you got that chip, or those braces, or that cavity, or that fever. They are little capsules of our time, a record of ourselves that we share every time they are unveiled at an archeological site, or in a friendly smile.

REFERENCES

Adams, W.R., 1950. Food animals used by the Indians at the Angel site. Proc. Indiana Acad. Sci. 59, 19–24.

Adovasio, J., Gunn, J.D., Donahue, J., Stuckenrath, R., 1975. Excavations at Meadowcroft Rock Shelter. 1973–1974: A Prog. Report. Pa. Archaeologist 45, 1–30.

Allegretto, K., Schmidt, C.W., van der Merwe, N., 2006. A comparison of stable isotope and dental evidence for maize consumption at Albee Phase sites in Indiana. Paper presented at the 71st Annual Meeting of the Society for American Archaeology, San Juan, Puerto Rico.

Alt, S., 2012. Making Mississippian at Cahokia. In: Pauketat, T.R. (Ed.), The Oxford Handbook of North American Archaeology. Oxford University Press, Oxford, pp. 497–508.

Anderson, D.L., Popovich, F., 1977. Dental reductions and dental caries. Am. J. Phys. Anthropol 47, 381–386.

Anderson, D.G., Sassaman, K.E., 2012. Recent Developments in Southeastern Archaeology: From Colonization to Complexity. SAA Press, Washington, D.C.

Anslinger, M., 1990. The Akers site: a Late Woodland Albee phase burial mound in Warren County, West Central, Indiana. Technical Report 10. Anthropology Laboratory, Indiana State University, Terre Haute.

Applegate, D., 2008. Woodland Period. In: Pollack, D. (Ed.), The Archaeology of Kentucky: An Update. Kentucky Heritage Council, Frankfort, KY, pp. 339–604.

Araujo, A.G.M., Neves, W.A., Kipnis, R., 2012. Lagoa Santa revisited: an overview of the chronology, subsistence, and material culture of Paleoindian sites in eastern central Brazil. Lat. Am. Antiquity 23, 533–550.

Arman, S., Brown, C., Ungar, P.S., DeSantis, L., Schmidt, C.W., Prideaux, G., 2016. Minimising inter-microscope variability in Dental Microwear Texture Analysis. Surf. Topography: Metrology Prop. Available from: https://doi.org/10.1088/2051-672X/4/2/024007.

Asch, N.B., Asch D.L., 1976. Paleoethnobotany of the Koster site: an interim report. Northwestern University Archaeobotanical Laboratory Report, 10.

Asch, N.B., Asch, D.L., 1980. Archeobotany of Napoleon Hollow, a multicomponent site in Pike County, Illinois: initial report. In: Wiant, M.D. (Ed.), Napoleon Hollow Interim Report. Northwestern University Archaeobotanical Laboratory Report.

Basso, K.H., 1996. Wisdom Sits in Places: Landscape and Language among the Western Apache. University of New Mexico Press, Albuquerque.

Beard, T., 1997. The Mound. General Electric Company. General Electric Company, Mount Vernon IN, Hopewell in Mt. Vernon: A Study of the Mt. Vernon Site (12-Po-885).

Behrend, G.D., 1978. The epidemiology of dental caries and subsistence pattern change. Am. J. Phys. Anthropol 48, 380.

Bellwood, P., 2005. First Farmers: The Origins of Agricultural Societies. Blackwell Publishing, Oxford.

Benz, B.F., 2009. Maize in the Americas. In: Staller, J., Tykot, R., Benz, B. (Eds.), Histories of Maize. Left Coast Press, Walnut Creek, CA, pp. 9–21.

Bergman, C.A., Peres Lemons, T., Schmidt, C.W., 2014. Scientific recovery investigations at the Kramer Mound (12Sp7): prehistoric artifact assemblages, faunal and floral remains, and human osteology. Indiana Archaeol 9, 13–101.

Black, G.A., 1933. The archaeology of Greene County. Indiana Hist Bull. 10, 183–346.

Black, G.A., 1934. Archaeological survey of Dearborn and Ohio Counties. Indiana Hist Bull. 11, 173–260.

Black, G.A., 1936. Excavations of the Nowlin Mound, Dearborn County site 7, 1934–1935. Indiana Hist Bull. 13, 197–342.

Black, G.A., 1943. The Angel mounds and related sites in southwestern Indiana. Proceedings of the 24th Annual Indiana History Conference, Indiana History Bulletin. 20, 108–115.

Black, G.A., 1967. Angel site. Indiana Historical Society, Indianapolis, IN.

Boldsen, J.L., Milner, G.R., Konigsberg, L.W., Wood, J.W., Hoppa, R.D., Vaupel, J.W., 2002. Transition analysis: a new method for estimating age from skeletons. In: Hoppa, R.D., Vaupel, J.W. (Eds.), Paleodemography: Age Distributions from Skeletal Samples. Cambridge University Press, Cambridge, pp. 73–106.

Boldurian, A.T., 2008. Clovis type-site, blackwater draw, New Mexico: a history, 1929–2009. North. Am. Archaeol 29, 65–90.

Boldurian, A.T., Cotter, J.L., 1999. Clovis Revisited: New Perspectives on Paleoindian Adaptations from Blackwater Draw, New Mexico. University of Pennsylvania, Philadelphia, University of Pennsylvania Museum Publications, Monograph 103.

Braun, D.P., 1987. Coevolution and sedentism, pottery technology, and horticulture in the Central Midwest, 200 B.C.–A.D. 600. Emergent Horticultural Economies of the Eastern Woodlands, Center for Archaeological Investigations Occasional Papers No. 7., Southern Illinois University, Carbondale, pp. 153–173.

Broca, P., 1879. Instructions relative à l'étude anthropologique du système dentaire. Bull. et. Memoires de. la. Societe d'Anthropologie de Paris. 2, 128–152.

Brose, D.S., Greber, N., 1979. Hopewell Archaeology. Kent State University Press, Kent, OH.

Brothwell, D.R., 1981. Digging Up Bones. Cornell University Press, Ithaca, NY.

Brown, J.A., 1977. The northeastern extension of the Havana Tradition. In: Caldwell, J.R., Hall, R.C. (Eds.), Hopewell Studies. Illinois State Museum, Springfield, Illinois State Museum Scientific Papers No. 12.

Brown, J.A., 2010. Cosmological layouts of secondary burials as political instruments. In: Sullivan, L.P., Mainfort, R.C. (Eds.), Mississippian Mortuary Practices: Beyond Hierarchy and the Representationist Perspective. University Press, Florida, Gainesville, pp. 30–53.

Buikstra, J.E., 1984. The lower Illinois River region: A prehistoric context for the study of ancient diet and health. In: Cohen, M.N., Armelagos, G.J. (Eds.), Paleopathology at the Origins of Agriculture. Academic Press, Orlando.

Buikstra, J.E., 1992. Diet and disease in late prehistory. In: Verano, J.W., Ubelaker, D.H. (Eds.), Disease and Demography in the Americas. Smithsonian Institution Press, Washington D.C.

Buikstra, J.E., Cook, D.C., 1980. Paleopathology: an American account. Annu. Rev. Anthropol 9, 433–470.

Buikstra, J.E., Ubelaker, D.H., 1994. *Standards for Data Collection from Human Skeletal Remains*. Arkansas Archaeological Survey Research Series No. 44.

Burkett, F., Cochran, D.R., 1985. The Commissary site (12-Hn-2) revisited. Proc. Indiana Acad. Sci. 94, 93.

Burdin, S.R., 2002. Report of Investigations: An Archaeological Assessement of site 12Fl73 in Floyd County, Indiana. Prepared for the Indiana Department of Natural Resources, Division of Historic Preservation and Archaeology, and the National Park Service.

Bush, L.L., 1994. Botanical remains from the Morell-Sheets site, 12 My 87. In: Redmond, B. (Ed.), Current Research in Indiana Archaeology and Prehistory. Glenn A. Black Laboratory of Archaeology, Research Reports No. 15.

Bush, L.L., 2003. Patterns of change in botanical remains from southern Indiana during the Late Woodland and Late Prehistoric. In: Redmond, B.G., Jones III, J.R. (Eds.), Facing the Final Millennium: Studies in the Late Prehistory of Indiana, A.D. 700 to 1700. Indiana Department of Natural Resources Division of Historic Preservation and Archaeology, Indianapolis, pp. 114–140.

Bush, L.L., 2004. Boundary Conditions. The Macrobotanical Remains of the Oliver Phase of Central Indiana, AD 1200-1450. The University of Alabama Press, Tuscaloosa.

Byers, A.M., 2005. The mortuary "Laying-In" crypts of the Hopewell Site: Beyond the funerary paradigm. In: Rakita, G.F.M., Buikstra, J.E., Beck, L.A., Williams, S.R. (Eds.), Interacting with the Dead. Gainesville. University Press, Florida.

Byers, A.M., 2005. The mortuary 'laying-in' crypts of the Hopewell site: beyond the funerary paradigm. In: Rakita, G.F.M., Buikstra, J.E., Beck, L.A., Williams, S.R. (Eds.), Interacting with the Dead: Perspectives on Mortuary Archaeology for the New Millennium. University of Florida Press, Gainesville, FL, pp. 124–141.

Byers, A.M., 2006. Cahokia: A World-Renewal Cult Heterarchy. University Press, Gainesville, FL.

Calandra, I., Schulz, E., Pinnow, M., Krohn, S., Kaiser, T.M., 2012. Teasing apart the contributions of hard dietary items on 3D dental microtextures in primates. J. Hum. Evol 63, 85–98.

Calandra, I., Zub, K., Szafrańska, P.A., Zalewski, A., Merceron, G., 2016. Silicon-based plant defences, tooth wear and voles. J. Exp. Biol. 219, 501–507. Available from: https://doi.org/10.1242/jeb.134890.

Cantin, M.E., 2000. Comparative analysis of thebes and kirk lithic technology and home range implications in southwestern Indiana. M.A. Thesis, Indiana State University, Terre Haute.

Carr, C., 2005. Historical insight into the directions and limitations of recent research on Hopewell. In: Carr, C., Case, T.D. (Eds.), Gathering Hopewell: Society, Ritual, and Ritual Interaction. Kluwer Academic/Plenum Publishers, New York, pp. 51–72.

Carr, C., 2006. The question of ranking in Havana Hopewellian societies: a retrospective in light of multi-cemetery ceremonial organization. In: Carr, C., Case, T.D. (Eds.), Gathering Hopewell: Society, Ritual, and Ritual Interaction. Springer, New York, pp. 238–257.

Carr, C., Case, T.D., 2005. Gathering Hopewell: Society, Ritual, and Ritual Interaction. Kluwer Academic/Plenum Publishers, New York.

Carskadden, J., 2008. Observations on the early woodland cultural landscape in the central Muskingum valley of eastern Ohio. In: Otto, M.P., Redmond, B.G. (Eds.), Transitions: Archaic and Early Woodland Research in the Ohio Country. Ohio University Press, Athens, pp. 232–270.

Casserly, A., Van Sessen, B., Schmidt, C.W., 2014. Determining onset of significant facial pathology using dental wear and microwear texture analysis: a case study from the Middle Archaic (~5500 BP) of Indiana. Dental Anthropol 27, 5–8.

Cassidy, C.M. 1972. A Comparison of Nutrition and Health in Preagricultural and Agricultural Amerindian Skeletal Populations. Ph.D. Dissertation. University of Wisconsin, Madison.

Cassidy, C.M., 1984. Skeletal evidence for prehistoric subsistence adaptation in the central Ohio River valley. In: Armelagos, G.J., Cohen, M.N. (Eds.), Paleopathology at the Origins of Agriculture. Academic Press, Orlando.

Chapman, J., Watson, P.J., 1993. The Archaic period and the flotation revolution. In: Scarry, C.M. (Ed.), Foraging and Farming in the Eastern Woodlands. University Press, Florida, Gainesville, Florida.

Charles, D.K., Buikstra, J.E., 1983. Archaic mortuary sites in the central Mississippi drainage: distribution, structure and behavior. In: Phillips, J.L., Brown, J.A. (Eds.), Archaic Hunters and Gatherers in the American Midwest. Academic Press, New York, pp. 117–146.

Charles, D.K., Buikstra, J.E., 2006. Recreating Hopewell. Gainesville. University Press, Florida.

Chiappe, L.M., Witmer, L.M., 2002. Mesozoic Birds. University of California Press, Berkeley, CA.

Chiu, L.W., Schmidt, C.W., Mahoney, P., McKinley, J.I., 2012. Dental microwear texture analysis of Bronze and Iron Age agriculturalists from England. American Association of Physical Anthropologists. Abstracts 115. Available from: https://doi.org/10.1002/ajpa.22032.

Claassen, C., 2005. An analytical study of shellfish from DeWeese Mound, Kentucky. In: Marquardt, W.H., Watson, P.J. (Eds.), Archaeology of the Middle Green River Region, Kentucky. Gainesville. University Press, Florida.

Clay, R.B., 1990. Essential Features of Adena Ritual. Glenn A. Black Laboratory of Archaeology, Research Reports. Indiana University, No. 16.

Clay, R.B., 2009. Where have all the houses gone? Webb's Adena house in historical context. Southeast. Archaeol 28 (1), 43–63.

Cochran, D.R., 1992. Adena and Hopewell cosmology: new evidence from east central Indiana. In: Hicks, R. (Ed.), Native American Cultures in Indiana. Minnetrista Cultural Center and Ball State University, Muncie.

Cochran, D.R., McCord, B.K., 1988. The Hesher site: a Late Albee cemetery in east central Indiana. Ball State University Archaeological Resources Management Service, Reports of Investigations No. 24.

Cochran, D.R., Knight, K.P., Bush, L., McCord, B., Rotman, D., 1997. McCullough's Run (12-B-1036): A Prehistoric Cremation Cemetery, Bartholomew County, Indiana. Archaeological Resources Management Service, Ball State University, Muncie, IN.

Cole, S.E., 2017. Ceremonial "killing" of Hopewell items recovered from redeposit pits in Mann mound 3, Posey County, Indiana. M.S. Thesis. Kent State University.

Cohen, M.N., Armelagos, G.J. (Eds.), 1984. Paleopathology at the Origins of Agriculture. Academic Press, Orlando.

Conaty, G.T., 1983. The significance of seeds in Eastern Woodlands prehistoric economy: a contextual analysis. North. Am. Archaeologist 4, 277–291.

Cook, D.C., 1984. Subsistence and health in the lower Illinois valley: osteological evidence. In: Armelagos, G.J., Cohen, M.N. (Eds.), Paleopathology at the Origins of Agriculture. Academic Press, Orlando.

Cook, R.A., 2007. Single component sites with long sequences of radiocarbon dates: the Sunwatch Site and Middle Fort Ancient village growth. Am. Antiquity 72, 439–460.

Cook, D.C., Buikstra, J.E., 1979. Health and differential survival in prehistoric populations: prenatal dental defects. Am. J. Phys. Anthropol 51, 649–664.

Cook, R.A., Price, D., 2015. Maize, mounds, and the movement of people: isotope analysis of a Mississippian/Fort Ancient region. J. Archaeol Sci. 61, 112–128.

Cook, D.C., Parker, S.K., McCullough, R.G., Barone, T.L., Cook, T.L., Blank, D.S., et al., 1986. Little Pigeon Creek cemetery (12W340): an Archaic midden-mound in Warrick County, Indiana. Research Report. Glenn A. Black Laboratory of Archaeology. <https://gbl.indiana.edu/research/reports/1986-abstracts.html>.

Cook, R.A., Schurr, M.R., 2009. Eating between the lines: Mississippian migration and stable carbon isotope variation in Fort Ancient populations. Am. Anthropol 111 (3), 344–359.

Cowan, C.W., 1985. Understanding the evolution of plant husbandry in eastern North America: lessons from botany, ethnography, and archaeology. In: Ford, R.I. (Ed.), Prehistoric Food Production in North America. Museum of Anthropology, University of Michigan, Ann Arbor, MI, pp. 205–243. Anthropological Papers No. 75.

Crawford, G.W., 1982. Late Archaic plant remains from west-central Kentucky: a summary. Midcontinental J. Archaeology 7, 205–224.

Cross, P.G., 1983. Vertebrate faunal remains from the Turner and DeMange Sites. In: Milner, G.R. (Ed.), The Turner and DeMange Sites. University of Illinois Press, Urbana, American Bottom Archaeology FAI-270 Site Reports.

Cross, P.G., 1984. Vertebrate faunal remains from the Julien Site. In: Milner, G.R. (Ed.), The Julien Site. University of Illinois Press, Urbana, American Bottom Archaeology FAI-270 Site Reports.

Da Gloria, P., Schmidt, C.W., 2019. Dental microwear texture analysis of the Paleoamericans of Lagoa Santa, central-eastern Brazil. In: Schmidt, C.W., Watson, J.T. (Eds.), Dental Wear in Evolutionary and Biocultural Perspectives. Academic Press, London.

Danielson, D.R., Reinhard, K.J., 1998. Human dental microwear caused by calcium oxalate phytoliths in prehistoric diet of the lower Pecos region, Texas. Am. J. Phys. Anthropol 107, 297–304.

Davis, B.M., 2011. Evolution of the tribosphenic molar pattern in early mammals, with comments on the "dual-origin" hypothesis. J. Mammal. Evol. 18, 227–244.

Daegling, D.J., Hu, L.-C., Ungar, P.S., 2016. The role of food stiffness in dental microwear feature formation. Arch. Oral. Biol. 71, 16–23.

Delcourt, P.A., Delcourt, H., Ison, C.R., Sharp, W., Gremillion, K.J., 1998. Prehistoric Human Use of Fire, the Eastern Agricultural Complex, and Appalachian Oak-ChestnutForests: Paleoecology of Cliff Palace Pond, Kentucky. Am. Antiquity 63, 263–278.

Delezene, L., Teaford, M.F., Ungar, P.S., 2016. Canine and incisor microwear in pitheciids and Ateles reflects documented patterns of tooth use. Am. J. Phys. Anthropology 161, 6–25.

Delezene, L., Zolnierz, M., Teaford, M.F., Grine, F.W., Ungar, P.S., 2013. Premolar microwear and tooth use in *Australopithecus afarensis*. J. Hum. Evol 65, 282–293.

Dennell, R.W., 1979. Prehistoric diet and nutrition: some food for thought. World Archaeol 2, 121–135.

DeSantis, L.R.G., Schubert, B.W., Scott, J.R., Ungar, P.S., 2012. Implications of diet for the extinction of saber-toothed cats and American lions. PLoS One 7 (12), e52453. Available from: https://doi.org/10.1371/journal.pone.0052453.

Detty, B.L., 2019. The Relationship of Cusp Placement and Tooth Size. MS Thesis. University of Indianapolis.

Digangi, E.A., Moore, M.K., 2012. Research Methods in Human Skeletal Biology. Academic Press, Oxford.

Dillehay, T., 1989. Monte Verde: A Late Pleistocene Settlement in Chile, vol. 1. Smithsonian, Washington, D.C., Smithsonian Series in Archaeological Inquiry.

Dillehay, T., 1997. Monte Verde: A Late Pleistocene Settlement in Chile, vol. 2, The Archaeological Context and Interpretation. Smithsonian, Washington, D.C.

Dorwin, J.T., 1971. The Bowen Site: An Archaeological Study of Culture Process in the Late Prehistory of Central Indiana. Indiana Historical Society, Indianapolis, IN.

Dragoo, D.W., 1949. Casual observations on angel mounds skeletal material. Proc. Indiana Acad. Sci. 58, 50–52.

Dragoo, D.W., 1955. An Archaeological Survey of Gibson County, Indiana. Indiana Historical Society, Indianapolis, IN.

Dragoo, D.W., 1963. Mounds for the dead: an analysis of the Adena Culture. Annals of the Carnegie Museum No. 37. Pittsburgh, PA.

Driver, H.E., 1952. The acorn in North American Indian diet. Proc. Indiana Acad. Sci. 62, 56–62.

Dye, D.H., 2006. The transformation of Mississippian warfare. In: Arkush, E.N., Allen, M.W. (Eds.), The Archaeology of Warfare: Prehistories of Raiding and Conquest. University Press, Florida, Gainesville, pp. 101–147.

Edgar, H.J.H., 2017. Dental Morphology for Anthropology: An Illustrated Manual. Routledge, New York.

Edgar, H.J.H., Jolie, E.A., Powell, J.F., Watkins, J.E., 2007. Contextual issues in Paleoindian repatriation: spirit cave man as a case. J. Soc. Archaeol 7, 101–122.

El Zaatari, S., 2008. Occlusal molar microwear and the diets of the Ipiutak and Tigara populations (Point Hope) with comparisons to the Aleut and Arikara. J. Archaeol Sci. 35, 2517–2522.

El Zaatari, S., 2010. Occlusal microwear texture analysis and the diets of historical/prehistoric hunter-gatherers. Int. J. Osteoarchaeol 20, 67–87.

El Zaatari, S., Grine, F.E., Ungar, P.S., Hublin, J.-J., 2016. Neandertal versus modern human dietary responses to climate fluctuations. PLoS One 11 (4), e0153277. Available from: https://doi.org/10.1371/journal.pone.0153277.

El Zaatari, S., Hublin, J.-J., 2014. Diet of upper paleolithic modern humans: Evidence from microwear texture analysis. Am. J. Phys. Anthropology 153, 570–581.

Emerson, T.E., Emerson, K.E., Hedman, K.M., Fort, M.A., 2019. Mortuary practices, cultural context, Bayesian chronology, and maize consumption among terminal Late Woodland societies in northeastern Illinois. Midcontinental J. of Archaeology. Available from: https://doi.org/10.1080/01461109.2019.1565359.

Emerson, T.E., McElrath, D.L., 1983. A settlement-subsistence model of the terminal Late Archaic adaptation in the American Bottom, Illinois. In: Phillips, J.L., Brown, J.A. (Eds.), Archaic Hunters and Gatherers in the American Midwest. Academic Press, New York.

Emerson, T.E., Titelbaum, A., 2000. The Des Plaines complex and the Late Woodland stage of Illinois. In: McEltrath, D.L., Emerson, T.E., Fortier, A.C. (Eds.), Late Woodland Societies. University of Nebraska Press, Lincoln, pp. 413–428.

Emerson, T.E., Hedman, K.M., Simon, M.L., 2005. Marginal horticulturalists or maize agriculturalists? Archaeobotanical, paleopathological, and isotopic evidence relating to Langford tradition maize consumption. Midcont J. Archaeol 30, 67–118.

Emerson, T.E., Hedman, K.M., Hargrave, E.A., Cobb, D.E., Thompson, A.R., 2016. Paradigms lost: reconfiguring Cahokia's mound 72 beaded burial. Am. Antiquity 81, 405–425.

Erickson, D.L., Smith, B.D., Clarke, A.C., Sandweiss, D.H., Tuross, N., 2005. An Asian origin for a 10,000-year-old domesticated plant in the Americas. Proc. Natl Acad. Sci. 102, 18315–18320.

Estalrrich, A., Rosas, A., 2015. Division of labor by sex and age in Neandertals: an approach through the study of activity-related dental wear. J. Hum. Evol 80, 51–63.

Faulkner, C.H., 1960. Walkerton: a point peninsula-like focus in Indiana, Indiana Hist Bull, 37. pp. 122–136.

Faulkner, C.H., 1961. An Archaeological Survey of Marshall County. Indiana Historical Society, Indianapolis, IN.

Fields, M., Herschaft, E.E., Martin, D.L., Watson, J.T., 2009. Sex and the agricultural transition: dental health of early farming females. J. Dent. Oral. Hyg. 1, 42–51.

Fiorenza, L., Benazzi, S., Estalrrich, A., Kullmer, O., 2019. Diet and cultural diversity in Neanderthals and modern humans from dental macrowear analyses. In: Schmidt, C.W., Watson, J.T. (Eds.), Dental Wear in Evolutionary and Biocultural Perspectives. Elsevier, Amsterdam, pp. 39–72.

Fortier, A.C., 1983. Settlement and subsistence at the Go-Kart north site: a Late Archaic Titterington occupation in the American Bottom, Illinois. In: Phillips, J.L., Brown, J.A. (Eds.), Archaic Hunters and Gatherers in the American Midwest. Academic Press, New York.

Fowler, M.L., 1974. Cahokia: ancient capital of the midwest. Addison Wesley Module in Anthropology, No. 48.

Fowler, M.L., 1975. A pre-Columbian urban center on the Mississippi. Sci. Am. 233, 92–101.

Fowler, M.L. (Ed.), 1977. Explorations into Cahokia Archaeology, Bulletin No. 7. Illinois Archaeological Survey.

Fowler, M.L., Rose, J.C., Vander Leest, B., Ahler, S.R., 1999. The Mound 72 Area: Dedicated and Sacred Space in Early Cahokia. Illinois State Museum, Reports of Investigation, No. 54.

Fox, C.L., Pérez-Pérez, A., Juan, J., 1994. Dietary information through the examination of plant phytoliths on the enamel surface of human dentition. Science 21, 29–34.

Fox, C.L., Juan, J., Albert, R.A., 1996. Phytolith analysis on dental calculus, enamel surface, and burial soil: information about diet and paleoenvironment. Am. J. Phys. Anthropol 101, 101–113.

Fraser, J., Cerny, R., Soukup, V., Bronner-Fraser, M., Streelman, J.T., 2010. The odontode explosion: The origin of tooth-like structures in vertebrates. Bioessays. 32, 808–817. Available from: https://doi.org/10.1002/bies.200900151.

Frazer, L., 2012. Dental Microwear Texture Analysis of Early/Middle Woodland and Mississippian Populations from Indiana. MS Thesis, University of Indianapolis.

Fritz, G.J., 1993. Early and Middle Woodland period paleoethnobotany. In: Scarry, C.M. (Ed.), Foraging and Farming in the Eastern Woodlands. University Press, Florida, Gainesville, Florida.

Fritz, G.J., 2000. Levels of native biodiversity in eastern North America. In: Minnis, P.E., Elisens, W.J. (Eds.), Biodiversity & Native America. University of Oklahoma Press, Norman, pp. 223–247.

Glenn, E.J., 1973. Analysis of human skeletal remains. In: Swartz, B.K. (Ed.), Mound Three, White Site Hn-10 (IAS-BSU). The Final Report on a Robbins Manifestation in East Central Indiana. Ball State University, Muncie, Contributions to Anthropological History No. 1.

Glenn, E.J., 1976. Skeletal material. In: Swartz, B.K. (Ed.), The New Castle Site: A Hopewell Ceremonial Complex in East Central Indiana. Ball State University, Muncie, Contributions to Anthropological History, No. 3.

Glenn, E.J., 1982. Skeletal material. In: Swartz, B.K. (Ed.), The Commissary Site: An Early Late Woodland Cemetery in East Central Indiana. Ball State University, Muncie, Contributions to Anthropological History No. 3.

Glenn, E.J., 1992. Miami and Delaware trade routes and relationships in northern Indiana. In: Hicks, R. (Ed.), Native American Cultures in Indiana. Minnetrista Cultural Center and Ball State University, Muncie.

Goldstein, M.S., 1932. Caries and attrition in the molar teeth of the Eskimo mandible. Am. J. Phys. Anthropol 16, 421–430.

Goldstein, L.G., 1980. Mississippian Mortuary Practices. Northwestern University Archaeological Program, Evanston.

Goldstein, P.S., 2003. From stew-eaters to maize-drinkers, the *Chicha* economy and Tiwanaku. In: Bray, T.L. (Ed.), The Archaeology and Politics of Food and Feasting in Early States and Empire. Kluwer Academic/Plenum Publishers, New York, pp. 143–172.

Goodyear, A.C., 2005. Evidence of pre-clovis sites in the eastern United States. Paleoamerican Origins: Beyond Clovis. Texas A & M University, College Station, TX, pp. 103–112.

Gordon, K.D., 1984. Pitting and bubbling artefacts in surface replicas made with silicone elastomers. J. Microsc 134, 183–188.

Górka, K., Romero, A., Pérez-Pérez, A., 2016. Dental-macrowear and diet of Tigara foragers from Point Hope, northern Alaska. Anthropologischer Anz. 73, 257–264.

Goslin, R.M., 1952. Cultivated and Wild Plant Food from Aboriginal Sites in Ohio. OhioArcheologist 2, 9–29.

Gosman, J.H., Ketcham, R.A., 2009. Patterns in ontogeny of human trabecular bone from SunWatch village in the prehistoric Ohio valley: general features of microarchitectural change. Am. J. Phys. Anthropol 138, 318–332.

Green, T.J., Cochran, B., Fenton, T., Woods, J.C., Titums, G., Tieszen, L., et al., 1998. The Buhl burial: A Paleoindian woman from southern Idaho. Am. Antiquity 63, 437–456.

Greene, D.L., 1972. Dental anthropology of Early Egypt and Nubia. J. Hum. Evol 1, 315–324.

Gregg, M.L., 1975. A population estimate for Cahokia. Perspectives in Cahokia Archaeology. Ill. Archaeological Survey, Bull. 10 .

Gremillion, K.J., 1993. The evolution of seed morphology in domesticated Chenopodium: an archaeological case study. J. Ethnobiol 13, 149–169.

Gremillion, K.J., 1996. Early agricultural diet in eastern North America: evidence from two Kentucky rockshelters. Am. Antiquity 61, 520–536.

Gremillion, K.J., 2004. Seed processing and the origins of food production in eastern North America. Am. Antiquity 69, 215–234.

Gremillion, K.J., 2015. Prehistoric Upland Farming, Fuelwood, and Forest Composition on the Cumberland Plateau, Kentucky, USA. J. Ethnobiology 35, 60–84.

Griffin, J.B., 1983. The midlands. In: Jennings, J.D. (Ed.), Ancient North Americans. W.H. Freeman and Co, New York.

Griffin, J.B., 1978. The Midlands and Northeastern United States. In: Jennings, J.D. (Ed.), Ancient Native Americans. San Francisco, pp. 221–279.

Grine, F.E., Ungar, P.S., Teaford, M.F., El Zaatari, S., 2013. Molar microwear evidence for diet in a purported hominin species lineage from the pliocene of east Africa. In: Fleagle, J.C., Reed, K. (Eds.), Palaeoecology of Australopithecus. Springer-Verlag, New York, pp. 213–223.

Guatelli-Steinberg, D., 2016. What Teeth Reveal About Human Evolution. Cambridge University Press, Cambridge.

Guernsey, E.Y., 1924. Archaeological survey of Lawrence County. Indiana Hist Bull.

Gügel, I.L., Grupe, G., Kunzelmann, K.H., 2001. Simulation of dental microwear: Characteristic traces by opal phytoliths give clues to ancient human dietary behavior. Am. J. Phys. Anthropol 114, 124–138.

Harris, E.F., 2016. Odontogenesis. In: Irish, J.D., Scott, G.R. (Eds.), A Companion to Dental Anthropology. Wiley-Blackwell, West Sussex, UK, pp. 142–158.

Harmon, A.M., Rose J.C., 1988. The role of dental microwear analysis in the reconstruction of prehistoric diet. In: Kennedy, B.V., LeMoine, G.M. (Eds.) Diet and Subsistence: Current Archaeological Perspectives, Proceedings of the 19th Annual Conference of the Archaeological Association of the University of Calgary.

Havill, L.M., White, A.A., Murphy, K.A., 2003. Skeletal Biology and Cemetery Use at the Albee Mound, Bucci, Shaffer, and Shepherd Sites. In: Redmond, B.G., Jones, J.R. (Eds.), Facing the Final Millennium: Studies in the Late Prehistory of Indiana, A.D. 700 to 1700. Indiana Department of Natural Resources Division of Historic Preservation and Archaeology, Indianapolis, pp. 95–113.

Heilman, J.M., Hoefer, R., 1981. Possible astronomical alignments in a Fort Ancient settlement at the incinerator site in Dayton, Ohio. In: Williamson, R. (Ed.), Archaeoastronomy in the Americas. Ballena Press, Menlo Park, CA.

Henderson, A.G., Pollack, D., 2001. Fort Ancient. In: Peregrine, P.N., Ember, M. (Eds.), Encyclopedia of Prehistory, vol. 6. Kluwer Academic/Plenum Publishers, New York, pp. 174–194.

Henry, E.R., Barrier, C.R., 2016. The organization of dissonance in Adena-Hopewell societies of eastern North America. World Archaeol 48 (1), 87–109.

Herrala, E.A., 1961. Change of incidence of dental caries with dietary change in prehistoric Indian populations. Proceedings of the Indiana Academy of Science for 1960. 70, 46.

Hicks, R., 1992. Native American Cultures in Indiana. Minnetrista Cultural Center and Ball State University, Muncie.

Hilgeman, S.L., 1988. Artificial cranial deformation and porotic hyperostosis at Angel Site, Vanderburgh County, Indiana. Proc. Indiana Acad. Sci. 98, 83–91.

Hill, M.K., 2004. Dental reduction and diet in the prehistoric Ohio river valley. Dental Anthropol 17, 34–44.

Hillson, S.W., 1979. Diet and dental disease. World Archaeol 2, 147–162.

Hillson, S.W., 1986. Teeth. Cambridge University Press, Cambridge.

Hillson, S., 1996. Dental anthropology. Cambridge University Press, Cambridge.

Hillson, S., 1997. Dental Anthropology. Cambridge, Cambridge.

Hillson, S., 2014. Tooth Development in Human Evolution and Bioarchaeology. Cambridge University Press, Cambridge.

Hinton, R.J., Smith, M.O., Smith, F.H., 1980. Tooth size changes in prehistoric Tennessee Indians. Hum. Biol. 52, 229–245.

Hoffecker, J.F., Elias, S.A., O'Rourke, D.H., Scott, G.R., Bigelow, N.H., 2016. Beringia and the global dispersal of modern humans. Evol. Anthropol 25, 64–78.

Hollenbach, K.D., 2009. Foraging in the Tennessee River Valley, 12,500 to 8,000 Years Ago. University of Alabama Press, Tuscaloosa.

Holt, J.Z., 2009. Rethinking the Ramey State: was Cahokia the center of a theater state? Am. Antiquity 74, 231–254.

Houck, G.K., Swartz, B.K., 1972. The Commissary site: a Woodland cemetery. Proc. Indiana Acad. Sci. 81, 56–57.

Householder, J.C., 1945. The Oliver Farm site. Proc. Indiana Acad. Sci. 1944 54, 29–32.

Hua, L.-C., Brandt, E.T., Meullenet, J.F., Zhou, Z.-R., Ungar, P.S., 2015. Technical note: an in vitro study of dental microwear formation using the Bitemaster II chewing machine. Am. J. Phys. Anthropology 158, 769–775.

Huffman, Antoine, D., 2010. Analysis of cementum layers in archaeological material. Dental Anthropol 23, 67–73. Available from: https://doi.org/10.26575/daj.v23i3.79.

Hylander, W.L., 1977. The adaptive significance of Eskimo craniofacial morphology. In: Dahlberg, A. A., Graber, T.M. (Eds.), Orofacial Growth and Development. Mouton, The Hague.

Irish, J.D., Nelson, G., 2008. Technique and Application in Dental Anthropology. Cambridge University Press, Cambridge.

Irish, J.D., Scott, G.R., 2016. A Companion to Dental Anthropology. Wiley-Blackwell, West Sussex.

Janzen, D.E., 1977. An examination of the late Archaic development in the falls of the Ohio River area. In: Cleland, C.E. (Ed.), For the Director: Research Essays in Honor of James B. Griffin, vol. 61. Anthropological Papers of the University of Michigan Museum of Anthropology, pp. 122–143.

Jefferies, R.W., 1997. Middle Archaic bone pins: evidence of Mid-Holocene regional-scale social groups in the southern Midwest. Am. Antiquity 62, 464–487.

Jefferies, R.W., 2008. Holocene Hunter-Gatherers of the Lower Ohio River Valley. University of Alabama Press, Tuscaloosa.

Jefferies, R.W., Butler, B., 1982. The Carrier Mills Project: Human Adaptation in the Saline Valley, Illinois. Center for Archaeological Investigations, Southern Illinois University at Carbondale, Research Paper No. 33.

Johannessen, S., 1981. Plant Remains from the Go-Kart North Site.The Go-Kart North Site: A Late Archaic, Titterington Occupation in the American Bottom. Department of Anthropology, University of Illinois, Urbana-Champaign, pp. 164–177, UIUC FAI-270 Archaeological Mitigation Project Report No. 32.

Johannessen, S., 1984a. Paleoethnobotany. In: Baries, C.J., Porter, J.W. (Eds.), American Bottom Archaeology. University of Illinois Press, Urbana, IL.

Johannessen, S., 1987. Floral remains. The Range Site: Archaic Through Late Woodland Occupation. University of Illinois Press, Urbana, IL.

Jenkins, D.L., Davis, L.G., Stafford, T.W., Campos, P.F., Hockett, B., Jones, G.T., et al., 2012. Clovis Age Western Stemmed Projectile Points and Human Coprolites at the Paisley Caves. Science 337, 223–228.

Karriger, W.M., Schmidt, C.W., Smith, F.H., 2016. Dental microwear texture analysis of Croatian Neandertal molars. Paleoanthropology 172–184. Available from: https://doi.org/10.4207/PA.2016.ART102.

Kay, R.F., Covert, H.H., 1983. True grit: a microwear experiment. Am. J. Phys. Anthropol 61, 33–38.

Kay, R.F., Hiiemae, K.M., 1974. Jaw movement and tooth use in recent and fossil primates. Am. J. Phys. Anthropol 40, 227–256.

Kellar, J.H., 1960. C.L. Lewis Stone mound and the stone mound problem, Prehistory Research Series, Indiana Historical Society, vol. 3. pp. 357–481.

Kellar, J.H., 1967. Material remains. In: Black, G.A. (Ed.), Angel Site. Indiana Historical Society, Indianapolis, IN.

Kelly, L.S., Cross, P.G., 1984. Zooarchaeology. In: Baries, C.J., Porter, J.W. (Eds.), American Bottom Archaeology. University of Illinois Press, Urbana.

Kelley, M.A., Larsen, C.S., 1991. Advances in Dental Anthropology. Wiley-Liss, New York.

Kelly, C.D., Schmidt, C.W., D'Anastasio, R., 2019. Dental microwear textura analysis in deciduous teeth. In: Schmidt, C.W., Watson, J.T. (Eds.), Dental Wear in Evolutionary and Biocultural Perspectives. Academic Press, London.

Keiser, J.A., 1990. Human Adult Odontometrics. Cambridge University Press, Cambridge.

Kellar, J.H., 1983. An Introduction to the Prehistory of Indiana. Indianapolis: Indiana Historical Society.

Kemp, B.M., et al., 2007. Genetic analysis of early holocene skeletal remains from Alaska and its implications for the settlement of the Americas. Am. J. Phys. Anthropol 132, 605–621.

King, F.B., 1993. Climate, Culture, and Oneota Subsistence in Central Illinois. In: Scarry, C.M. (Ed.), Foraging and Farming in the Eastern Woodlands. University Press, Florida, Gainseville, pp. 232–254.

King, F.B., 1985. Presettlement vegetation and plant remains from the Alexander Site (3CN117), Conway County, Arkansas. In: Hemmings, E.T., House, J.H. (Eds.), The Alexander Site, Conway County, Arkansas. Arkansas Archaeological Survey, pp. 49–57. , Research Series No. 24.

Knight Jr., V.J., Steponaitis, V.P., 1998. A New History of Moundville. In: Knight Jr, V.J., Steponaitis, V.P. (Eds.), Archaeology of the Moundville Chiefdom. Smithsonian Institution Press, Washington DC, pp. 1–25.

Konigsberg, L.W., 1985. Demography and mortuary practice at Seip Mound One. Midcont J. Archaeol 10, 123–148.

Krueger, K.L., Ungar, P.S., 2010. Incisor microwear textures of five bioarcheological groups. Int. J. Osteoarchaeol 20 (5), 549–560.

Krueger, K.L., Chwa, E., Peterson, A., Delong, R., Fok, A., Van Heel, B., et al., 2018. Experimental dental microwear textures with implications for Neandertal diet Poster presented at the 87th annual meeting of the American Association of Physical Anthropologists, Abstract Book, p. 147.

Krueger, K.L., Chwa, E., Peterson, A., Delong, R., Fok, A., 2019. The role of grit in dental microwear textures: evidence from Artificial Resynthesis Technology (ART). American Journal of Physical Anthropology. Abstract Book, p. 131.

Krueger, K.L., Ungar, P.S., 2012. Anterior dental microwear texture analysis of the Krapina Neandertals. Cent. Eur. J. Geosci. 4, 651–662.

Krueger, K.L., Ungar, P.S., Guatelli-Steinberg, D., Hublin, J.-J., Perez-Perez, A., Trinkaus, E., 2017. Anterior dental microwear textures show climate-driven variability in Neandertal behavior. J. Hum. Evol 105, 13–23.

Kulkarni, B.V., Mattes, R.D., 2014. Lingual lipase activity in the orosensory detection of fat in humans. Am. J. Physiol. Regulatory, Integr. Comp. Physiol. 306, 879–885. Available from: https://doi.org/10.1152/ajpregu.00352.2013.

Kullmer, O., Benazzi, S., Fiorenza, L., Schulz, D., Bacso, S., Winzen, O., 2009. Technical note: occlusal fingerprint analysis: quantification of tooth wear pattern. Am. J. Phys. Anthropol 139, 600–605.

Lagan, E.M., Cook, R.A., Schmidt, C.W., 2018. What they ate: a biological perspective at the Guard site. Paper Presented at the Annual Meeting of the Midwest Archaeology Conference, Notre Dame, IN.

Larsen, C.S., 1984. Health and disease in prehistoric Georgia: the transition to agriculture. In: Armelagos, G.J., Cohen, M.N. (Eds.), Paleopathology at the Origins of Agriculture. Academic Press, Orlando.

Larsen, C.S., 1985. Dental modifications and tool use in the western Great Basin. Am. J. Phys. Anthropol 67, 393–402.

Larsen, C.S., 1992. Transitions in health, diet, and behavior: bioarchaeology in Spanish colonial Florida. Paper presented to the 25th Annual Chacmool Conference, Calgary.

Larsen, 2015. Bioarchaeology, 2nd Ed. Cambridge University Press, Cambridge.

Larsen, C.S., 1990. The Archaeology of Mission Santa Catalina De Guale: 2. Biocultural Interpretations of a Population in Transition. Anthropological Papers No. 68. American Museum of Natural History, New York.

Larsen, C.S., Griffin, M.C., Hutchinson, D.L., Noble, V.E., Norr, L., Pastor, R.F., et al., 2001. Frontiers of contact: bioarchaeology of Spanish Florida. J. World Prehist 15, 69–123.

Larsen, C.S., Schoeninger, M.J., Hutchinson, D.L., Russell, K.F., Ruff, C.B., 1990. Beyond demographic collapse: biological adaptation and change in native populations of La Florida. Columbian Consequences, Volume 2, Archaeological and Historical Perspectives on the Spanish Borderlands. Smithsonian Institution Press, Washington, pp. 409–428.

Larsen, C.S., Shavit, R., Griffin, M.C., 1991. Dental caries evidence for dietary change: an archaeological context. In: Kelley, M.A., Larsen, C.S. (Eds.), Advances in Dental Anthropology. Wiley-Liss, New York.

Legge, S.S., Hardin, A.M., 2016. The pulp cavity and its contents. In: Irish, J.D., Scott, G.R. (Eds.), A Companion to Dental Anthropology. Wiley-Blackwell, West Sussex, UK, pp. 191–203.

Leigh, R.W., 1925. Dental pathology of Indian tribes of varied environmental and food conditions. Am. J. Phys. Anthropol 8, 179–199.

Leigh, R.W., 1928. Dental pathology of aboriginal California, vol. 23. University of California Publications on American Archaeology and Ethnology, pp. 399–440.

Lewis, R.L., 2006. Pre-contact fish weirs: a case study from southwestern Nova Scotia. M.S. Thesis. Memorial University, St. John's Newfoundland.

Lin, Q., Fan, S., Zhang, Y., et al., 2016. The seahorse genome and the evolution of its specialized morphology. Nature 540, 395–399.

Liversidge, H.N., 2009. Permanent tooth formation as a method of estimating age. Front. Oral. Biol. 13, 153–157.

Lovejoy, C.O., 1985. Dental wear in the Libben population: its functional pattern and role in the determination of adult skeletal age at death. Am. J. Phys. Anthropol 68, 47–56.

Lucas, S.L., 1973. Round lake: remnants of a Late Woodland site in Starke County, Indiana. Proc. Indiana Acad. Sci. 82, 91–96.

Lukacs, J.R., 2008. Fertility and agriculture accentuate sex differences in dental caries rates. Curr. Anthropol 49, 901–914.

Lukacs, J.R., 2010. Sex differences in dental caries experience: clinical evidence, complex etiology. Clin. Oral. Investig 15, 649–656. Available from: https://doi.org/10.1007/s00784-010-0445-3.

Lukacs, J.R., 2016. Oral health in past popuations: context, concepts, and controversies. In: Grauer, A.L. (Ed.), A Companion to Paleopathology. Wiley, Malden, MA, pp. 553–581.

Lunt, D.A., 1974. The prevalence of dental caries in the permanent dentition of Scottish prehistoric and medieval populations. Arch. Oral. Biol. 19, 431–437.

Lunt, D.A., 1978. Molar attrition in medieval Danes. In: Butler, P.M., Joysey, K.A. (Eds.), Development, Function, and Evolution of Teeth. Academic Press, London.

Luo, Z.X., Kielan-Jaworowska, Z., Cifelli, R.L., 2004. Evolution of dental replacement in mammals. Bull. Carnegie Mus. Nat. Hist 36, 159–175.

McCord, B.K., Cochran, D.R., 1994. Morell-Sheets: An Albee Phase Habitation. Reports of Investigations 38. Archaeological Resources Management Service. Ball State University, Muncie, Indiana.

McCord, B.K., Cochran, D.R., 1996. Windsor Mound: A Synthesis of an Adena Mound in Randolph County. Ball State University: Report of Investigation 37.

McCord, B.K., Cochran, D.R., 2003. The Morell-Sheets Site: Refining the definition of the Albee Phase. In: Redmond, B.G., Jones III, J.R. (Eds.), Facing the Final Millennium: Studies in the Late Prehistory of Indiana, A.D. 700 to 1700. Indiana Department of Natural Resources Division of Historic Preservation and Archaeology, Indianapolis, pp. 32–60.

MacLean, J.A., 1931. Excavation of Albee mound 1926-1927. Indiana Hist Bull. 8, 87–176.

Mahoney, P., Schmidt, C.W., Deter, C., Remy, A.J., Slavin, P., Johns, S.E., et al., 2016. Deciduous enamel 3D microwear texture analysis as an indicator of childhood diet in medieval Canterbury, England. J. Archaeological Sci. 66, 128–136.

Martin, F.P., 1954. A Vanderburgh County site with southern affinities. Proc. Indiana Acad. Sci. 1953 63, 57–58.

Martin, K.A., 2009. Eastern Agricultural Complex Tradition in Small Fort Ancient Communities—The Wildcat Example. M.S. Thesis. The Ohio State University, Columbus.

Mason, R.J., Irwin, C., 1960. An Eden-Scottsbluff burial in Northeastern Wisconsin. Am. Antiquity 26 (1), 43–57.

Massey, F.P., Ennos, A.R., Hartley, S.E., 2007. Herbivore specific induction of silica-based plant defences. Oecologia 152 (4), 677–683.

Matternes, H.B., 1994. Demographic features of Wickliffe's mound C cemetery: a model for defining the presence of post-Classic Mississippian peoples in western Kentucky. Wickliffe Mounds Research Center Report No. 5.

McAllister, J.G., 1932. The archaeology of Porter County. Indiana Hist Bull. 10, 1–94.

McCord, B.K., Cochran, D.R., 2014. Redefining the New Castle phase: Middle Woodland landscapes in east central Indiana. Indiana Archaeol 9 (1), 137–156.

McCullough, R.G., 1992. An overview of the Oliver phase: a Late Woodland manifestation from central Indiana. In: Hicks, R. (Ed.), Native American Cultures in Indiana. Minnetrista Cultural Center and Ball State University, Muncie.

McCullough, R.G., 2003. Cultural interaction along the West Fork of the White river during the Late Prehistoric period. Facing the Final Millennium: Studies in the Late Prehistory of Indiana, A.D. 700 to 1700. Indiana Department of Natural Resources Division of Historic Preservation and Archaeology, Indianapolis, pp. 141–171.

McElrath, Emerson, Fortier, 2000. Social evolution or social response? A fresh look at the "Good Gray Cultures" after four decades of Midwest research. In: McEltrath, D.L., Emerson, T.E., Fortier, A.C. (Eds.), Late Woodland Societies. University of Nebraska Press, Lincoln, pp. 3–36.

Meltzer, D.J., 2015. Pleistocene overkill and North American mammalian extinctions. Annu. Rev. Anthropol 44 (1), 33–53.

Meltzer, D.J., Smith, B.D., 1986. Paleoindian and Early Archaic subsistence strategies in eastern North America, Foraging, Collecting, and Harvesting: Archaic Period Subsistence and Settlement in the Eastern Woodlands, Vol. 6. Southern Illinois University, Carbondale, pp. 3–31, Center for Archaeological Investigations Occasional Paper.

Meier, W., Schneck, G., 1982. Functional morphology of hominoid dentitions. J. Hum. Evolution 11, 693–696.

Mikkola, M.L., 2009. Molecular aspects of hypohidrotic ectodermal dysplasia. Am. J. Med. Genet. Part. A 149A, 2031–2036.

Miles, A.E.W., 1963. The dentition in the assessment of individual age in skeletal material. In: Brothwell, D.R. (Ed.), Dental Anthropol. Pergamon Press, New York, pp. 191–208.

Miller, H.E., Schmidt, C.W., 2018. Craniometric indicators of ancestry among French Americans. Proc. Indiana Acad. Sci. 127, 97–106.

Milner, G.R., 1984. Dental caries in the permanent dentition of a Mississippian period population from the American Midwest. Coll Antropol 1, 77–91.

Milner, G.R., 1985. The East St. Louis Stone Quarry Site Cemetery. University of Illinois Press, Urbana.

Milner, G.R., 1998. The Cahokia Chiefdom. Smithsonian Institution Press, Washington, D.C.

Milner, G.R., 1991. American Bottom Mississippian culture: Internal developments andexternal relations. In: Stoltman, J.B. (Ed.), New Perspectives on Cahokia: Views from the Periphery, Monographs in World Archaeology. WI: Prehistory Press, Madison, pp. 29–47. , No. 2.

Milner, G.R., Anderson, E., Smith, V.G., 1991. Warfare in Late Prehistoric West-Central Illinois. Am. Antiquity 56, 581–603.

Mochanov, J.U.A., 1970. Djuktai cave–new palaeolithic site of northeastern Asia (results of works in 1967). Trudy prilenskoi arheologicheskoi ekspedicii. Yakutsk.

Molnar, S., 1968. Some functional interpretations of tooth wear in prehistoric and modern man. Ph.D. Dissertation. University of California at Santa Barbara.

Molnar, S., 1971a. Human tooth wear, tooth function and cultural variability. Am. J. Phys. Anthropol 34, 27–42.

Molnar, S., 1971b. Sex, age, and tooth position as factors in the production of tooth wear. Am. Antiquity 36, 182–188.

Molnar, S., 1972. Tooth wear and culture: a survey of tooth functions among some prehistoric populations. Coll Antropol 13, 511–526.

Molnar, S., 1972. Tooth wear and culture: A survey of tooth functions among some prehistoric populations. Curr. Anthropology 13, 511–526.

Molnar, S., Richards, R., McKee, J., Molnar, I., 1989. Tooth wear in Australian aboriginal populations from the River Murray valley. Am. J. Phys. Anthropol 79, 185–196.

Moore, C.R., 2008. Raw material utilization in Carroll County, Indiana: a small-scale analysis of diachronic patterns in the usage of Attica, Kenneth, and Wyandotte Cherts. Midcont J. Archaeol 33 (1), 73–106.

Moore, C.R., 2010. A macroscopic investigation of technological style and the production of Middle to Late Archaic fishhooks at the Chiggerville, Read and Baker Sites, Western Kentucky. Southeast. Archaeol. 29, 197–221.

Moore, C.R., Schmidt, C.W., 2009. Paleoindian and Early Archaic organic technologies: a review and analysis. North. Am. Archaeol 30, 57–86.

Moore, C.R., Thompson, V.D., 2012. Animism and green river persistent places: a dwelling perspective of the Shell Mound Archaic. J. Soc. Archaeol 12 (2), 264–284.

Muller, J., 1983. The Southeast. In: Jennings, J. (Ed.), Ancient North Americans (372–419). San Francisco, Freeman.

Muller, J., 1986. Archaeology of the Lower Ohio River Valley. Academic Press, Orlando.

Muller, J., 1997. Mississippian Political Economy. Plenum Press, New York.

Munson, C.A., Cook, D.C., 2001. Residential mortuary practices and skeletal biology at the Late Mississippian Hovey Lake site, Posey County, Indiana. Midcont. J. Archaeol 26 (1), 1–52.

Murphy, T., 1959. The changing pattern of dentine exposure in human tooth attrition. Am. J. Phys. Anthropol 17, 167–178.

Nawrocki S.P., Schmidt C.W., 1995. Analysis of human remains from the Behem Site (12-Vi-688), Vigo County, Indiana. Report Submitted to the Division of Historic Preservation and Archaeology, Indiana Department of Natural Resources, Indianapolis, IN. Report of Investigation No. 34. Archeology and Forensics Laboratory, University of Indianapolis.

Nealis, S.E., Seeman, M.F., 2015. Dental attrition at the Indian Knoll (15OH2) and Black Earth (11SA87) sites: extreme wear as a stressor in Late Archaic populations of the Ohio Valley. Southeast. Archaeology 34, 57–70.

Nelson, C.T., 1938. The teeth of the Indians of the Pecos Pueblo. Am. J. Phys. Anthropol 23, 261–292.

Neumann, G.K., 1952. Archaeology and Race in the American Indian. In: Griffin, J.B. (Ed.), Archaeology of the Eastern United States. University of Chicago Press, Chicago.

Neumann, G.K., 1960. Origins of the Indians ofthe Middle Mississippi area. Proc. Indiana Acad. Sci. 1959 69, 66–68.

Neumann, G.K., 1961. The physical types occurring in the Historic Illinois (Peoria), Miami, Sauk, and Shawnee tribes. Proc. Indiana Acad. Sci. 1960 70, 46.

Neumann, H.W., 1961. The identification of a sample of unmodified faunal remains from the Angel Site. Proc. Indiana Acad. Sci. 70, 46.

Neumann, G.K., Tomak, C.H., 1965. The Early Woodland manifestation in Greene County, Indiana. Proc. Indiana Acad. Sci. 74, 90–98.

Neumann, G.K., 1966. Racial history of the Indians. In: Lindsey, A.A. (Ed.), Natural Features of Indiana. Indianapolis: Indiana Academy of Science. .

Newbrun, E., 1982. Sugar and dental caries: a review of human studies. Science. 217, 418–423.

Newman, J.E., 1966. Bioclimate. In: Lindsey, A.A. (Ed.), Natural Features of Indiana. Indiana Academy of Science, Indianapolis, IN.

Organ, J.M., Teaford, M.F., Larsen, C.S., 2005. Dietary inferences from dental occlusal microwear at Mission San Luis de Apalachee. Am. J. Phys. Anthropol 128, 801–811.

Ortner, D.J., Putschar, W.G.J., 1985. Identification of pathological conditions in human skeletal remains. Smithsonian Institution Press, Washington.

Osterholt, A.E., 2019. The Bioarchaeology of Instability: Violence and EnvironmentalStress During the Late Fort Ancient (AD 1425 –1635) Occupations of Hardin Village. Doctoral Dissertation, University of Nevada, Las Vegas.

Pace, R.E., Thiel, D.P., 1983. Albee component at the Cooke Site (12-P-5) Parke County, Indiana Late Woodland in the Central Wabash Valley. Proc. Indiana Acad. Sci. 92, 78.

Parmalee, P.W., 1975. A general survey of the vertebrate fauna from Cahokia. Perspectives in Cahokia archaeology. Ill. Archaeol Surv. Bull. 10, 137–155.

Pastor, R.F., 1993. Dental microwear among prehistoric inhabitants of the Indian subcontinent: A quantitative and comparative analysis. Ph.D. dissertation. University of Oregon.

Patch, D.C., 2005. The freshwater molluscan fauna: identification and interpretation for archaeological research. In: Marquardt, W.H., Watson, P.J. (Eds.), Archaeology of the Middle Green River Region, Kentucky. University of Florida Press, Gainesville, pp. 257–278.

Pauketat, T.R., 2007. Chiefdoms and Other Archaeological Delusions. AltaMira Press, Lanham, Maryland.

Pauketat, T.R., 2010. The missing persons in Mississippian mortuaries. In: Sullivan, L.P., Mainfort, R.C. (Eds.), Mississippian Mortuary Practices: Beyond Hierarchy and the Representationist Perspective. Gainesville: University Press, Florida, pp. 14–29.

Pearsall, D., 1989. Paleoethnobotany. Academic Press, Orlando, FL.

Perzigian, A.J., Tench, P.A., Braun, D.J., 1984. Prehistoric health in the Ohio River valley. In: Armelagos, G.J., Cohen, M.N. (Eds.), Paleopathology at the Origins of Agriculture. Academic Press, Orlando.

Petersen, J.B., Robinson, B.S., Belknap, D.F., Stark, J., Kaplan, L.K., 1994. An Archaic and Woodland period fish weir complex in central Maine. Archaeol East. North. Am. 22, 197–222.

Peterson, R.J., Nawrocki, S.P., Williamson, M.A., Schmidt, C.W., Tomak, C.H.,1996. An Archaic Rockshelter burial from Daviess County, Indiana. Paper presented at the 3rd Annual Meeting of the Midwest Bioarchaeology and Forensic Anthropology Association, Kalamazoo, MI.

Peyer, B., 1968. Comparative Odontology. University of Chicago, Chicago, IL.

Pindborg, J.J., 1970. Pathology of Dental Hard Tissues. WB Saunders, Philadelphia, PA.

Piperno, D.R., 1984. A comparison and differentiation of phytoliths from maize and wild grasses: use of morphological criteria. Am. Antiquity 49, 361–383.

Piperno, D.R., 1985. Phytolith analysis and tropical paleo-ecology: production and taxonomic significance of siliceous forms in New World plant domesticates and wild species. Rev. Palaeobotany Palynol 45, 185–228.

Piperno, D.R., 2006. Phytoliths. A Comprehensive Guide for Archaeologists andPaleoecologists. Altamira Press, Oxford.

Pollack, D., 2004. Caborn-Welborn: Constructing a New Society after the Angel Chiefdom Collapse. University of Alabama Press, Tuscaloosa.

Pollack, D., Henderson, A.G., 1992. Toward a model of Fort Ancient society. Fort Ancient Cultural Dynamics in the Middle Ohio Valley. Prehistory Press, Madison, WI., pp. 281–294.

Potter, B.A., Irish, J.D., Reuther, J.D., Gelvin-Reymiller, C., Holliday, V.T., 2011. A terminal Pleistocene child cremation and residential structure from eastern Beringia. Science 331, 1058–1062.

Potter, B.A., Irish, J.D., Reuther, J.D., McKinney, H.J., 2015. New insights into eastern Beringian mortuary behavior: a terminal Pleistocene double infant burial at Upward Sun River. Proc. Natl Acad. Sci. 111, 17060–17065.

Potter, B.A., Baichtal, J.F., Beaudoin, A.B., Fehren-Schmitz, L., Haynes, C.V., Holliday, V.T., et al., 2018. Current evidence allows multiple models for the peopling of the Americas. Sci. Adv. 4, 1–8.

Powell, M.L., 1981. Late prehistoric community health in the central deep south: biological and social dimensions of the Mississippian chiefdom at Moundville, Alabama. In: Levy, J. E. (Ed.), Skeletal Analysis in Southeastern Archaeology. North Carolina Archaeology Council, Publication No. 24.

Powell, M.L., 1985. The analysis of dental wear and caries for dietary reconstruction. In: Gilbert, R.I., Mielke, J.H. (Eds.), The Analysis of Prehistoric Diets. Academic Press, Orlando, FL.

Powell, M.L., 1988. Status and Health in Prehistory. Smithsonian Institution Press, Washington.

Prentice, G., 1986. An analysis of the symbolism expressed by the Birger Figurine. Am. Antiquity 51, 239–266.

Purdue, A.H., 1896. Some mounds of Vanderburgh County, Indiana. Proceedings of the Indiana Academy of Science. 6, 68–71.

Purnell, M.A., Darras, L.P., 2016. 3D tooth microwear texture analysis in fishes as a test of dietary hypotheses of durophagy. Surf. Topography: Metrol Prop. 4, 014006.

Quataert, R., 2018. Steele: Analysis of an Early Archaic Cremation Site from Southern Indiana. M.S. Thesis, University of Indianapolis. Indianapolis, IN.

Ragni, A.J., Teaford, M.F., Ungar, P.S., 2017. A molar microwear texture analysis of pitheciid primate. Am. J. Primatol 79 (12). Available from: https://doi.org/10.1002/ajp.22697.

Redmond, B.G., 1994. The archaeology of the Clampitt Site (12Lr329), An Oliver Phase Village in Lawrence County. Glenn A. Black Laboratory of Archaeology, Research Reports. Indiana University, Indiana, p. 16.

Redmond, B.G., 2000. The Oliver Phase occupation of the east Fork White river valley in south central Indiana. Facing the Final Millennium:Studies in the Late Prehistory of Indiana, A.D.700 to 1700. Indiana Department of Natural Resources, Division of Historic Preservation and Archaeology, Indianapolis, IN, pp. 201–254.

Redmond, B.G., 2003. The Oliver Phase occupation of the East Fork of the White River Valley in south central Indiana. In: Redmond, B.G., Jones III, J.R. (Eds.), Facing the Final Millennium: Studies in the Late Prehistory of Indiana, A.D. 700 to 1700. Indiana Department of Natural Resources Division of Historic Preservation and Archaeology, Indianapolis, pp. 201–254.

Redmond, B.G., McCullough, R.G., 2000. The Late Woodland to Late Prehistoric occupations of central Indiana. Late Woodland Societies: Tradition and Transformation across the Midcontinent. University of Nebraska Press, Lincoln, pp. 643–683.

Reinhard, K.J., Danielson, D.R., 2005. Pervasiveness of phytoliths in prehistoric southwestern diet and implications for regional and temporal trends for dental microwear. J. Archaeol Sci. 32, 981–988.

Reinhard, K.J., Bryant Jr., V.T., 2008. Pathoecology and the future of coprolite studies in bioarchaeology. In: Stodder, A.L.W. (Ed.), Reanalysis and Reinterpretation in Southwestern Bioarchaeology. Arizona State Anthropological Research Papers No. 59.

Reinhard, K.J., Hamilton, D.L., Hevly, R.H., 1991. Use of pollen concentration in paleopharmacology: coprolite evidence of medicinal plants. J. Ethnobiol 11, 117–132.

Remy, A.J., Schmidt, C.W., 2016. What ancient people ate. Phys. Today 69, 78–81.

Remy, A.J., Schmidt, C.W., D'Anastasio, R., Reinhardt, G.A., 2014. Dental microwear texture analysis of the people of Herculaneum. American Association of Physical Anthropologists. Abstracts 220. Available from: https://doi.org/10.1002/ajpa/22487.

Richards, R.L., 1988. Faunal remains. In: Cochran, D.R. (Ed.), The Hesher Site: A Late Albee Cemetery in East Central Indiana. Archaeological Resources Management Service, Ball State University, Reports of Investigations 24.

Rick, T., Barber, M., Lowery, D., Wah, J., Madden, M., 2015. Early Woodland Coastal Foraging at the Savage Neck Shell Midden (44NH478), Chesapeake Bay, 43. Archaeology of Eastern North America, Virginia, pp. 22–38.

Rose, J.J., 1983. A replication technique for scanning electron microscopy: applications for anthropologists. Am. J. Phys. Anthropol 62, 255–261.

Rose, J.C., 1984. Bioarchaeology of the Cedar Grove site. In: Trubawitz (Ed.), Cedar Grove. Arkansas Archeological Research, Fayetteville, AR, pp. 227–256. Series No. 23.

Rose, J.C., Marks, M.K., 1985. Bioarchaeology of the Alexander site. In: Hemmings, E.T., House, J.H. (Eds.), The Alexander Site, Conway County, Arkansas. Arkansas Archeological Research, Fayetteville, AR, pp. 76–98. Series No. 24.

Rose, J.C., Marks, M.K., Tieszen, L.L., 1991. Bioarchaeology and subsistence in the central and lower portions of the Mississippi river. In: Powell, M.L., Bridges, P.S., Wagner Mires, A.M. (Eds.), What Mean These Bones? Studies in Southeastern Bioarchaeology. The University of Alabama Press, Tuscaloosa.

Roth, B.J., 2006. The role of gender in the adoption of agriculture in the southern southwest. J. Anthropol Res. 62, 513–538.

Ruby, B.J., 1993. An archaeological investigation of Mann phase settlement patterns in southwestern Indiana. Glenn A. Black Laboratory of Archaeology, Indiana University, Bloomington, Reports of Investigations 93–18.

Ruby, B.J. (1997). The Mann phase: Hopewellian subsistence and settlement adaptations in the Wabash lowlands of southwestern Indiana. Ph.D. Dissertation, Indiana University, Bloomington.

Ruby, B.J., 2006. The Mann phase: Hopewellian community organization in the Wabash lowland. Recreating Hopewell. University Press of Florida, Gainesville, pp. 190–205.

Ruff, C.B., Larsen, C.S., Hayes, W.C., 1984. Structural changes in the femur with the transition to agriculture on the Georgia coast. Am. J. Phys. Anthropol 64, 125–136.

Ruby, B.J., Shriner, C.M., 2006. Ceramic vessel compositions and styles as evidence of the local and nonlocal social affiliations of ritual participants at the Mann Site, Indiana. In: Carr, C., Case, T. (Eds.), Gathering Hopewell. Springer, New York, pp. 533–552.

Ruby, B.J., Carr, C., Charles, D.K., 2006. Community Organizations in the Scioto, Mann, and Havana Hopewellian Regions: A Comparative Perspective. In: Carr, C., Case, T. (Eds.), Gathering Hopewell. Springer, New York, pp. 119–176.

Ryan, A.S., 1979. Wear striation direction on primate teeth: a scanning electron microscope examination. Am. J. Phys. Anthropol 50, 155–168.

Rybin, E., 2014. Tools, beads, and migrations: Specific cultural traits in the Initial Upper Paleolithic of Southern Siberia and Central Asia. Quaternary Int. 347, 39–52.

Sanson, G.D., Kerr, S.A., Gross, K.A., 2007. Do silica phytoliths really wear mammalian teeth? J. Archaeol Sci. 34, 526–531.

Sassaman, K.E., 2005. Poverty point as structure, event. Process. J. Archaeol Method. Theory 12, 355–364.

Saunders, R., 1988. Excavations at 8NA41: two mission period sites on Amelia island, Florida. Department of Anthropology, Miscellaneous Project Report Series No. 35, Florida State Museum.

Scarry, C.M., 2003. Patterns of wild plant utilization in the prehistoric eastern woodlands. In: Minnis, P.E. (Ed.), People and Plants in Ancient Eastern North America. Smithsonian Books, Washington, D.C., pp. 50–104.

Schmidt, C.W., 1993. Paleodemographic analysis of the Santa Catalina de Guale de Santa Maria Ossuary. M.S. Thesis. Purdue University.

Schmidt, C.W., 1998. Dietary Reconstruction in Prehistoric Humans from Indiana: An Analysis of Dental Macrowear, Dental Pathology, and Dental Microwear. PhD dissertation. Purdue University.

Schmidt, C.W., 2001. Dental microwear evidence for a dietary shift between two nonmaize-reliant prehistoric human populations from Indiana. Am. J. Phys. Anthropol 114, 139–145.

Schmidt, C.W., 2003. Results of 12D468 skeletal analysis. Report Submitted to Landmark Archeological and Environmental Services, Sheridan, IN.

Schmidt, C.W., 2008. Analysis of human remains from 12GR1647. Submitted to Indiana Department of Natural Resources, Division of Reclamation.

Schmidt, C.W., 2010. On the relationship of dental microwear to dental macrowear. Am. J. Phys. Anthropol 142, 67–73.

Schmidt, C.W., 2015. Estimating age, sex, and individual ID from teeth. In: Irish, J.D., Scott, G. R. (Eds.), A Companion to Dental Anthropology. Wiley-Liss, New York.

Schmidt, C.W., Helmkamp, R.C., 1994. Preliminary scanning electron microscopic analysis of human dental microwear from two late woodland sites in northwest Indiana. In: Redmond, B. (Ed.), Current Research in Indiana Archaeology and Prehistory, 1994. Glenn A. Black Laboratory of Archaeology, Research Reports, No. 15.

Schmidt, C.W., Helmkamp, R.C., 1997. Analysis of the human dental remains. Hopewell in Mt. Vernon: A Study of the Mt. Vernon Site (12-Po-885). General Electric Company, Mount Vernon, IN.

Schmidt, C.W., Greene, T.R., Megyesi, M., 1999a. Analysis of skeletal remains. Report Submitted to the Forensic Pathology Division, University Clinical Pathology Associates, Indiana University School of Medicine, Indianapolis, IN.

Schmidt, C.W., Greene, T.R., Nawrocki, S.P., Kuba, C., 1999b. Analysis of faunal remains from 12Hr6. Report Submitted to Landmark Archaeological and Environmental Services, Sheridan, IN.

Schmidt, C.W., Moore, C.R., 2003. Survey and Testing of an Early Holocene Site in Carroll County, Indiana (12C180). University of Indianapolis Indiana Prehistory Laboratory Archeology Research Report No. 1. Submitted to the Division of Historic Preservation and Archaeology, Indiana Department of Natural Resources, Indianapolis IN.

Schmidt, C.W., Tomak, C.H. 1999. A Preliminary Report of the 1997 Archaeological Excavation at the Late Archaic Scherschel Site, 12Mo152, Monroe County, Indiana. Report submitted to the Division of Historic Preservation and Archaeology, Indiana Department of Natural Resources, Indianapolis IN.

Schmidt, C.W., Watson, J.T., 2019. Dental Wear in Evolutionary and Biocultural Perspectives. Elsevier, Amsterdam.

Schmidt, C.W., 2021. 12Fl73. Middle/Late Archaic trophy-taking from the Indiana aspect of the Falls of the Ohio river region, In: Pollack D., Bader A. (Ed.) Falls of the Ohio Archaeology. Kentucky Heritage Council.

Schmidt, C.W., Williamson, M.A., 1998. Paleopathology at the Late Woodland, Albee phase, Commissary site (12Hn2): implications for sedentism and maize consumption. Indiana Archaeol 2, 43–69.

Schmidt, C.W., Hill, M.K. 2000. Osteology report. Report submitted to Algonquin Archeological Services, Cincinnati, OH.

Schmidt, C.W., Greene, T.R., 2003. Dental evidence for maize consumption during the Albee phase in Indiana. In: Redmond, B., Jones III, J.R. (Eds.), Facing the Final Millennium: Studies in the Late Prehistory of Indiana, A.D. 700 to 1700. Indiana Department of Natural Resources, Division of Historic Preservation and Archeology, Indianapolis, IN.

Schmidt, C.W., Hill, M.K. 2003b. Preliminary osteological analysis of the 12B1051 human skeletal remains. Archeology Research Report No. 2, Indiana Prehistory Laboratory, University of Indianapolis. Submitted to the Division of Historic Preservation and Archaeology, Indiana Department of Natural Resources, Indianapolis, IN and Gray and Pape, Inc, Cincinnati, OH.

Schmidt, C.W., Sharkey, R.A., 2012. Ethical and political ramifications of the reporting/non-reporting of Native American ritualized violence. In: Chacon, R., Mendoza, R. (Eds.), The Ethics of Anthropology and Amerindian Research: Reporting on Environmental Degradation and Warefare. Springer Press.

Schmidt, C.W., Osterholt, A.E., 2014. Middle and Late Archaic trophy taking in Indiana. In: Allen, M.W., Jones, T.L. (Eds.), Violence and Warfare among Hunter Gatherers. Left Coast Press, Walnut Creek, CA.

Schmidt, C.W., Remy, A.J., 2016. Dietary nuances of Late Pre-Contact agriculturists determined via dental microwear texture analysis. Poster presented at the 85th Annual Meeting of the American Association of Physical Anthropologists, Atlanta, GA. 159, 281–282. Available from: https://doi.org/10.1002/ajpa.22955.

Schmidt, C.W., Greene, T.R., Megyesi, M., 1998. Analysis of an isolated human mandible recovered on the Lake Michigan National Lakeshore. Report Submitted to the Indiana Dunes National Lakeshore, Chesterton, IN.

Schmidt, C.W., Lockhart, R.A., Bowman, D.R., 2006. Analysis of the human remains from 12D563. The Firehouse Site, Dearborn Co., Greendale, IN, University of Indianapolis Indiana Prehistory Laboratory, Archeology Research Report, No. 6. Submitted to Landmark Archaeological and Environmental Services, Inc.

Schmidt, C.W., Lockhart, R.A., Newman, C., Serrano, A., Zolnierz, M., Bader, A., et al., 2010. Skeletal evidence of cultural variation: Mutilation related to warfare and mortuary treatment. In: Auerbach, B.M. (Ed.), Human Variation in the Americas: The Integration of Archaeology and Biological Anthropology. Center for Archaeological Investigations, Carbondale, IL, Occasional Paper No. 38.

Schmidt, C.W., Remy, A.J., Van Sessen, R., Willman, J.C., Scott, R.M., Mahoney, P., et al., 2019. Dental microwear texture analysis of Homo sapiens sapiens: foragers, farmers, and pastoralists. Am. J. Phys. Anthropol 169, 207–226. Available from: https://doi.org/10.1002/ajpa.23815.

Schmidt, C.W., Tomak, C.H., Lockhart, R.A., Greene, T.R., Reinhardt, G.A., 2008. Early Archaic cremations from southern Indiana. In: Schmidt, C.W., Symes, S. (Eds.), Analysis of Burned Human Remains. Academic Press, Orlando, FL.

Schmidt, C.W., Ousley, S.D., Schmidt, M.K., 2011. Addressing inaccuracy when determining two-dimensional occlusal area in human molars. Am. J. Phys. Anthropol 145, 327–332.

Schmidt, C.W., Beach, J.J., McKinley, J., Eng, J.T., 2016. Distinguishing dietary indicators of pastoralist and agriculturists via dental microwear texture analysis. Surf. Topography: Metrol Prop. 4. Available from: https://doi.org/10.1088/2051-672X/4/1/014008.

Schmidt, C.W., El Zaatari, S., Van Sessen, R., 2019. Dental microwear texture analysis in bioarchaeology. In: Schmidt, C.W., Watson, J.T. (Eds.), Dental Wear in Evolutionary and Biocultural Perspectives. Academic Press, London.

Schmucker, B.J., 1985. Dental attrition: a correlative study of dietary and subsistence patterns in California and New Mexico Indians. In: Merbs, C.F., Miller, R.J. (Eds.), Health and Disease in the Prehistoric Southeast, 34. Arizona State University, pp. 275–323. , Anthropological Research Papers.

Schoeninger, M.J., 2009. Stable isotope evidence for the adoption of maize agriculture. Curr. Anthropol 50, 633–640.

Schulz, E., Calandra, I., Kaiser, T.M., 2013. Feeding ecology and chewing mechanics in hoofed mammals: 3D tribology of enamel wear. Wear 300, 169–179.

Schurr, M.R., 1992. Isotopic and mortuary variability in a Middle Mississippian population. Am. Antiquity 57, 300–320.

Schwarcz, H.P., Schoeninger, M.J., 1991. Stable isotope analyses in human nutritional ecology. Yearb. Phys. Anthropol 34, 283–321.

Schwarcz, H.P., Schoeninger, M.J., 2012. Stable isotopes of carbon and nitrogen as tracers for paleo-diet reconstruction. In: Baskaran, M. (Ed.), Handbook of Environmental Isotope Geochemistry. Advances in Isotope Geochemistry. Springer, Berlin, Heidelberg.

Sciulli, P.W., Cook, R.A., 2016. Intracemetery Biological Variation at the Fort Ancient SunWatch Village. Am. J. Phys. Anthropology 160, 719–728.

Scott, E.C., 1979. Dental scoring technique. Am. J. Phys. Anthropol 51, 213–218.

Scott, E.C., 1982. Replica production for scanning electron microscopy: a test of materials suitable for use in field settings. J. Microsc 125, 337–341.

Scott, R., Halcrow, S.E., Standen, V., Arriaza, B.,. Schmidt, C.W., 2016. The Inka Expansion and Diet at the Empire's Periphery. Paper presented at the Australasian Society for Human Biology. Otago, New Zealand.

Scott, G.R., Turner, C.G., 1997. Anthropology of Modern Human Teeth. Cambridge University Press, Cambridge.

Scott, R.S., Ungar, P.S., Bergstrom, T.S., Brown, C.A., Grine, F.E., Teaford, M.F., et al., 2005. Dental microwear texture analysis shows within-species diet variability in fossil hominins. Nature 436, 693–695.

Scott, R.S., Ungar, P.S., Bergstrom, T.S., Brown, C.A., Childs, B.E., Teaford, M.F., et al., 2006. Dental microwear texture analysis: technical considerations. J. Hum. Evol 51, 339–349.

Scott, R.S., Teaford, M.F., Ungar, P.S., 2012. Dental microwear texture and anthropoid diets. Am. J. Phys. Anthropol 147, 551–579.

Scott, R., Halcrow, S.E., Standen, V., Arriaza, B., Schmidt, C.W., 2016. The Inka expansion and diet at the empire's periphery. Paper presented at the Australasian Society for Human Biology. Otago.

Seeman, M.F., 1986. Adena "Houses" and the Implications for Early Woodland Settlement Models in the Ohio Valley. In: Farnsworth, K.B., Emerson, T.E. (Eds.), Early Woodland Archaeology. Kampsville Seminars in Archaeology 2. Center for American Archaeology, Kampsville, Illinois, pp. 564–580.

Seeman, M.F., 1979. The Hopewell Interaction Sphere: The Evidence for Interregional Trade and Structural Complexity. Indiana Historical Society, Indianapolis, IN.

Setzler, F.M., 1930. The archaeology of Whitewater valley. Indiana Hist Bull. 7, 351–549.

Setzler, F.M., 1932. The archaeology of Randolf County and the Fudge Mound. Indiana Hist Bull. 9, 1–35.

Shearer, B.M., Ungar, P.S., McNulty, K.P., Harcourt-Smith, W., Dunsworth, H.M., Teaford, M. F., 2015. Dental microwear profilometry of African non-cercopithecoid catarrhines of the Early Miocene. J. Hum. Evol 78, 33–43.

Simek, J.F., Cressler, A., 2010. Caves as mortuary contexts in the southeast. In: Sullivan, L.P., Mainfort, R.C. (Eds.), Mississippian Mortuary Practices: Beyond Hierarchy and the Representationist Perspective. University Press, Florida, Gainesville, pp. 270–292.

Simon, M.L., 2009. A regional and chronological synthesis of Archaic period plant use in the midcontinent. In: Emerson, T.E., McElrath, D.L., Fortier, A.C. (Eds.), Archaic Societies: Diversity and Complexity across the Midcontinent. State University of New York Press, Albany, pp. 81–114.

Slobodin, S., 1999. Northeast Asia in the Late Pleistocene and Early Holocene. World Archaeology. 30, 484–502.

Smith, P., 1972. Diet and attrition in the Natufians. Am. J. Phys. Anthropol 37, 233–238.

Smith, B.H., 1984. Patterns of molar wear in hunter-gatherers and agriculturalists. Am. J. Phys. Anthropol 62, 39–56.

Smith, B.D., 1985a. The role of *Chenopodium* as a domesticate in pre-maize garden systems of the eastern United States. Southeast. Archeol 4, 51–71.

Smith, B.D., 1985b. *Chenopodium Berlandieri ssp. Jonesianum*: evidence for a Hopewellian domesticate from Ash Cave, Ohio. Southeast. Archeol 4, 107–133.

Smith, B.D., 1986. The archaeology of the Southeastern United States: from Dalton to de Soto, 10,500-500 B.P. Adv. World Archaeol 5, 1–92.

Smith Jr., E.E., 1995. The Swan's landing site (12Hr304): an early Archaic (Kirk Horizon) site in Harrison County, south-central Indiana. Midcont J. Archaeol 20, 192–238.

Smith, R.J., 2018. The continuing misuse of null hypothesis significance testing in biological anthropology. Am. J. Phys. Anthropology. Available from: https://doi.org/10.1002/ajpa.23399.

Smith, R.J., 2020. P > .05: The incorrect interpretation of "not significant" results is a significant problem. Am. J. Phys. Anthropology 172, 521–527.

Smith, B.D., Cowan, C.W., 1987. Domesticated *Chenopodium* in prehistoric eastern North America: new accelorator dates from eastern Kentucky. Am. Antiquity 52, 355–357.

Sokal, R.R., Rohlf, F.J., 1995. Biometry. W. H. Freeman & Company, New York.

Spengler, P., Da Gloria, P., Schmidt, C.W., 2018. Dental microwear texture analyses of the Paleoamericans of Lagoa Santa, Central Brazil. Poster Presented at the 87th annual Meeting of the American Association of Physical Anthropologists. Abstract Book. p. 262.

Stafford, C.R., Cantin, M., 2009. Archaic period chronology in the hill country of southern Indiana. Archaic Societies: Diversity and Complexity across the Midcontinent. State University of New York Press, Albany, pp. 287–313.

Stewart, T.D., 1931. Dental caries in Peruvian skulls. Am. J. Phys. Anthropol 15, 315–326.

Stojanowski, C., 2005. Biocultural Histories of La Florida. University of Alabama Press, Tuscaloosa.

Stoltman, J.B., 1978. Temporal models in prehistory: an example from eastern North America. Curr. Anthropol 19, 703–744.

Stone, A.L., Krueger, K.L., 2015. Telling the whole story: How dentalmicrowear texture analysis can add to the archaeology of the Fort Ancientindividuals. Poster presented at the Undergraduate Research Symposium associated with the annual meeting of the American Association of Physical Anthropologists.

Strait, S.G., 1991. Dietary reconstruction in small-bodied fossil primates. Ph.D. Dissertation. State University of New York at Stony Brook.

Strathern, A., 1971. The Rope of Moka: Big-men and Ceremonial Exchange in Mount Hagen New Guinea. Cambridge University Press.

Styles, B.W., Ahler, S.R., Fowler, M.L., 1983. Modoc Rock Shelter revisited. In: Phillips, J.L., Brown, J.A. (Eds.), Archaic Hunters and Gatherers in the American Midwest. Academic Press, New York.

Sullivan, L.P., Mainfort Jr., R.C., 2010. Mississippian Mortuary Practices. University Press, Gainesville, FL.

Svendsen, J.I., Pavlov, P., 2004. Mamontovaya Kurya—an enigmatic, nearly 40,000 years old Palaeolithic site in the Russian Arctic. In: Zilhão, J., d'Ericco, F. (Eds.), The Chronology of the Aurignacian and the Transitional Technocomplexes—Dating, Stratigraphies, Cultural Implications. Trabalhos de Archaeologia, Lisbon.

Swartz, B.K., 1973. Mound Three, White Site Hn-10 (IAS-BSU). The Final Report on a Robbins Manifestation in East Central Indiana. Ball State University, Muncie, Contributions to Anthropological History No. 1.

Swartz, B.K., 1976. The New Castle Site: A Hopewell Ceremonial Complex in East Central Indiana. Ball State University, Muncie, Contributions to Anthropological History No. 2.

Swartz, B.K., 1982. The Commissary Site: An early Late Woodland Cemetery in East Central Indiana. Contributions to Anthropological History No. 3. Muncie: Ball State University.

Swartz, B.K., 1983. The Commissary Site: An early Late Woodland Cemetery in East Central Indiana. Contributions to Anthropological History No. 3. Ball State University, Muncie.

Talalay, L., Keller, D.R., Munson, P.J., 1984. Hickory nuts, walnuts, butternuts, and hazelnuts: observations and experiments relevant to their aboriginal exploitation in eastern North America. In Munson PJ (Ed.) Experiments and Observations on Aboriginal Wild Plant Food Utilization in Eastern North America, Indiana Historical Society, Indianapolis, IN pp. 338–359.

Tang, N., Le Cebec, A., Antione, D., 2016. Dentine and cementum structure and properties. In: Irish, J.D., Scott, G.R. (Eds.), A Companion to Dental Anthropology. Wiley-Blackwell, West Sussex, UK, pp. 204–222.

Tankersley, K.B., 1992. The archaeology of early Paleoindians: a view from Indiana. In: Hicks, R. (Ed.), Native American Cultures in Indiana. Minnetrista Cultural Center and Ball State University, Muncie.

Tankersley, K.B., Adams, W.R., 1991. Holocene Bison remains (Bison bison), from Greene County, Indiana. Proc. Indiana Acad. Sci. 99, 229–236.

Teaford, M.F., 1988a. A review of dental microwear and diet in modern mammals. Scanning Microsc 2, 1149–1166.

Teaford, M.F., 1988b. Scanning electron microscope diagnosis of wear patterns versus artifacts on fossil teeth. Scanning Microsc 2, 1167–1175.

Teaford, M.F., 1991. Dental Microwear: what can it tell us about diet and dental function? In: Kelley, M.A., Larsen, C.S. (Eds.), Advances in Dental Anthropology. Wiley-Liss, New York, pp. 341–356.

Teaford, M.F., 1994. Dental microwear and dental function. Evolut. Anthropology 3, 17–30.

Teaford, M.F., Walker, A., 1984. Quantitative differences in dental microwear between primate species with different diets and a comment on the presumed diet of *Sivapithecus*. Am. J. Phys. Anthropol 64, 191–200.

Teaford, M.F., Ungar, P.S., 2014. Dental adaptations of African apes. In: Henke, W., Tattersall, I. (Eds.), Handbook of Paleoanthropology. Springer, Heidelberg, pp. 1–26. Available from: http://doi.org/10.1007/978-3-642-27800-6_36-4.

Teaford, M.F., Larsen, C.S., Pastor, R.F., Noble, V.E., 2001. Pits and scratches: microscopic evidence of tooth use and masticatory behavior in La Florida. In: Larsen, C.S. (Ed.), Bioarchaeology of Spanish Florida: The Impact of Colonialism. University Press of Florida, Gainesville.

Teaford, M.F., Ungar, P.S., Taylor, A.B., Ross, C.F., Vinyard, C.J., 2017. In vivo rates of dental microwear formation in laboratory primates fed different food items. Biosurf Biotribol 3, 166–173.

Ten Cate, A.R., 1998. Oral Histology. Moseby, St. Louis.

Tomak, C.H., 1970. Aboriginal occupations in the vicinity of Greene County, Indiana. MA Thesis, Indiana University. Bloomington, IN.

Tomak, C.H., 1979. Jerger: an early archaic mortuary site in southwestern Indiana. Proc. Indiana Acad. Sci. 88, 62–69.

Tomak, C.H., 1980. Alton: a paleo-Indian site in southern Indiana. Proc. Indiana Acad. Sci. 89, 84–90.

Tomak, C.H., 1983. A proposed prehistoric cultural sequence for a section of the valley of the west fork of the White River in southwestern Indiana. Tennesse Anthropol 8, 67–94.

Tomak, C.H., 1994a. The Mount Vernon site: a remarkable Hopewell mound in Posey County. Indiana. Archaeol East. North. Am. 22, 1–46.

Tomak, C.H., 1994b. The paleoindian Alton site, Perry County, Indiana. In: Dancey, W.S. (Ed.), The First Discovery of America. The Ohio Archaeological Council, Inc.

Tomak, C.H., 1994c. An archaeological research project at Swan's Landing, a buried Early Archaic site in Harrison County, Indiana. Tenn. Anthropologist 19, 180–191.

Tomak, C.H., 1994d. The Mount Vernon Mound Site: a remarkable Hopewell mound in Posey County. Indiana. Archeol East. North. Am. 22, 1–46.

Tomak, C.H., O'Connor, N.J., 1978. An early woodland burial from Greene County, Indiana. Proc. Indiana Acad. Sci. 87, 90–97.

Tsartsidou, G., Lev-Yadun, S., Albert, R.M., Miller-Rosen, A., Efstratiou, N., Weiner, S., 2007. The phytolith archaeological record: strengths and weaknesses evaluated based on a quantitative modern reference collection from Greece. J. Archaeol Sci. 34, 1262–1275.

Turner, C.G., 1979. Dental anthropological indications of agriculture among the Jomon people of Central Japan. Am. J. Phys. Anthropol 51, 619–636.

Tykot, 2006. Isotope analysis and the histories of Maize. In: Staller, J.E., Tykot, B.H., Benz, R. F. (Eds.), Histories of Maize. Routledge, London.

Ungar, P.S., 1994. Incisor microwear of Sumatran anthropoid primates. Am. J. Phys. Anthropol 94, 339–364.

Ungar, P.S., 1995. A semiautomated image analysis procedure for the quantification of dental microwear II. Scanning 17, 57–59.

Ungar, P.S., 2010. Mammal Teeth. Johns Hopkins University Press, Baltimore.

Ungar, P.S., 2012. Dental evidence for diet in early Homo. Curr. Anthropol 53, S318–S329.

Ungar, P.S., 2015. Mammalian dental function and wear: a review. Biosurf Biotribol 1, 25–41.

Ungar, P.S., 2016. Origins and functions of teeth: from "toothed" worms to mammals. In: Irish, J.D., Scott, G.R. (Eds.), A Companion to Dental Anthropology. Wiley-Blackwell, West Sussex, pp. 21–37.

Ungar, P.S., 2017. Evolution's Bite. Princeton University Press, Princeton.

Ungar, P.S., Spencer, M.A., 1999. Incisor microwear, diet, and tooth use in three Amerindian populations. Am. J. Phys. Anthropol 109, 387–396.

Ungar, P.S., Scott, R.S., 2009. Dental evidence for diets of early Homo. In: Grine, F.E., Leakey, R.E., Fleagle, J.G. (Eds.), The First Humans: Origins of the Genus Homo. Springer, New York, pp. 121–134.

Ungar, P.S., Sponheimer, M.J., 2011. Early hominin diets. Science 334, 190–193.

Ungar, P.S., Grine, F.E., Teaford, M.F., 2008. Dental microwear indicates that *Paranthropus boisei* was not a hard object feeder. PLoS One 3 (4), 1–6.

Ungar, P.S., Krueger, K.L., Blumenschine, R.J., Njao, J., Scott, R.S., 2012. Dental microwear texture analysis of hominins recovered by the Olduvai landscape paleoanthropology project, 1995-2007. J. Hum. Evol 63, 429–437.

Ungar, P.S., Scott, J.R., Steininger, C.M., 2016. Dental microwear differences between eastern and southern African fossil bovids and hominins. South. Afr. J. Sci. 112, 1–5.

Ungar, P.S., Livengood, S.V., Crittendon, A.N., 2019. Dental microwear of living Hadza foragers. Am. J. Phys. Anthropol 169, 356–367.

van Reenan, J.F., 1982. The effects of attrition in the tooth dimensions of San Bushmen. In: Kurten, B. (Ed.), Teeth, Form Function and Evolution. Columbia University Press, New York.

Van Sessen R., 2013. Transition at Tell Dothan: dietary Evidence from the Late Bronze Age and Early Iron Age. MS Thesis. University of Indianapolis.

Viciano, J., Alemán, I., D'Anastasio, R., Capasso, L., Botella, M.C., 2011. Odontometric sex discrimination in the herculaneum sample (79 AD, Naples, Italy), with application to juveniles. Am. J. Phys. Anthropology 145, 97–106.

Vickery, K.D., 1970. Preliminary report on the excavation of the "Great Mound" at Mounds State Park in Madison County, Indiana. Proc. Indiana Acad. Sci. 79, 75–81.

Vorberger, T.V., Raja, J., 1990. Surface finish metrology tutorial, U.S. Department of Commerce, URL: <http://www.nist.gov/calibrations/upload/89-4088.pdf>

Wagner, G.E., 1987. Uses of Plants by the Fort Ancient Indians. UnpublishedPhD dissertation, Washington University, St. Louis.

Walker, P.L., 1978. A quantitative analysis of dental attrition rates in the Santa Barbara Channel Area. Am. J. Phys. Anthropol 48, 101–106.

Walker, P.L., Dean, G., Shapiro, P., 1991. Estimating age from tooth wear in archaeological populations. In: Kelley, M.A., Larsen, C.S. (Eds.), Advances in Dental Anthropology. Wiley-Liss, New York, pp. 341–356.

Walker, P.L., Erlandson, J.M., 1986. Dental evidence for prehistoric dietary change on the northern Channel Islands, California. Am. Antiquity 51, 375–383.

Walker, A., Teaford, M.F., 1989. Inferences from quantitative analysis of dental microwear. Folia Primatol 53, 177–189.

Walker, A., Hoeck, H.N., Perez, L., 1978. Microwear of mammalian teeth as an indicator of diet. Science. 201, 908–910.

Walthall, J.A., 1999. Mortuary behavior and early Holocene land use in the North American midcontinent. North. Am. Archaeol 20, 1–30.

Waters, B.T., Savage, D.E., 1971. Making duplicates of small vertebrate fossils for teaching and for research collections. Curator 14, 123–132.

Watson, J.T., 2008. Prehistoric dental disease and the dietary shift from cactus to cultigens in northwest Mexico. Int. J. Osteoarchaeol 18, 202–212.

Watson, P.J., Kennedy, M.C., 1991. The development of horticulture in the eastern woodlands of North America: women's role. In: Gero, J.M., Conkey, M.W. (Eds.), Engendering Archaeology. Basil Blackwell, Oxford, pp. 255–275.

Watson, J.T., Schmidt, C.W., 2019. Introduction to dental wear in evolutionary and biocultural contexts. In. In: Schmidt, C.W., Watson, J.T. (Eds.), Dental Wear in Evolutionary and Biocultural Perspectives. Elsevier, Amsterdam, pp. 1–10.

Webb, W.S., 1946. Indian Knoll. University of Kentucky, Reports in Anthropology 4 (Part 1).

Webb, W.S., 1946. Indian Knoll, Site Oh 2, Ohio County, Kentucky. Univ. Kentucky. Rep. Anthropol Archaeol 4 (3), part I.

Webb, W.S., Snow, C., 1945. The Adena people. University of Kentucky Report in Anthropology and Archaeology No. 6.

Weer, P.W., 1935. Sweeping a prehistoric floor. Proceedings of the 16th Annual Indiana History Conference, Indiana History Bulletin 12, 161–168.

Welch, P.D., Scarry, C.M., 1995. Status-related Variation in foodways in the Moundville Chiefdom. Am. Antiquity 60, 397–419.

Whalley, L.A., 1983. Plant remains from the Turner site. In: Milner, G.R. (Ed.), The Turner and DeMange Sites. University of Illinois Press, Urbana, IL, American Bottom Archaeology FAI-270 Site Reports.

White, A.A., 1998. Early and Late Albee mortuary components in west central Indiana. Indiana Archaeology 2, 70–143.

White, A.A., 2013. Functional and stylistic variability in paleoindian and early Archaic projectile points from midcontinental North America. North. Am. Archaeol 34, 71–108.

Williams, S.A., Curzon, M.E.J., 1986a. Observations on dental caries in primary teeth in some medieval British skull material. In: Cruwys, E., Foley, R.A. (Eds.), Teeth and Anthropology. B. A.R. International, Oxford, Series 291.

Williams, D.R., Woodhead, C.M., 1986b. 'Attrition'—a contemporary dental viewpoint. In: Cruwys, E., Foley, R.A. (Eds.), Teeth and Anthropology. B.A.R. International, Oxford, Series 291.

Williamson, M.A., 1998. Regional variation in health and lifeways among late prehistoric Georgia agriculturalists. Ph.D. Dissertation, Purdue University, West Lafayette, IN.

Williams, F.E., Droke, J., Schmidt, C.W., Willman, J.C., Becam, G., de Lumley, M.-A., 2018a. Dental microwear texture analysis of Neandertals from Hortus cave, France. Comptes Rendus Palevol 17, 545–556.

Willman, J.C., Schmidt, C.W., Remy, A., Shackleford, L., Demeter, F., 2018b. Dental microwear texture analysis of the Late Upper Paleolithic/Neolithic humans at Tam Hang (Northern Laos). Poster presented at the 87th annual meeting of the American Association of Physical Anthropologists. Abstract Book. p. 303.

Winkler, D.E., Schulz-Kornas, E., Kaiser, T.E., Codron, D., Leichliter, J., Hummel, J., et al., 2020a. The turnover of dental microwear texture: testing the "last supper" effect in small mammals in a controlled feeding experiment. Palaeogeogr, Palaeoclimatol, Palaeoecol 557, 109930. ISSN 0031-0182. Available from: https://doi.org/10.1016/j.palaeo.2020.109930.

Winkler, D.E., Tütken, T., Schulz-Kornas, E., Kaiser, T.E., Müller, J., Leichliter, J., et al., 2020b. Shape, size, and quantity of ingested external abrasives influence dental microwear texture formation in guinea pigs. Proceedings of the National Academy of Sciences, 202008149; Available from: https://doi.org/10.1073/pnas.2008149117.

Winters, H.D., 1967. An archaeological survey of the Wabash Valley in Illinois. Illinois State Museum Reports of Investigations, No. 10. Springfield.

Winters, H.D., 1969. The Riverton Culture: A Second Millenium Occupation in the Central Wabash Valley. Illinois State Museum Reports of Investigations, No. 13. Springfield.

Wymer, D.A., 1993. Cultural change and subsistence: The Middle Woodland and LateWoodland transition in the Mid-Ohio Valley. In: Scarry, C.M. (Ed.), Foraging and Farming in the Eastern Woodlands. Gainesville. University Press, Florida, Florida.

Xia, J., Zheng, J., Huang, D., Tian, Z.R., Chen, L., Zhou, Z., et al., 2015. A new model to explain tooth wear with implications for microwear formation and diet reconstruction. Proc. Natl Acad. Sci. 112, 10669–10672.

Xia, J., Tian, Z.R., Hua, L., Chen, L., Zhou, Z., Qian, L., et al., 2017. Enamel crystallite strength and wear: nanoscale responses of teeth to chewing loads. J. R. Soc. Interface 14 (135), 0456.

Yarnell, R.A., 1993. The importance of native crops during the Late Archaic and Woodland periods. In: Scarry, C.M. (Ed.), Foraging and Farming in the Eastern Woodlands. University Press, Florida, Gainesville, Florida.

Young, D., Patrick, S., Steele, D.G., 1987. An analysis of the Paleoindian double burial Horn Shelter No. 2 in central Texas. Plains Anthropol 32, 275–298.

Zalzala, F., Quataert, R., Droke, J., Gonzalez, A., 2015. Analysis of a Late Archaic group grave from southern Indiana. Paper Presented at the Annual Meeting of the Midwest Bioarchaeology and Forensic Anthropology Association, Chicago, Illinois.

Zhu, M., Yu, X., Ahlberg, P.E., Choo, B., Lu, J., Qiao, T., et al., 2013. A Silurian placoderm with osteichthyan-like marginal jaw bones. Nature 503, 188–194.

Further reading

Addington, J.E., 1973. Collectors or farmers: dental attrition and pathology related to subsistence in the Ohio Valley. Paper Presented to the Annual Meeting of the American Anthropological Association, New Orleans, LA.

Agresti, A., 2012. Categorical Data Analysis. Wiley, New York.

Ambrose, S.H., 1986. Stable carbon and nitrogen isotopic analysis of human and animal diet in Africa. J. Hum. Evol 15, 707–731.

Ambrose, S.H., 1987. Chemical and isotopic techniques of diet reconstruction in Eastern North America. In: Keegan, W.F. (Ed.), Emergent Horticultural Economies of the Eastern Woodlands. Southern Illinois University, Carbondale, IL, Center for Archaeological Investigations Occasional Papers No. 7.

Aufderheide, A.C., 1989. Chemical analysis of chemical remains. In: Iscan, M.Y., Kennedy, K.A. R. (Eds.), Reconstruction of Life from the Skeleton. Wiley-Liss, New York.

Asch, D.L., Asch, N.B., Farnsworth, K.B., 1979. Woodland subsistence and settlement in west central Illinois. In: Brose, D.S., Greber, N. (Eds.), Hopewell Archaeology. Kent State University Press, Kent, OH.

Barnes, G., 2015. Archaeology of East Asia: The Rise of Civilization in China, Korea and Japan. Oxbow Books, New York.

Bartram, W., 1940. The Travels of William Bartram. Barnes and Noble Inc, New York.

Benfer, R.A., 1984. The challenges and rewards of sedentism: the preceramic village of Paloma, Peru. In: Armelagos, G.J., Cohen, M.N. (Eds.), Paleopathology at the Origins of Agriculture. Academic Press, Orlando, FL.

Benfer, R.A., Edwards, D.S., 1991. The principal axis method for measuring rate and amount of dental attrition: estimating juvenile or adult tooth wear from unaged adult teeth. In: Kelley, M.A., Larsen, C.S. (Eds.), Advances in Dental Anthropology. Wiley-Liss, New York.

Beynon, A.D., 1987. Replication technique for studying microstructure in fossil enamel. Scan. Microsc. 1, 663–669.

Bhussry, B.R., 1980. Development and growth of teeth. In: Bhaskar, S.N. (Ed.), Orban's Oral Histology and Embryology. Mosby, St. Louis, pp. 46–106.

Black, G.A., 1935. Excavations of a Blackford County site. Proceedings of the 16th Annual Indiana History Conference, Indiana History Bulletin. 12, 148–160.

Black, G.A., 1940. Work on the Angel Mound site. Proceedings of the 21st Annual Indiana History Conference, Indiana History Bulletin. 17.

Brace, C.L., Molnar, S., 1967. Experimental studies in human tooth wear: I. Am. J. Phys. Anthropol 27, 213–222.

Brothwell, D.R., 1963. The macroscopic dental pathology of some earlier human populations. In: Brothwell, D.R. (Ed.), Dental Anthropology. Pergamon Press, New York.

Bullington, J., 1991. Deciduous dental microwear of prehistoric juveniles from the lower Illinois river valley. Am. J. Phys. Anthropol 84, 59–73.

Burns, P.E., 1979. Log-linear analysis of dental caries occurrence in four skeletal series. Am. J. Phys. Anthropol 51, 637–648.

Burns, P.E., 1982. A study of sexual dimorphism in the dental pathology of ancient peoples. Ph. D. Dissertation. Arizona State University.

Bush, L.L., 1995. Historical and archaeological evidence for indigenous plant use: an example from the Forks of the Wabash. Paper Presented at the 111th Annual Meeting of the Indiana Academy of Science, Indianapolis, IN.

Bush, L.L., 1996. Botanical remains from the Crouch site. Paper Presented at the 113th Annual Meeting of the Indiana Academy of Science, Greencastle, IN.

Campbell, T.D., 1939. Food, food values and food habits of the Australian Aborigines in relation to their dental conditions. Aus Dental J. 43, 45–55.

Carr, C., Goldstein, B.J., Weets, J.D., 2006. Estimating the sizes and social compositions of mortuary-related gatherings at Scioto Hopewell earthwork-mound sites. In: Carr, C., Case, T.D. (Eds.), Gathering Hopewell: Society, Ritual, and Ritual Interactions. Springer, New York, pp. 480–532.

Clarke, N.G., Hirsch, R.S., 1991. Physiological, pulpal, and periodontal factors influencing alveolar bone. In: Kelley, M.A., Larsen, C.S. (Eds.), Advances in Dental Anthropology. Wiley-Liss, New York.

Clay, R.B., 2002. Deconstructing the Woodland sequence from the heartland: a review of recent research directions in the upper Ohio valley. The Woodland Southeast. University of Alabama Press, Tuscaloosa, pp. 162–184.

Clay, R.B., 2005. Adena: rest in peace? Woodland Period Systematics in the Middle Ohio Valley. The University of Alabama Press, Tuscaloosa, pp. 94–110.

Clementa, A.F., Hillson, S.W., Aiello, L.C., 2012. Tooth wear, Neanderthal facial morphology and the anterior dental loading hypothesis. J. Hum. Evol 62, 367–376.

Cole, F.C., 1951. Kincaid. University of Chicago Press, Chicago, IL.

Conover, W.J., Iman, R.L., 1981. Rank transformations as a bridge between parametric and non-parametric statistics. Am. Stat 35, 124–133.

Cook, R.A., 2017. Continuity and Change in the Native American Village: Multicultural Origins and Descendants of the Fort Ancient Culture. Cambridge University Press, Cambridge.

Coon, M.S., 2009. Variation in Ohio Hopewell political economies. Am. Antiquity 74 (1), 49–76.

Costa, R.L., 1980a. Incidence of caries and abscesses in archaeological Eskimo skeletal samples from Point Hope and Kodiak Island, Alaska. Am. J. Phys. Anthropol 52, 501–514.

Costa, R.L., 1980b. Age, sex, and antemortem loss of teeth in Prehistoric Eskimo samples from Hope and Kodiak Island, Alaska. Am. J. Phys. Anthropol 53, 579–587.

Costa, R.L., 1982. Periodontal disease in the prehistoric Ipiutak and Tigara skeletal remains from Point Hope, Alaska. Am. J. Phys. Anthropol 59, 97–110.

Crothers, G.M., 2008. From foraging to farming: the emergence of exclusive property rights in Kentucky prehistory. Economies and the Transformation of Landscape. AltaMira Press, Lanham, MD, pp. 127–147.

Deagan, K., 1985. Spanish-Indian interaction in sixteenth century Florida and Hispaniola. In: Fitzhugh, W.W. (Ed.), Cultures in Contact. Smithsonian Institution Press, Washington.

Deagan, K., 1990. Accommodation and resistance: the process and impact of Spanish colonization in the southeast. In: Thomas, D.H. (Ed.), Columbian Consequences, Volume 2, Archaeological and Historical Perspectives on the Spanish Borderlands East. Smithsonian Institution Press, Washington.

Dobney, K., Brothwell, D.R., 1986. Dental calculus: its relevance to ancient diet and oral ecology. In: Cruwys, E., Foley, R.A. (Eds.), Teeth and Anthropology. B.A.R. International Series 291.

Doolittle, W.E., Frederick, C.D., 1991. Phytoliths as indicators of prehistoric maize (*Zea mays* subsp.mays, Poaceae) cultivation. Plant. Syst. Evol 177, 175–184.

Driver, H.E., 1953. The acorn in North American Indian diet. Proc. Indiana Acad. Sci. 1952 62, 56–62.

Farnsworth, K.B., 1986. Black sand culture origins and distribution. Early Woodland Archeology. Center for American Archeology, Kampsville, IL, pp. 634–641, Kampsville Seminars in Archeology No. 2.

Fiedel, S.J., 1999. Older than we thought: implications of corrected dates for Paleoindians. Am. Antiquity 64, 95–115.

Ford, R.I., 1979. Gathering and gardening: trends and consequences of Hopewell subsistence strategies. In: Brose, D.S., Greber, N. (Eds.), Hopewell Archaeology. Kent State University Press, Kent, Ohio.

Ford, R.I., 1985. Prehistoric Subsistence in North America. University of Michigan, Ann Arbor, MI, Anthropological Papers No. 75, Museum of Anthropology.

Fowler, M.L., 1991. Mound 72 and Early Mississippian at Cahokia. In: Stoltman, J.B. (Ed.), New Perspectives on Cahokia Views from the Periphery. Prehistory Press, Madison, WI, Monographs of World Archaeology No. 2.

Gilbert, R.I., Mielke, J.H., 1982. The Analysis of Prehistoric Diets. Academic Press, San Diego, CA.

Goldstein, M.S., 1948. Dentition of Indian crania from Texas. Am. J. Phys. Anthropol 6, 63–84.

Goodman, A.H., Armelagos, G.J., 1985. Factors affecting the distribution of enamel hypoplasias within the human permanent dentition. Am. J. Phys. Anthropol 68, 479–493.

Goodman, A.H., Armelagos, G.J., Rose, J.C., 1980. Enamel hypoplasias as indicators of stress in three prehistoric populations from Illinois. Hum. Biol. 52, 515–528.

Gordon, K.D., 1982. A study of microwear on Chimpanzee molars: implications for dental microwear analysis. Am. J. Phys. Anthropol 59, 195–215.

Gordon, K.D., 1986. Dental microwear analysis to detect human diet. Am. J. Phys. Anthropol 69, 206–207.

Gordon, K.D., 1988. A review of methodology and quantification in dental microwear analysis. Scanning Microsc Int. 2, 1139–1147.

Green, T.J., Munson, C.A., 1978. Mississippian settlement pattern in southwestern Indiana. In: Smith, B.D. (Ed.), Mississippian Settlement Patterns. Academic Press, New York.

Greene, T., Schmidt, C.W., Tomak C.H., 1996. Preliminary analysis of the Archaic period Jerger site human skeletal remains. Paper Presented at the 112th Annual Meeting of the Indiana Academy of Science, Greencastle, IN.

Gremillion, K.J., Piperno, D.R., 2009. Human behavioral ecology, phenotypic (developmental) plasticity, and agricultural origins: insights from the emerging evolutionary synthesis. Curr. Anthropol 50, 615–619.

Gremillion, K.J., Sobilik, J.D., 1996. Dietary variability among prehistoric forager-farmers of eastern North American. Curr. Anthropol 37, 529–538.

Griffin, J.B., 1967. Eastern North American archaeology: a summary. Science 156, 175–191.

Griffin, J.B., 1984. Observations on the FAI-270 project. In: Baries, C.J., Porter, J.W. (Eds.), American Bottom Archaeology. University of Illinois Press, Urbana, IL.

Grine, F.E., 1987. Quantitative analysis of occlusal microwear in *Australopithecus* and *Paranthropus*. Scanning Microsc Int. 1, 647–656.

Guernsey, E.Y., 1931. Skeletal material from the Albee mound excavation, summer of 1926. In MacLean JA, Excavation of Albee Mound 1926-1927. Indiana Hist Bull. 8, 128–130.

Guernsey, E.Y., 1934. Successive stages of occupation of a notable prehistoric site. Proceedings of the 15th Annual Indiana History Conference, Indiana History Bulletin. 11, 124–130.

Guernsey, E.Y., 1939. Relationships among various Clark County sites. Proc. Indiana Acad. Sci. 48, 27–32.

Guernsey, E.Y., 1941. The cultural sequence of the Ohio Falls sites. Proc. Indiana Acad. Sci. 51, 60–67.

Hartnady, P., Rose, J.C., 1991. Abnormal tooth loss patterns among Archaic period inhabitants of the lower Pecos region, Texas. In: Kelley, M.A., Larsen, C.S. (Eds.), Advances in Dental Anthropology. Wiley-Liss, New York.

Heithersay, G.S., 1960. Attritional values for Australian Aborigines, Haast's Bluff. Australian Dental J. 5, 84–88.

Hemmings, E.T., 1985. Analysis of materials. In: Hemmings, E.T., House, J.H. (Eds.), The Alexander Site. Arkansas Archaeological Survey, Research Series No. 24.

Hemmings, E.T., House, J.H., 1985. Physical context of the Alexander site. In: Hemmings, E. T., House, J.H. (Eds.), The Alexander Site. Arkansas Archaeological Survey, Research Series No. 24.

Hiiemae, K., 1984. Functional aspects of primate jaw morphology. In: Chivers, D.J., Wood, B. A., Bilsborough, A. (Eds.), Food Acquisition and Processing in Primates. Plenum Press, New York.

Hildebolt, C.F., Molnar, S., 1991. Measurement and description of periodontal disease in anthropological studies. In: Kelley, M.A., Larsen, C.S. (Eds.), Advances in Dental Anthropology. Wiley-Liss, New York.

Hillson, S.W., 2005. Teeth, *second ed.* Cambridge University Press, Cambridge.

Hinton, R.J., 1981. Form and patterning of anterior tooth wear among aboriginal human groups. Am. J. Phys. Anthropol 51, 555–564.

Hrdlicka, A., 1916. Physical anthropology of the Lenape or Delawares, and of the Eastern Indians in general. Bureau of American Ethnology, Bulletin 62.

Hudson, C., 1976. The Southeastern Indians. University of Tennessee Press, Knoxville, TN.

Janis, C.M., 1984. Prediction of primate diets from molar wear patterns. In: Chivers, D.J., Wood, B. A., Bilsborough, A. (Eds.), Food Acquisition and Processing in Primates. Plenum Press, New York.

Janzen, D.E., 1971. Excavations at the Falls of the Ohio river region. Filson Club Historical Q. 45, 373–380.

Johannessen, S., 1984b. Plant remains from the Julien site. In: Milner, G.R. (Ed.), The Julien Site. University of Illinois Press, Urbana, American Bottom Archaeology FAI-270 Site Reports.

Jones, J.S., 1996. The Anzick Site: Analysis of a Clovis Burial Assemblage. Oregon State University, Corvallis.

Jurmain, R., 1990. Paleoepidemiology of a central California prehistoric population from CA-AlA-329: dental disease. Am. J. Phys. Anthropol 81, 333–342.

Katzenberg, M.A., Saunders, S.R., Fitzgerald, W.R., 1993. Age differences in stable carbon and nitrogen isotope ratios in a population of prehistoric maize horticulturalists. Am. J. Phys. Anthropol 90, 267–282.

Kay, R.F., 1987. Analysis of primate dental microwear using image processing techniques. Scanning Micr Int. 1, 657–662.

Kay, R.F., Grine, F.E., 1988. Early hominid diets from quantitative image analysis of dental microwear. Nature. 333, 765–768.

Keegan, W.F., 1989. Stable isotope analysis of prehistoric diet. In: Iscan, M.Y., Kennedy, K.A. R. (Eds.), Reconstruction of Life from the Skeleton. Wiley-Liss, New York.

Kelley, M.A., Levesque, D.R., Weidl, E., 1991. Contrasting patterns of dental disease in five early northern Chilean groups. In: Kelley, M.A., Larsen, C.S. (Eds.), Advances in Dental Anthropology. Wiley-Liss, New York.

Kestle, S., 1988. Subsistence and sex roles. In: Blakely, R.L. (Ed.), The King Site: Continuity and Contact in Sixteenth Century Georgia. University of Georgia Press, Athens.

King, M.M., 2017 Gender, lithics, and perishable technology: searching for evidence of split-cane technology in the archaeological record at the Mussel Beach site (40MI70). Ph.D. Dissertation. Knoxville, TN: University of Tennessee.

Lalueza, F.C., Perez-Perez, A., 1993. The diet of the Neanderthal child Gibralter 2 (Devil's Tower) through the study of the vestibular striation pattern. J. Hum. Evol. 24, 29–41.

Lalueza, C., Perez-Perez, A., Turbon, D., 1993. Microscopic study of the Banyoles mandible (Girona, Spain): diet, cultural activity and toothpick use. J. Hum. Evol. 24, 281–300.

Larsen, C.S., 1982. The anthropology of St. Catherines Island. 3. Prehistoric human biological adaptation. Anthropol Pap. Am. Mus. Nat. Hist. 57, 155–270.

Larsen, C.S., Creekmore, A., Hutchinson, D.L., Joyce, C., Legge, S.S., McNeil, J., et al. (Clarence Bloomfield), 1852–1936, 2002. Bioarchaeology of the late prehistoric Guale: South End Mound I, St. Catherines Island, Georgia. Anthropological Papers of the American Museum of Natural History, No.84.

Larsen, C.S., Schoeninger, M.J., van der Merwe, N.J., Moore, K.M., Lee-Thorp, J.A., 1992. Carbon and nitrogen stable isotopic signatures of human dietary change in the Georgia Bight. Am. J. Phys. Anthropol 89, 197–214.

Lopinot, N., Brussell, D.E., 1982. Assessing uncarbonized seeds from open-air sites in mesic environments: an example from southern Illinois. J. Archaeol Sci. 9, 95–108.

Lovell, N.C., 2014. Occlusal macrowear, antemortem tooth loss, and temporomandibular joint arthritis at predynastic Naqada. In: Metcalfe, R., Cockitt, J. (Eds.), Palaeopathology in Egypt and Nubia: a century in review. Achaeopress, Oxford, pp. 95–106.

Lukacs, J.R., 1989. Dental paleopathology: Methods for reconstructing dietary patterns. In: Iscan, M.Y., Kennedy, K.A.R. (Eds.), Reconstruction of Life from the Skeleton. Wiley-Liss, New York.

Lukacs, J.R., 1992. Dental paleopathology and agricultural intensification in South Asia: new evidence from Bronze Age Harappa. Am. J. Phys. Anthropol 87, 133–150.

Mayhall, J.T., 1970. The effect of culture change upon the Eskimo dentition. Arct. Anthropol 7, 117–121.

McCullough, R.G., 1994. Climatic change and swidden agriculture: implications for the late prehistoric period of Indiana. 110th Meeting of the Indiana Academy of Science, Programs and Abstracts.

Meyer-Rochow, V.B., 2009. Food taboos: their origins and purposes. J. Ethnobiology Ethnomedicine 5, 18. Available from: https://doi.org/10.1186/1746-4269-5-18.

Million, M., 1975. Ceramic technology of the Nodena phase peoples (ca. A.D. 1400-1700). Southeastern Archaeological Conference Bulletin 18, 201–208.

Moore-Jansen, P.H., 1982. Observations of human dental enamel using light and scanning electron microscopy as means for dietary reconstruction in prehistoric populations: a study in experimental bioarchaeology. M.A. Thesis, University of Arkansas, Fayetteville.

Morse, D.F., Morse, P.A., 1983. Archaeology of the central Mississippi Valley. Academic Press, New York.

Mountford, C.P., 1960. Records of the American-Australian Scientific Expedition to Arnhem Land 2. Anthropology and Nutrition. University of Melbourne Press, Victoria.

Newman, M.T., Snow, C.E., 1942. Preliminary report on the skeletal material from the Pickwick Basin, Alabama. Bur. Am. Ethnol Bull. 129, 469.

O'Brien, P.J., 1972. A formal analysis of Cahokia ceramics from the Powell tract. Illinois Archaeological Survey, Monograph No. 3.

Osborn, J.W., 1982. Heliocoidal plane of dental occlusion. Am. J. Phys. Anthropol 57, 273–281.

Petruzo, K.M., Wickens, J.M., 1984. The acorn in aboriginal subsistence in eastern North America: a report on miscellaneous experiments. In: Munson, P.J. (Ed.), Experiments and Observations on Aboriginal Wild Plant Food Utilization in Eastern North America. pp. 360–377.

Pettitt, P., 2011. The Palaeolithic Origins of Human Burial. Routledge, London.

Pfeiffer, S., 1979. The relationship of buccal pits to caries formation and tooth loss. Am. J. Phys. Anthropol 50, 35–38.

Price, T.D., 1985. Late Archaic subsistence in the midwestern United States. J. Hum. Evol 14, 449–459.

Price, T.D., Kavanagh, M., 1982. Bone composition and the reconstruction of diet: examples from the midwestern United States. Midcont J. Archeol 7, 61–79.

Pollack, D.A., Henderson, G., Begley, C.T., 2002. Fort Ancient/Mississippian interaction on the northeastern periphery. Southeast. Archaeol 21 (2), 206–220.

Reinhardt, G.A., 1983. Relationship between attrition and lingual tilting in human teeth. Am. J. Phys. Anthropol 61, 227–237.

Richards, L.C., 1984. Principal axis analysis of dental attrition data from two Australian aboriginal populations. Am. J. Phys. Anthropol 65, 5–13.

Richards, L.C., Brown, T., 1981. Dental attrition and age relationships in Australian Aboriginals. Archaeol Ocean. 16, 94–98.

Rose, J.C., Condon, K.W., Goodman, A.H., 1985. Diet and dentition: developmental disturbances. In: Gilbert, R.I., Mielke, J.H. (Eds.), The Analysis of Prehistoric Diets. Academic Press, Orlando, FL.

Rose, J.C., Clancy, P.M., Moore-Jansen, P.H., 1981. Bioarchaeology of the Roden site. In: Perino, G. (Ed.), Archaeological Investigations at the Roden Site (Mc-215), McMurtain County, Oklahoma. Potsherd Press, Museum of the Red River, Publication No. 1.

Scheidegger, E., 1962. The Crib mound. Cent. S Archaeol J. 9, 4–14.

Schoeninger, M.J., DeNiro, M.J., 1984. Nitrogen and carbon isotopic composition of bone collagen from marine and terrestrial animals. Geochimica et. Cosmochim Acta 48, 625–639.

Schoeninger, M.J., van der Merwe, N.J., Moore, K., Lee-Thorp, J., Larsen, C.S., 1990. Decrease in diet quality between the prehistoric and contact period. In: Larsen, C.S. (Ed.), The

Archaeology of Mission Santa Catalina de Guale: 2. Biocultural Interpretations of a Population in Transition. Anthropological Papers of the American Museum of Natural History, No. 68.

Schurr, M.R., 1987. A 'partial cremation' from the Angel site, Vanderburgh County, Indiana. Proc. Indiana Acad. Sci. 96, 91–93.

Schurr, M.R., Schoeninger, M.J., 1995. Associations between agriculture intensification and social complexity: an example from the prehistoric Ohio valley. J. Anthropol Archaeol 14, 315–339.

Sciulli, P.W., 1982. The Williams (33Wo7a) Red Ocher cemetery: preliminary descriptive and comparative analysis of acquired dental pathology. Pa. Archaeol 52, 18–24.

Seeman, M.F., 1992. Woodland traditions in the midcontinent: a comparison of three regional sequences. Res. Econ Anthropol Suppl. 6, 3–46.

Sillen, A., Kavanagh, M., 1982. Strontium and paleodietary research: a review. Yearb. Phys. Anthropol 25, 67–90.

Smith, C.E., 1982. Recovery and processing of botanical remains. In: Gilbert, R.I., Mielke, J.H. (Eds.), The Analysis of Prehistoric Diets. Academic Press, San Diego.

Smith, B.H., 1986. Development and evolution of the helicoidal plane of dental occlusion. Am. J. Phys. Anthropol 69, 21–35.

Smith Jr., E.E., 1986b. An Archaeological Assessment of the Swan's Landing Site (12Hr304), Harrison County, Indiana. Glenn A. Black Laboratory of Archaeology, Bloomington, IL.

Smith, B.H., 1991. Standards of human tooth formation and dental age assessment. In: Kelley, M.A., Larsen, C.S. (Eds.), Advances in Dental Anthropology. Wiley-Liss, New York.

Sobolik, K.D., Gremillion, K.J., Whitten, P.L., Watson, P.J., 1996. Technical note: sex determination of prehistoric human paleofeces. Am. J. Phys. Anthropol 101, 283–290.

Steponaitis, V., 1983. Ceramics, Chronology, and Community Patterns. Academic Press, New York.

Stuart-MaCadam, P., 1992. Porotic hyperostosis: a new perspective. Am. J. Phys Anthropol 87, 39–47.

Suchey, J.M., Owings, P.A., Wiseley, D.V., Noguchi, T.T., 1984. Skeletal aging of unidentified persons. In: Buikstra, J.E., Rathbun, T.A. (Eds.), Human Identification: Case Studies in Forensic Anthropology. C.C. Thomas Publisher Co, Springfield, IL.

Swanton, J.R., 1942. Source material on the history and ethnology of the Caddo Indians. Bur. Am. Ethnol Bull. 132.

Swanton, J.R., 1946. Indians of the southeastern United States. Bur. Am. Ethnol Bull. 137.

Teaford, M.F., Robinson, J.G., 1989b. Seasonal or ecological differences in diet and molar microwear in *Cebus nigrivittatus*. Am. J. Phys. Anthropol 80, 391–401.

Teaford, M.F., Oyen, O.J., 1989a. In vivo and in vitro turnover in dental microwear. Am. J. Phys. Anthropol 80, 447–460.

Thomas, D.H., 1990. The Spanish missions of La Florida. In: Thomas, D.H. (Ed.), Columbian Consequences, Volume 2, Archaeological and Historical Perspectives on the Spanish Borderlands East. Smithsonian Institution Press, Washington.

Turner, J.C., 2011. Macrobotanical analysis of two Hopewll mound samples from the Mann site (12Po2) in Indiana. Southeast. Archaeol 30, 365–376.

Turner, C.G., Machado, L.M.C., 1983. A new dental wear pattern and evidence for high carbohydrate consumption in a Brazilian Archaic skeletal population. Am. J. Phys. Anthropol 61, 125–130.

Ubelaker, D.H., 1989. Human Skeletal Remains: Excavation, Analysis, Interpretation, second edition Taraxacum, Washington.

Ungar, P.S., Grine, F.E., 1991. Incisor size and wear in *Australopithecus africanus* and *Paranthropus robustus*. J. Hum. Evol 20, 313–340.

Vogel, J.O., 1975. Trends in Cahokia ceramics: preliminary study of the collections from tracts 15A and 15B. Perspectives in Cahokia Archaeology. Illinois Archaeological Survey Bulletin 10.

Walker, P.L., Hewlett, B.S., 1990. Dental health and social status among central African foragers and farmers. Am. Anthropol 92, 383–398.

Watson, J.T., Arriaza, B., Standen, V., Munoz, I., Ovalle, I.M., 2011. Tooth wear related to marine foraging, agro-pastoralism and the formative transition on the northern Chilean Coast. Int. J. Osteoarcheol . Available from: https://doi.org/10.1002/oa.1247.

Webb, W.S., 1936. Indiana's prehistoric southern neighbors. Proceedings of the 17th Annual Indiana History Conference, Indiana History Bulletin. 13, 58–64.

Webb, W.S., Baby, R.S., 1957. The Adena People #2. The Ohio Historical Society, Columbus, OH.

White, T.D., 1991. Human Osteology. Academic Press, San Diego, CA.

Williamson, M.A., 1996. Patterns of osteoarthritis in Mississippian period populations from northern Georgia. Am. J. Phys. Anthropol (Suppl. 22), 245–246.

Yaeger, J.A., 1980. Enamel. In: Bhaskar, S.N. (Ed.), Orban's Oral Histology and Embryology. C.V. Mosby Company, St. Louis, pp. 46–106.

FSC
www.fsc.org
MIX
Papier | Fördert
gute Waldnutzung
FSC® C083411

Kolibri 360 GmbH
Ferdinand-Jühlke-Straße 7
99095 Erfurt, Deutschland
produktsicherheit@kolibri360.de